Elements of Semiotics

Semaphores and Signs

General Editors: Roberta Kevelson and Marcel Danesi

SENSING SEMIOSIS
Toward the Possibility of Complementary Cultural "Logics"
Floyd Merrell

THE SENSE OF FORM IN
LITERATURE AND LANGUAGE
Michael Shapiro

ARCHITECTONICS OF SEMIOSIS
Edwina Taborsky

OF CIGARETTES, HIGH HEELS,
AND OTHER *INTERESTING* THINGS
The Semiotics of Everyday Life
Marcel Danesi

ART, CULTURE, AND THE SEMIOTICS OF MEANING
Culture's Changing Signs of Life in
Poetry, Drama, Painting, and Sculpture
Jackson Barry

ELEMENTS OF SEMIOTICS
David Lidov

Elements of Semiotics

David Lidov

St. Martin's Press
New York

ISBN 0-312-21413-8

Some passages of this book are adapted from materials originally published in the *Encyclopedia of Semiotics,* edited by Paul Bouissac (New York: Oxford University Press,
1998), and are used by permission of the publisher.

Library of Congress Cataloging-in-Publication Data

Lidov, David, 1941–
    Elements of semiotics / by David Lidov.
        p.   cm.—(Semaphores and signs)
    Includes bibliographical references and index.
    ISBN 0-312-21413-8
    1. Semiotics.   I. Title.   II. Series.
P99.L52   1999
302.2—DC21   98-44712
                                                                          CIP

Design by Letra Libre, Inc.

First edition: June, 1999
10   9   8   7   6   5   4   3   2   1

CONTENTS

Tables and Figures   ix

Foreword   xi

Part I. The Provenance of Semiotics

Introduction   1

1. What Is Semiotics About?   3
2. Consciousness of Signs   15
3. Concepts of Sign   25
4. Critical Phenomena of Semiosis   37

Part II. Sign Systems

Introduction   45

5. Vocabulary   47
6. Function   57
7. Syntax   67
8. The Reality of System in a Universe of Change   77

Part III. Analysis of the Sign

Introduction   85

9. Peirce's Problematics for the Sign   87
10. Psychological Aspects of Signification   97
11. What Is a Sign?   103
12. Boundaries of Semiosis   117

Part IV. Elaborations of the Sign

Introduction   127

13. Comparative Articulation   131

14. The Elaboration of Reference   147

15. Double Structure—Grammar and Pattern in Texts   153

16. The Text in Context   171

17. Processive Signs—Ritual, Symbol, and Art   181

Part V. Topics in Comparative Semiotics

Introduction   191

18. Artful and Artificial Languages   193

19. Signs in the Visual Arts   205

20. Melody   215

21. Concept and Expressivity in Art   229

Part VI. Consequences

Introduction   251

22. Semiotics and the Problem of Free Will   253

23. Semiotics and the Aims of Education   261

Notes   269

References   275

Index   283

2.1 We make to ourselves pictures of facts. . . .

2.2 The picture has the logical form in representation with what it pictures. . . .

3. The logical picture of the facts is the thought. . . .

—Ludwig Wittgenstein, Tractatus

"That's called a cheese?" asks Josette. "Then people are going to think it's made of cheese."

"No," says papa, "because cheese isn't called cheese. It's called music box. And the music box is called a rug. The rug is called a lamp. The ceiling is called floor. The floor is called ceiling. The wall is called a door."

So papa teaches Josette the real meaning of words. A chair is a window.

. . . Josette is doubtful about one thing. "What are pictures called?" she asks. "Pictures?" says papa. "What are pictures called? One mustn't say *pictures!* One must say *pictures.*"

—Eugene Ionesco, Story Number 2

Wherefore let him that speaketh in an unknown tongue pray that he may interpret.

—I Corinthians, 14:13

TABLES AND FIGURES

Table 1.1: Varieties of signs according to various authors   6
Figure 1.1: Range of the word "sign" in ordinary and in technical
    language   8
Table 1.2: Signs shown as two factors   9
Table 1.3: Terms for sign factors   10

Figure 3.1: Frege's manner of graphing logic   31

Figure 7.1: Representation of mental data required to interpret
    grammatical structures   71
Figure 7.2: Inclusion hierarchy   73

Figure 9.1: Stipulated indexical icon   95

Figure 13.1: Articulation of representamen and articulation
    of object   132
Figure 13.2: Color oppositions   135
Table 13.1: Chess pieces as complexes of distinctive features   136
Figure 13.3: Greimassian square   137
Figure 13.4: Dual articulation   138
Figure 13.5: Varieties of markedness   142

Figure 15.1: Hemiola   165
Figure 15.2: Grammatical hierarchy of meter (tree graph)   165
Figure 15.3: Grammatical hierarchy of tonality (net graph)   166
Figure 15.4: Pattern in the tune (array)   168
Figure 15.5: Additional pattern in the hemiola   169

Figure 16.1: Rhetorical figures   178

Figure 18.1: Tree graph and two net graphs   200
Figure 18.2: Net graph of plot   201

Figure 20.1: Effort and momentum represented by melody   220
Figure 20.2: Sentic expression forms   225

Figure 21.1: Beginnings of march melody and trio.
    Beethoven, Op. 55, ii   232
Figure 21.2: Overall form of the Funeral March   234
Figure 21.3: Articulation contrasts in the Funeral March   237
Figure 21.4: Frame pattern in the windows   242
Figure 21.5: Sketch of compositional elements of "Joseph"   243

FOREWORD

This book has six parts. Each part is proceeded by an introduction that sets its outline. Part I is itself introductory, and the plan of the whole book is sketched at its end.

Perhaps it will serve the reader to know something of the history of this book, an on-and-off project of 15 years. I teach music theory in a university music department, all I was trained to do, but this book concerns general semiotics—not music, except by example. By telling how this came to be I will be able to thank some friends and colleagues for their ideas or support and also to indicate the orientation of my work.

I entered Canada with my wife in 1965 to avoid the Vietnam War, and we spent some years quite isolated, without academic contacts. In 1968 a clipping from the *New York Times* sent me off to find Noam Chomsky's *Aspects of Syntax*. Its effect on me was explosive. Without having the simple good sense to hunt up background reading, I struggled to decode its jargon and master its logic. I nearly memorized it, attracted at the outset by what I mistook for an obvious parallel between Chomsky's description of sentences and Heinrich Schenker's descriptions of musical compositions. Shortly after my first academic appointment, I devised a grammar (programmed by James Gabura) exploiting those "parallels" to compose melodies with a computer.

The output didn't include any hit tunes, but in 1972, after I read a paper on the project to an ethnomusicology conference, a big man in a blue suit tapped me on the shoulder and informed me that I was committing semiotics. It was not a policeman, but Jean-Jacques Nattiez, the leading animateur then and for further decades of the semiotics of music. Thus accused, I thought I should find out what semiotics might be. On his clue, I looked up the Toronto Semiotic Circle. Paul Bouissac was its leading spirit. His projects over the years provided a mentorship that remains a splendid impetus. Having attended a couple of exciting and confusing meetings of the circle, I asked Professor Bouissac how one could get the basics of this field.

To my great fortune, he told me no one had figured that out yet. He suggested—as the best place to start—that I read Ferdinand de Saussure's *Course in General Linguistics,* which I did, and he invited me read a paper on it for the circle with application to music (which I also did—on a song of Schubert). The host of fascinating and helpful people I met through the circle included David Savan, whose work soon had me thinking that the best place to start must be Charles Peirce, and Lubomir Dolezel, by whom I felt persuaded one must really start with the Prague Circle.[1] President Carter's amnesty, in 1977, allowed me to attend (by coincidence in my hometown of Denver, Colorado) the second annual meeting of the Semiotics Society of America. There must only have been about 30 of us, but we spanned all generations and seemed to each other to be terribly bright. It was exciting to find art historians, film critics, philosophers doing it too, even if none of them knew beans about music. (Modestly enlarged, the society continues to attract a diversity of professions—even musicologists—and to inspire fascinating work. I am very indebted to its collegiality.)

At that time and for some years my interest in semiotics was its bearing on music. By 1980 I was ready to set the world straight. The Toronto Semiotic Circle published my monograph, *Structure and Significance in Music,* billed too ambitiously as the first of two volumes, and then I got stuck.

Added together, my bits of Peirce, bits of Saussure, bits of Prague semiotics, and bits of much else just made too much ad hocary. How could there be an intelligible semiotics of *music* if one did not start with a unified theory of semiotics in general, comprehensive, noncontradictory, and economical, as Louis Hjelmslev demanded? Umberto Eco had tried to pull it all together, but had produced, I then thought, more of a critical compilation than a synthesis with clear primary principles. How could it be otherwise? He was grounded in literature. Wasn't the job of a truly *general* semiotics—a theory for all signs and media—hopeless unless someone would try who was not from the start sufficiently distanced from linguistics and verbal art? Surely the job for a musician! Well, it happened that I needed to spend a summer in a New York suburb in 1983 while my daughter received medical treatment, and we were in circumstances that were impossible for doing music but great for doing words. Nearly a whole summer, just what it would take to write out my neat, clear, general theory. The draft didn't quite tally. This book, several interruptions and second thoughts later, is what I came up with.

This is a book that attempts to draw the foundational problems of semiotics into a unified focus. Because its ideas emerge in part through dialogue with previous writings, it provides a cursory and biased introduction to semiotic literature, but it is not a history. It offers neither a comprehensive nor a balanced survey of that literature. As a book that formulates a basis for semiotics, I hope it will be useful to readers new to the subject, but it is not a textbook. It pretends to no such anonymous certainty.

It will seem old-fashioned to some readers that I look for unity or foundations. I cannot accept the grandly reductive idea that such ambitions ignore a great international dateline that puts us in a new "postmodern" age. When I started the work, I did not know what all my graduate students know today: that Hilary Putnam says foundations are out of the question, that Jacques Derrida shows us the foundations always weep, that Hans-Georg Gadamer warns we cannot build castles in the air and must shore up best we can the foundations of our ancestors. Yet the alternative of blind faith in a consensual discourse risks too much that our terms will be hostage to fashion. I would prefer that we understand construction and deconstruction as a dialectic and not a brandnew one. Deconstruction is liveliest when it targets formulated systems, and in this sense it depends on them. The salute my title directs to Euclid is no more old-fashioned than would be one in the opposite direction, say to Plato's *Symposium,* where Socrates and Alcibiades can protest too much that their matter is independent of their manner, only because the dependence of thought on figures has been so blatantly problematized. Those who find that system is inherently totalitarian need to think more about the politics of exaggerated chaos. Those who argue that systematic thinking is inherently supportive of male dominance could have argued the same about voting 100 years ago. Better to share these resources than reject them.

In the end, I don't think you will find my constructions excessively weighty. My ideal for universals is Snap-On tools, portable and adaptable, not the lever with which Alchemides offered to move the world. More often than not my elements do not arise from full definitions but from exploratory distinctions within categories already established by common speech. These are not rigorously formal but lend themselves, I believe, to the pragmatic test (in the pure Peircean sense of the term) of having intellectual consequences that discipline their continuing development.

A recurring conceit in this book is that I avoid philosophy. Credit me please for knowing well that in reality I have no special dispensation. In the rest of my life, I accept Alfred North Whitehead's dictum that there is no escaping metaphysical first principles. What not doing philosophy means, in the present context, is sometimes doing some philosophy shoddily, sometimes closing my eyes, sometimes taking evasive tactics, and then showing if I can that it doesn't matter. One thing Charles Morris got right: Every special study depends on pretending that a range of neighboring problems are unproblematic. My hope is to demonstrate that foundational semiotics has rich problems which do not require broad philosophical agreement among those who cooperate in investigating them. Our situation is parallel to that in sociology or psychology. Each field has substantial issues of its own. The issues of the philosophy of mind, the philosophy of society, and the philosophy of the sign are not entirely separate from their specialized offshoots, but they are enormously different. I hope I convince my readers that the tasks of semiotics are no more tasks of philosophy than they are tasks of linguistics, both of which have vital relations with it.

By comparison to other theories of semiotics, what I might list on a patent application for this one would include its emphasis on a comparative perspective; its category of "elaborated signs" and some contributions to their structural analysis; its principle that semiotics emerges as a distinctive, unified, and insightful study when (and only when) its purview is strictly limited to consciousness; a definition of sign derived from Peirce's but radically revised to evade his metaphysical commitments; and, above all, an insistence that structure both develops and opposes reference.

For most of the time of my professional career, theoretical semiotics has been largely a contest between structuralism and the broader philosophical tradition that we like to see as centering on Peirce. In his honor I use the label "pragmatism" for this alternative to structuralism, but I use it lightly, only as a label, without regard to its implications in other contexts. This received opposition sets a theory of significant structure against a theory of reference. The position I take in this book is that the dialectic does not properly belong to semiotic theory but to the use and development of signs themselves. In fewer words, the dialectic of structure and reference is constitutive of semiosis, not semiotics. "Wait there," my good readers will say. "You can't patent that! The idea is ubiquitous." And you are right in some measure. The idea is everywhere, in Prague School aesthetics, in the notion of "constructs," in Julia Kristeva's opposition of "significance" and "signifiance," in the postmodern critique of semiotics, and elsewhere, but only, I must observe, by implication or in fragments. The principle that semiotic elaboration both develops and supplants reference, as a primary, even "universal," constitutive principle of semiosis, has not been squarely confronted. If I can't patent the idea, it is because I haven't confronted it well enough. There is much more to say on the matter than I do.

Pragmatism provides tools to describe the sign as open. Structuralism provides the tools that describe closure. Far from exhausted, structuralism is a still new venture that begs further development in the face of many unsolved problems. My discussion of comparative articulation and my distinction between the syntax of structured objects (pattern) and the syntax of languages (grammar) are intended to remove roadblocks and keep that ball in play.

The shame of dilly-dallying with the preparation of a book is that you lose some of your favorite readers. I learned only when we talked in the 1980s that my late uncle, the painter and illustrator Arthur Lidov, had been a protégé of Charles Morris at the University of Chicago and was deeply immersed in semiotics. Despite a natural affinity, geography (and the Vietnam War) limited our times together, but I know now that my direction must really have been set by the trips to the dictionary that were obligatory interruptions of any meal one shared with Arthur, starting around age seven. In his last decade he was very supportive of my efforts, and he enormously broadened my awareness of my ignorance of philosophy.

No one has contributed so many unfootnoted ideas to this book as my wife, Marilyn Strauss Lidov, who, until her death in 1987, had become increasingly intrigued with its subject. Where music, visual art, history, or politics are concerned, I cannot begin to distinguish her thoughts from mine. I have wished generally to adhere to her precept that in the humanities, structural analysis is rarely of interest unless it is subordinated to appreciation.

Had it not been for my colleague Alan Lessem, I doubt that I would ever have been persuaded to regard analytical work as just as serious as artistic work and to take it fully to heart. I much regret that I have no recourse to his criticisms.

As this book was in production, we received the sad news of the death of Roberta Kevelson, our series editor. The energy, wisdom, and generosity of her scholarly activities were a model for her colleagues and our memories of her will continue as a bond among us and an inspiration.

Fortunately, I have more obligations to the quick, more than I will list, but a few more to mention that I have not yet. First off, to Mr. Oscar Radin, a businessman and extraordinary English teacher and probably the most well-read person I know, whose library, house, intellect, and enthusiasm were put at my disposal the summer of 1983 when I started and whose interest in the project has never flagged.

My thanks to my colleagues Eugen Baer, Paul Bouissac, Evan Cameron, Naomi Cumming, John Deely, Robert Hatten, Guy Metraux, Danuta Mirka, Raymond Monelle, and Jim Robbins for reading bits or all of earlier drafts and setting standards I have not met. I have benefited from the criticisms and ideas of, poached the research of, profited from the legwork of, and leaned on the moral support of several former students. All of the above in the case of Richard Stewardson who batted me in in the seventh, and also John Brownell, Christopher Ciepiela, Jeff Cupchik, William Echard, Anne-Marie Gallagher, Jason Stanley, Peter Sudbury, Matthew VanderWoude, and the others to whom I hereby offer yet more evidence of bad memory and worse filing.

At an early stage, I received assistance from the Social Sciences and Humanities Research Council of Canada and all along, nearly continuously, a trickle of grants from my faculty, reliable, essential, and ever more appreciated as they were apportioned from ever more straitened resources. I tip my professorial bonnet to the studious and insightful editors of St. Martin's Press. I can assure you, dear reader, that they have done us both some good turns.

D. L. 1998

The Provenance of Semiotics

Routinely, we hear that semiotics is the study of the sign and that a sign is something that stands for something else. These definitions are scant clues to the origins and motivations of semiotics as a characteristic intellectual movement of the twentieth century.

Charles Peirce wanted to find out how the progress of knowledge was possible and why it was occurring. Ferdinand de Saussure wanted a standpoint for a disciplined analysis of language, as Charles Morris did for the social sciences. Roman Jakobson wanted to show that the logical patterns he found in phonology unified all manifestations of culture, inspiring Claude Levi-Strauss to explicate structures common to scientific and pre-scientific thought and Tom Sebeok to insist on the unity of intellectual and biological processes. Umberto Eco shows us the life of thought in avant-garde culture. My own original motivation had been to understand how music without words could seem to mean something and could seem to advance its meaning phrase by phrase, but unraveling the logic behind that puzzle became a motivation in itself.

The premise each of these authors seized on was that their investigations hinged on a fuller conceptual mastery of the notion of sign. That there are conceptual problems is almost immediately obvious. What realm of existence do signs inhabit? Are they like houses and roses? Like the facts of arithmetic? Like images in the imagination? Or something quite other than these? What does it mean "to mean" or "to refer" ? These are not questions that philosophy had neglected before the twentieth century nor that it neglected during the twentieth century, when, in fact, they emerged as a chief theme. The interaction of this philosophical concern with a host of specialized studies was the novelty.

Part I is introductory but puts in play some notions and prejudices that are developed throughout the book. Chapter 1 regards our problems from the vantage of ordinary language. Chapter 2 traces the emergence of semiotics in our self-reflection. Chapter 3 is a cautionary sampler of historical sources. Chapter 4 situates the investigation to follow, closing with an overview of the book.

Bibliographic references for authors mentioned in passing here and in chapter 1 are provided in later chapters, where fuller discussions of their work appear.

1

WHAT IS SEMIOTICS ABOUT?

Semiotic theory constructs a comprehensive, comparative perspective of the artifacts of mental life. The method of semiotics is to regard these artifacts (stories, pictures, gestures, tunes, prices, etc.) as signs or sign systems. *Semiotic analysis* exploits the perspective of semiotic theory to enrich our understanding of particular signs. But these definitions, without a context, can serve here only as punctuation, like the illuminated capitals of a medieval manuscript or a fanfare.

For a first context, reflect briefly on the state of some of the artifacts of our present mental lives. In our epoch, we are informed to an unprecedented extent of the geographical and historical diversity of languages, artistic styles, rituals, costumes, and customs. On the other hand, the homogenizing influence of mass production on our environment is unsettling. The two factors pull in opposite directions with complementary results, one adding diversity that is too raw to signify very much, the other erasing differences to which we had attached a lot of meaning. Both make us more conscious of signs. Our new technologies for transporting and manipulating information, the media and the computers, transgress borders that used to offer security. We want to know if computers think or— if convinced that they will—whether there will still be anything special about our human thoughts. Television pretends to transport distant realities into our own homes. Two generations ago one could count on the fact that communication required the filtering and cushioning of verbal and pictorial style. If it is true that television gives us direct access to wars, poverty, boardrooms, bedrooms, and police stations with less elaborate filters, how are we to evaluate the languages and codes we worked so hard to learn? Has literacy become a foolish investment? Our imaginal and linguistic repertoires are subjected to continuous coercion. In at least three industries the main stock-in-trade is the forced-march revision of our symbols: the fashion industry (clothes, interior decorating, etc.), the advertising industry, and the fine arts avant gardes. We live in an age forced to interrogate its own modalities of representation; we witness a growth of signs and a loss of meanings.

The principle idea of semiotics is the category of *sign*. All the circumstances and social pressures alluded to in the preceding paragraph are said, in the perspective of semiotics, to center on *signs*.

"Semiotics" (or "semiotic," without the "s") and "semiology" are roughly equivalent terms. Semiotics is conventionally defined as "the study of signs," but simple definitions are pernicious. Not every study of signs is semiotics. Besides, to use that definition we may need to know what a sign is, and it is notoriously difficult to decide on a good definition of sign. Students of semiotics—"semioticians," to use a jargon that is all too easy a target for parody—do not agree about these matters. That is no failure: Semiotics is more a philosophical study than a technological one. We shall need to reflect on various definitions, but perhaps definitions are perhaps best viewed as experiments. You do not want to take your car to a maintenance shop where the experts are in doubt regarding what a carburetor is. Auto maintenance is a technology. In philosophical investigations, disagreement about basic concepts is the center attraction.

Many sciences were historically part of philosophy before their accumulations of information and their methods of observation and argument distinguished them as special fields. One aim of this book is to show that we can remove semiotics further from general philosophy by elaborating its special tools more clearly, but at present semiotics is half and half, partly specialized and partly philosophical. We take advantage of highly specialized research in linguistics, mathematical logic, music, anthropology, literary criticism, and elsewhere, but our extrapolations from these researches border philosophical problems.

Considering semiotics sociologically—that is to say, as a field of work in which actual human beings are presently engaged—we might note that like many other endeavors, semiotics is unified by the overlapping interests of those who work in it, not a consensus regarding terminology, concepts, or theories. To propose a definition is therefore a polemical or even political move with respect to this social activity. Before launching such an offensive, I prefer that we scout the territory. Definitions belong to *sys-*

tems. Sign systems are one of our chief concerns, but current practice actually takes the form of *dialogue*, an equal concern and resource. The investigation conducted in this book constructs a limited system framed by dialogue.

To introduce the dialogue I juxtapose three very preliminary discussions of the question of what semiotics is. The first of these contrasts the usage of the word "sign" in ordinary language with its usage in technical language. The second, more theoretical, considers traditional definitions. The third illustrates what semiotics is not.

"SIGN AS AN EVERYDAY TERM AND "SIGN" AS A TECHNICAL TERM

> And God said, this is the token of the covenant which I make between me and you and every living creature that is with you, for perpetual generations: I do set my bow in the cloud, and it shall be for a token of the covenant.
>
> —Genesis 9:12.

"Token," "mark," "sign," and "symbol" are common, everyday words, largely interchangeable, but their normal usages are inconsistent or at least very unsystematic. Generally semiotic scholarship ignores the everyday habits of these words in favor of more systematic ideas, but ordinary and technical language are related. What is it, in ordinary, nontechnical parlance, that we call tokens or signs or symbols?

For a sample, ordinary conversation speaks of signs and symbols in religions—the cross, the votive candle, and so on—but to tell a believer that a prayer or a ritual is *merely* a symbol may give offense. Psychoanalytic doctrine speaks of symbols, especially in dreams: Freud's trains for marriages, Jung's mythological personae, but if we say the "ego" or the "id" are "simply symbols," we seem to challenge the theory. We speak of the "sign language" of the deaf, but ordinarily we don't call our own spoken language a "sign language," although we may be dimly aware that oral words, too, are signs. In casual usage a totem pole is a sign but not the words "totem" or "pole" or "totem pole." Standard pictograms or ideograms, such as stick and circle drawings to indicate washrooms, baggage areas, taxi locations at airports, are readily called signs. We speak of traffic signs, political symbols and signs, storefront and office signs. On the other hand, the yellow line down the middle of the road is not generally referred to as a sign. (Ask some friends to name the six most common traffic signs, and see whether any include this one!) We speak of "symbolist poetry," suggesting thereby that some poetry features symbols and other poetry does not, but is there poetry without symbols?

From this short list it is evident that everyday language is selective and perhaps erratic in what it includes as a sign. The first requirement of technical language, by contrast, is consistency. To seek and exploit consistency, many semioticians cast the net very wide.

The items of table 1.1, according to the precepts of various authors, are all signs.

Does it make any sense to lump all these together? We are not yet in a position to say; however, as broad and open as the list is, it may be too selective. For each or most of its entries, the idea of sign relates to their *pri-*

Table 1.1   **Varieties of signs according to various authors**

Words
Sentences
Sounds or marks on paper which represent words or sentences
Computer programs (hard wired, electronically recorded or written out)
Pictures, diagrams, and graphs
Chemical and physics formulae
Finger prints
Objects made of other signs (Therefore, poems and fictions even if we don't
    consider them to "represent something else")
Objects which have the types of structure signs do. (Some persons—not this
    author—think music has no reference outside itself, but works of music or of
    abstract mathmatics are still signs by this criterion)
Fictitious scenes, beasts and characters
Ideas, thoughts, concepts, images
Self, God, personality
Sensations
Money
Postures and gestures
Manners and customs, costumes
Rules and values
The orienting dance of a honeybee, avian display, DNA

mary functions. The entries in the list are instrumental principally in some respect that concerns knowledge, information, and/or communication. Many other items will have other primary uses and yet possess signification *secondarily* by context or aesthetic design: Architecture, automobiles, and home furnishings, for example, have a communicative function that is secondary to their utility. As Umberto Eco points out, a relatively insignificant jar of fruit preserves takes on additional signification if it is a gift. These, too, can go on the list.

Thus technical usage of "sign" seems wider than the common usage, and we might wonder what the purpose could be of such a wide category. Inevitably, we flirt here with a premise that invites wariness: Everything is a sign, and the apparently consequent corollary—therefore, semiotics studies everything. Surely either an empty boast or a *reductio ad absurdum.* "Study" is misleading. We could say, "All objects are formed of chemicals; therefore, chemistry studies everything." There is a certain sense in such statements if they are rightly understood. The chemical study of a book will consider its color, weight, degradability, and chemical constituents. A chemist can study a book without reading it. This is the sense in which chemistry studies everything. Whether a semiotician can study a book without reading it I am not prepared to say, but the sense in which "semiotics studies everything" is, as with chemistry, very restricted.

Technical semiotics accords the concept of sign much wider scope than ordinary speech because it is not possible to convey a *unified* notion of "sign" that includes only the common usages unless we start with the wider, technical meaning. The dictionary definitions are compilations, not unities. They list several different senses of words. If there is an underlying unity in these families of sense, the dictionaries do not spell it out. The technical approach is an effort to explicate an intuition of unity. One attempt to construct such a unity is the medieval formula, "aliquid stat pro aliquo"—a sign is "something that stands for something else." Postponing, momentarily, the necessary criticism of that formula, we may note that with just a bit of interpretive argument, it will justify all the items of table 1.1.

Taking this definition as a starting point, the usage of "sign" in casual speech emerges by means of a restriction: The sign of everyday talk might be "something that stands for something else *and that catches our attention either because it is quite striking in itself or because its meaning is difficult or unclear.*" The difference is captured in two theoretical terms: Signs so

Figure 1.1   Range of the word "sign" in ordinary and in technical language

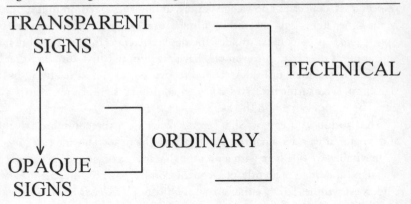

called in everyday speech are those signs that are more *opaque* (or the less *transparent*). (See figure 1.1.)

Transparency and opacity are relative and unstable. As we become accustomed to a sign, we tend to stop noticing that it is one; it becomes transparent. On the other hand, a sign that has become inconspicuous can be made opaque by a new context, as when a barber shop pole shows up in an ice cream parlor. Fluctuations of *sign consciousness* are a fundamental phenomenon for semiotics.

"SIGN" AS A FORMAL CONCEPT

"Signs" depend, as a rule, upon habits learnt by experience. . . . We may say that A is a "sign" of B if it promotes a behaviour that B would promote, but that has no appropriateness to A alone. It must be admitted, however, that some signs are not dependent upon experience. . . . The precise definition of "sign" is difficult . . . there is no satisfactory definition of "appropriate" behaviour. . . .

—Bertrand Russell, *An Inquiry into Meaning and Truth*

We move now from examples to definitions. The preceding discussion took a rough measure of what signs are as a collection. Can we now say more precisely what sign is as a concept? The problem is to construct a definition of "sign" (a) that permits all the applications which seem intuitively natural (which consistently excludes some of them) and (b) that is not narrowly circular—that is, which does not just substitute an equally slippery synonym. In the quotation, Russell acknowledges substantial difficulty here. The intention of the following discussion is to suggest why this is so, not to resolve the problem.

Sign is a relational construct bringing together at least two or three factors—for Russell, A and B, more generally:

A signifies B
or
A represents B as (or to) C.

Table 1.2 illustrates the possible minimum of just two factors.

Four pairs of terms are widely used in semiotics to label these two factors. Although each of these pairs of terms is associated with a different theory, any of the pairs in table 1.3 can designate these factors. Please note: Parts I and II of this book borrow *signifier* and *signified* as a default terminology; in part III an alternative is developed.

"Signam" and "signatum" are medieval terms. "Signifier" and "signified" are the rather awkward but now standard translations of Ferdinand de Saussure's French terms, "signifié" and "signifiant," which formed part of his novel and influential framework for linguistics at the beginning of this century. "Vehicle" and "object" are terms of Charles Morris, who founded a behavioral interpretation of semiotics extensively influenced by the very different philosophy of Charles Peirce. "Expression" and "content" are terms from Louis Hjelmslev, who, developing Saussure's suggestions for a

Table 1.2 Signs shown as two factors

	A		B
	word sound	. . .	word meaning
	red octagon	. . .	stop
♩		. . .	musical sound
	clock hands	. . .	time of day
	$	. . .	dollars

Table 1.3 Terms for sign factors

signam	signatum
signifier	signified
vehicle	object
expression	content

systematic approach to language, constructed a semiotic theory that is as abstract as geometry. These theories (see in chapter 3 and elsewhere) are entirely different from each other, reflecting their very different purposes, but they share their perception of "sign" as *relational*.

To say what *kind* of relation is entailed is more problematic.

In the medieval formula quoted earlier, aliquid stat pro aliquo (something that stands for something else), the three-letter word is the catch. What could "pro," or "for," or "stands for" mean in this context? Perhaps something on the order of "takes the place of" or "substitutes"? Some signs can be understood this way—for example, the ritual bread and wine of communion, which take the place of the body and the blood of Christ. The approval of a blueprint partially substitutes for the inspection of a house. But in general, a sign is *not* automatically permitted to substitute for its object. (We say: "No personal checks!" disallowing the sign to substitute for the cash it represents. Or "Easier said than done!" disallowing the word to substitute for the deed it represents.) The check and the boast are signs, but not because they are substitutes. They still "stand for" or "signify" or "mean" something. Clearly "stat pro" has a special sense: It means "means." And that is circular: Defining "meaning" is essentially the same problem and equally as difficult as defining sign. (The same examples invalidate Bertrand Russell's definition quoted earlier.)

Another medieval definition, sometimes credited to St. Augustine, explains a sign as "something which besides manifesting itself to the senses also indicates to the mind something beyond itself." This is a more careful formulation, but it begs a question about the status of thoughts, ideas, mental images, and concepts: Are these signs? These entities may seem to partake of a representational function, but they do not manifest themselves to the senses.[1]

This difficulty aside, the Augustinian definition is still circular. "Indicates to the mind" or, as some translations have it, "brings to mind" is not intended here in an exactly literal sense. H_2O is a sign that brings water to mind. But if water brings "H_2O" to mind, do we want to say that "water" is a sign of "H_2O"? Karl Bühler pointed out (see chapter 6), that saying the first three letters of the alphabet brings the fourth to mind, but *prima facie*, it seems ridiculous to regard the first three letters as a sign of the fourth. In the Augustinian definition, "indicates" and "brings to mind" are again merely synonyms for "means" or "represents." At bottom, the definition is circular.

There is a limit to what definitions accomplish. Now that we have considered ordinary and technical meanings, I will explain how I indicate my own usage. Formalization is a double problem for semiotics, emerging both as a topic and as a tactic. Can a formally elaborate semiotic discourse avoid losing touch with the phenomena we want to talk about? Alternately, can our language remain relaxed but still help to clarify the thoughts tangled in the inconsistencies of normal talking? Jargon for its own sake is ridiculous (the epigraphs at the head of this book advertise my sentiments in that regard), but when we need to insist on distinctions that ordinary language does not preserve, technical jargon is indispensable. I have not produced a tight, closed logic, but I try nevertheless to tidy up a bit in the corner of our language that semiotics investigates. Formally, my *elements* are system of technical usages. To identify these, key terms are *italicized* when they occur in statements which define, regulate or describe my own technical usage, be it borrowed, adapted, or invented. (See, for example, the first paragraph of this chapter.) These passages are also referenced by the Index of Terms at the end of the book. This convention does not apply when I discuss the usages of other authors but do not retain their terminology.

WHAT ISN'T SEMIOTICS?

There's rosemary, that's for remembrance. Pray you love, remember. And there is pansies. That's for thoughts.

—*Hamlet*, Act IV, Scene 5.

In the medieval courtly tradition of flower symbols, rosemary was a sign of fidelity or, as Ophelia has it in her "document of madness," of remembrance. How may we study this sign? Obviously there is, first, a practical knowledge of rosemary that is not part of semiotics. We may know that it is the flower of a southern European shrub or know how to cultivate it or know where to gather it or know when to use its pungent odor in culinary preparations. Such practical knowledge of rosemary is not the particular business of semioticians. Knowing what rosemary means—its interpretation—might seem more pertinent to semiotics. But Ophelia, who has that part down pat, is not a semiotician. (She is engaged in *semiosis*—a signifying activity—not semiotics—the analysis of that activity.)

Each field of knowledge rests on the comparisons it brings to bear on its subject. Culinary knowledge of rosemary compares tastes; botanical knowledge compares shrubs, growing conditions, and so on. Ophelia's comparative series requires the meanings of flowers *within one system*. (Though she disperses her flowers chaotically here, she still distinguishes their values.) The comparative frame of reference that is essential to semiotics is the comparison of the flower system with *other types of signs or sign systems*. Semiotics may ask how the European medieval system of flower symbols is like or unlike spoken languages or like or unlike melodies or like or unlike pictures. To demonstrate: Flower symbols are picturesque. Like pictures they are concretely visual and hold attention in themselves as well as in what they represent. But they are not really like pictures in their mode of signifying. Pictures typically resemble their objects. Flower symbols, like words, are attached to their meanings by largely arbitrary conventions. There is little more reason why "rosemary" should mean fidelity than why the sound "fidelity" should mean fidelity. Like words, flower symbols belong to a limited vocabulary, each unit distinct from the others. Yet for all this, it would be hasty to speak of a "language" of flower symbols. Languages have grammars as well as vocabularies. Words in grammatical combinations have meaning on plane quite apart from their isolated significations. In this respect, the flower symbols really are more like pictorial elements. They may be combined and thus qualify each other, but their combinations do not create a new plane of meanings.

And there are questions of dependency: Do flower symbols ultimately depend on language for their significance? Are they a surrogate system for words, or, once launched into orbit by the booster rockets of speech, do they establish a symbolic dynamic of their own that speech could not subsume? (Perhaps we could not answer that question in this case without an integrated study of the period's color symbols, heraldic symbols, allegorical roles for birds and beasts, and codes of manners.)

Ultimately, it is not the ubiquitous activity of interpreting signs that best characterizes semiotics, but these other questions that compare different genres of sign.

2

CONSCIOUSNESS OF SIGNS

So long as you look at *X, you are* not *attending* from *X to something else, which would be its meaning. In order to attend* from *X to its meaning, you must cease to look* at *X, and* the moment you look at X you cease to see its meaning. . . .*

We shall presently see that to attend from *a thing to its meaning is to* interiorize *it and that to look instead* at *the thing is to* exteriorize *or* alienate *it. We shall then say* that we endow a thing with meaning by interiorizing it and destroy its meaning by alienating it. . . .*

I have shown how our subsidiary awareness of our body is extended [into tools]. To use language in speech, reading and writing, is to extend our bodily equipment and become intelligent human beings. We may say that when we learn to use language, or a probe or a tool, and thus make ourselves aware of these things as we are of our body, we interiorize *these things and* make ourselves dwell in them. . . .

Interiorization bestows meaning, alienation strips of meaning, when the two are applied alternately, they can jointly develop *meaning. . . .*

—Michael Polanyi, *Knowing and Being*

Semiosis is the action of signs, the activities of representing or interpreting.

Semiotics as a formal study is rooted in our fluctuating awareness of semiosis in day-to-day experience. To be conscious of sign as something distinct from its referent is almost to move from semiosis to semiotics.

Sign consciousness develops as a function of the critical use of signs and involves us spontaneously in the puzzles that semiotics elaborates more formally.

When we see a throne not as a vesture of authority but only as an ornate chair, the flag just as colored cloth, the sign has split. The signifier is estranged from its signified. This splitting induces us to observe a process of semiosis which would not otherwise command attention. Such shifts of perspective are rarely free of emotional entailments. The evidence of spontaneous sign consciousness includes our memories of doubt, amusement, and fantasy connected with the status of signs in our thoughts. Our sense of belonging or alienation can be at stake.

A child distinguishing between dreaming and waking perceptions is checking up on representations. Some of our checking is automatic and doesn't involve sign consciousness, but much does. Language use, for example, is largely automatic and transparent, but it comes into view when we attend to a foreign accent or a rasping or mellifluous voice, encounter new slang, use a dictionary, search for the right phrase, or discover a pun. The fabric of social signs in our environment is sometimes more transparent and sometimes less. A major change in fashion, automobile design, or architecture can induce a dislocation. We attend to signs (the designs of dresses, cars, buildings, as the case may be) that we had the habit of ignoring. Roland Barthes compares the double perception in such moments to noticing a window glass that separates us from whatever we are looking at through it (1972, p. 123).

The passage cited to begin this chapter displays a very sensitive metaphor that Michael Polanyi invented to describe fluctuations of sign consciousness. He suggests that gaining or losing consciousness of signs is like gaining or losing consciousness of our bodies.

Like James H. Bunn (1981), Polanyi speaks here of "tools" rather than signs, but tool overlaps much of what we regard as "sign." Sign consciousness grows as a function of critical thought. Critical thought advances by discipline, by controlling signs. In the first examples that follow, from religion and medical science, the sign comes into awareness through inhibition. In the next section, with examples drawn from drama and song, the sign comes into awareness in a praxis of release.

RESTRAINING THE SIGN

We consider how religion limits the signifier and how science limits the signified. In both cases it appears that the societies involved in these movements of thought were quite conscious of semiotic issues.

Restricting the Signifier

In the absence of sign consciousness, the signifier and signified can seem equivalent. An insult to the flag is an injury to the nation; a deprecation of my mother is as hideous as a bodily hurt. In semiotically uncritical religious belief, no distinction of kind need occur between the divine being and its signifier; the representation is itself accorded a spiritual status. Without sign consciousness words and images can have magic powers; they are not simply stand-ins. In the following passage the adequacy of the sign relation is questioned; its critical posture is blatant.[1] "Thou shalt not make unto thee a graven image, nor any manner of likeness, of any thing that is in heaven above, or that is in the earth beneath, or that is in the water under the earth" (Exodus, 20:3). The commandment is ambiguous in its implications. It suggests on one hand that the image is inadequate as a representation and, on the other hand, that it could be used—but should not be—as a substitute for what it signifies. Lurking behind these slightly different interpretations is a third. The use of the sign is an act of power, not to be abused: "Thou shalt not take the name of the Lord thy God in vain." Unification of the one omnipotent and omniscient God is deeply enmeshed with the restriction of His signifiers. We can hardly doubt that the narrative of Moses, smashing the tablets of written law when he confronts idol worship, expresses an anxiety about the form of the medium as well as the content and the adequacy of their semiosis. Moses descends from the mountain bearing the first artifact of *written language* mentioned in the Bible. The repudiation of the golden sheep thus appears linked to an overall transformation in the semiotic status of his culture.

In biblical history the signifiers of faith become progressively more abstract. The injunction to Abraham to sacrifice a goat instead of his son was an earlier progress in this respect. Later the signs become almost invisible. "Who may enter the temple of the Lord? He that hath clean hands and a pure heart." In this liturgical formula the clean hands are already metaphorical. The pure heart is, of course, invisible. The signifier is being banished from view. It is of further interest that these metaphoric and invisible signs arise in competition with a plethora of explicit and concrete signs furnished by the myriad rules of conduct elaborated in the books that follow Exodus.

The progressive abstraction of symbols in Judaic, Christian, and Islamic tradition supports an increasingly specialized science of interpretation.

The New Testament debates between Jesus and the rabbis as well as the style of teaching by parable are both evidence of the conscious fascination with signs that finds further elaboration in religious commentary throughout the intertwined dialectical traditions of Jewish, Christian, and Islamic scholarship of the Middle Ages.

Of course, I don't mean to suggest that semiotic consciousness in religion is a unique achievement of the West. There is, for example, a passage of the Chandogya Upanishad that seems to beg a reading in same perspective, suggesting a very carefully considered analysis of hierarchical relations within the signifying process, a hierarchy of "name," "speech," "mind," and "will," which might bear comparison with speech, language, concept, and intention (Seventh Prapathaka, Khanda's 1–5, Muller, trans., 1962). I suggest that a common semiotic principle links the rejection of human sacrifice and then of the golden lamb in Genesis to the prescriptions for meditation inculcated here in the Upanishad. In both cases religious thought attempts to move closer to the content of its contemplation by progressively stripping away the layers of expression—the signifiers—which, merely standing for that content, seem to be poor substitutions. But as each signifier is displaced, another signifier is revealed, not the ultimate signified. I understand mysticism as the extreme pole in this direction, pursuing a perception of reality without signs.

It is hardly a surprise that a community intent on divine communion would carefully analyze its channel of communication. Centuries later the Hindu tradition gives rise to an explicit linguistic theory in the writings of Bahardini. He described the sentence as unpacking a unified concept, the *sphota*. (The term is etymologically related to "photon.") The receiver understands a sentence by repacking the separate words into the unified idea.

Restricting the Signified—The Techne Semiotika

The radical revision of medical practice in classical Greece was a restraint in interpretation, a limitation of signifieds. In science, meaning is restricted to lend signs greater precision and thereby to empower operations on them by more certainty. This is what technical language does generally. Early deliberations of semiotic problems in the Greek philosophical tradition arise in considering the symptom as a signifier.

Modern scientific medicine can trace both its power and its alienating character to the circumscription of the fullness of meaning that the symptom carried before the Athenian enlightenment. Although Hippocrates is called "the father of medicine," he was born into a tradition of medical practice that was, in its own terms, well developed. It included the practice of recording detailed case histories. This tradition was religious. Medicine was practiced by a priestly guild. The Hippocratic school broke with tradition in refusing to acknowledge religious signification in the symptom. It is not easy to recapture a sense of the rupture that this change heralded in epistemology. Previously, in Attic culture, the symptom was saturated with meanings, as it remains in cultures not inhibited by Western science.

In pre-Hippocratic medicine the symptom bears witness to the will of the gods; it may furnish prognosis of climate or provide a means of interaction with tribal enemies or prey. As a sign, the suffering body, if properly divined by the doctor-priest, was transparent: All of its significance lay without, in what it stood for. To quash these interpretations meant to invalidate important sources of knowledge and influence.

The Hippocratic revolution made the symptom more opaque. This change did not occur without considerable conscious reflection on the nature of signs. The new doctrine, exhibiting our verbal root, was called the Techne Semiotika, the knowledge of (or art of interpreting) signs. This doctrine insisted that the body's conditions be understood as *self*-evidence.

The symptom became an object to be *interpreted*—understood mediately through correlative evidence—rather than *divined*—understood immediately through spiritual revelation.

Eugen Baer (1975) analyzes the historical echoes of the alienation entailed in Greek scientific medicine and shows us that we have not yet banished its ghosts. Their echoes reverberate in the nineteenth-century appreciation of illness as a stigmata. Susan Sontag uncovers them in her analyses of the tubercular personality in the nineteenth century and the cancer personality in our century (1978). They rebound in full strength when psychoanalysis emerges as a complement to physiological medicine. The course of the patient in insight therapy reverses the discipline of scientific medicine. The patient confronts, in his or her symptoms, a complete opacity, gradually understanding that the symptom can become transparent and that its content can be addressed through alternate signifiers. Gladys Schmitt displays this logic with a sonnet that portrays the psychoanalyst as pre-Hypocratic, more diviner than scientist:

The innocent pigeons flown from lands long lost
With dead men's letters fastened to their feet—
. . . Their missives with their feathers fed the blaze
Yet here and there between the drifts of smoke
I saw a phrase: She sang . . . He wept . . . We spoke . . .
It bloomed . . . Forgive . . . They knew . . . a psalm of praise . . .
The rest is charred. I look at you aghast:
How, in these ashes, could you find my past?
(1979, p. 29)

RELEASING THE SIGN

"How can we know the dancer from the dance?"

—W. B. Yeats, "Among School Children"

When style matters, the sign is enlarged. Yeats's question makes patent
what we all know, that the fluctuation of sign awareness in art is itself a
continual topic of contemplation both for the artist and the audience. The
following examples play with an awareness not only of the sign per se but
also with its relation to our selves, with sign consciousness as self-consciousness.

"What do you read My Lord?"
"Words, words, words"
—*Hamlet* Act II, scene 2

In *Hamlet* semiotic ambiguities are foregrounded and are central to the
drama. From the outset the play's signs are cast in doubt, creating a world
that reflects Hamlet's ambivalence about his knowledge and perceptions.
We are frequently reminded that Elizabethan audiences did not meet
Claudius' ghost with any skepticism, but Hamlet and his friends do. They
see, yet they are not sure what to believe. The play within the play provides
further insecurity, not only because it is a sign of different things to different characters but also because we, the audience, cannot watch it without being reminded that we, ourselves, are watching a play. The tension of
that double perception is purely comic in *Midsummer's Night Dream,* but
here it involves us more deeply in Hamlet's doubt. Something of that edgy
experience is already evoked when Hamlet dwells in his soliloquy on the

possibilities of a life beyond, not a "dream"—false signifier—that will deny us eternal rest.

The pathos of Ophelia's flower scene depends on our recognition of the inadequacy of her signs. The orphaned daughter of a courtier, ruined and rejected by a prince, she is, by the codes of her court, absolutely without recourse. Her inability to influence the destiny of any of the characters who surround her is mirrored by semiotic incapacity. Her madness is the total indirection of her significations in a situation where they cannot obtain any object. They force a bifurcated perception. On one hand, we hear them as representing *that which cannot be expressed*—what is beyond conveying, too distant, too intense (Laertes: "Hadst thou thy wits. . . . It could not move thus. . . . This nothing's more than matter" IV:5, 184–189). On the other hand, we perceive the sign *as an end in itself,* her song, the flowers, the disjointed images are all pathetic and beautiful objects—absolutely opaque—wanting no translation but seeming inherently meaningful.

The ante can go higher. Self-reference in art is a real risk to its texture, something we can note in pictures of pictures of people painting, the play with a stage manager as a character (Thornton Wilder's *Our Town*). Yet many good stage magicians are able to sustain illusions even while reminding us, in their patter, that they are performing deceptions.

More commonly, art or artists refer to themselves in the frames of their work—signatures, picture frames, prologues, introductions, elaborated cadences, final morals, and bows and curtsies, formalities that are signs within or attached to the artwork that indicate the border between art and the rest of our reality. The effects available to art through the manipulation of these self-referential signs can be spectacular. The signature stanza that Huddie (Leadbelly) Ledbetter sings in "The Boll Weevil" is a case in point (Ledbetter, 1967).

> The first time I seen the boll weevil
> He's a-sittin' on the square
> The next time I seen the boll weevil
> He had his whole family there.
>
> Just lookin' for a home.
> Just lookin' for a home.

In form and style, this song is a sad but slightly playful complaint. The fictitious persona, the first person of the song, is—to begin—a cotton farmer who has lost his whole cotton crop to the boll weevil, a much more serious calamity than the understated tune acknowledges. The refrain, "He's lookin' for a home," refers immediately and sympathetically to the weevil, the villain. Here Ledbetter's performance raises the ditty to an artwork. He lengthens the vowel of "home," creating a color luminous and mournful; he makes it a moan but with no heaviness. This outburst of feeling focuses attention on the refrain, somewhat detaching it and making it universal. The farmer, strangely, empathizes with the weevil; we are all "lookin' for a home," villains and victims alike.

But then the performance ends with a formulaic signature stanza, a framing element:

> If they ask you who sung this song,
> Tell them Huddie Leadbelly did and gone.
> He's lookin' for a home. . . .

This partly metalinguistic stanza refers directly to the song itself and obliquely (because in third person) to the performer. The signature stanza, retaining the refrain, identifies Ledbetter himself with the weevil. The impact is double if you know Ledbetter was himself a convict, another homeless villain, finally rescued from jail to make recordings and sing university concerts. The formula could refer to the performer simply as a stage persona, but in this case the mask is off—one more sign is peeled back, we are reminded of his "real life." As this song, first presented as a narrative set elsewhere, expands to represent the here-and-now of performance, what listener does not, at least for a brief instant, become a self-conscious investigator of semiotic paradox?

The alienation Shakespeare and Ledbetter play with is the symptom of a deep disturbance. We are not at peace with our signs. This is the alienation expressed, in the extreme case, by thoughts like "Nobody understands me," "They don't know what I'm really like." This initial alienation gives rise to the illusion—still more alienating—that other people enjoy much more continuous and reliable relations to their own sign costumes and sign environments than ourselves, that others wear a comfortable cloth of signs while our own is constraining and does not show our "true self." In actuality, the signs we use are not good enough to keep us as close in touch with each other as we wish.

One of the attractions of art is the fantasy it sustains of healing the shortfall of our semiotic ability and anesthetizing the frequently painful alienation of semiotic consciousness. The perfected signs of art permit us to acknowledge our self -or semiotic consciousness without feeling cut off from others.

SIGN CONSCIOUSNESS TODAY

In moving our attention from the story it tells to the performance itself, the closing formula of Ledbetter's song is like a stone in a quick creek that throws up a spray and causes us to think "water" instead of "river"; the flow of signs has been turned back to reflect on itself. The sign consciousness induced in the arts dramatizes and enlarges but also typifies our normal sign experience, drawing us into the contemplations of signs, their natures and functions, which make some semiotic consciousness a recurrent element of any intellectual life.

Semiotic conscious waxes and wanes in the evolution of culture. Consciousness of these problems is very prominent in our own time because of the turbulence of our own semiotic environment. A striking witness of that heightened consciousness is the artistic movement known as postmodernism, an aesthetic that characteristically exaggerates sign consciousness.

The flowering of semiotic theory in the twentieth century is a counterpart of the radical revisions of our ideas in physics, the discoveries of unsuspected limitations in mathematics, the revolution in media, and the emergence of a real-world politics. It might even seem that we share a heightened level of sign consciousness today in which we no longer lose track of the boundaries between signs and their objects. I doubt it. Consider finance. Finance is a sign system, an imperfect representation of economic activity, but not the economy itself. Yet how well do we distinguish the two? Is the nation-state merely a construction? (For our academics, an easy yes. How about on the street?) Or advertising. We know advertisements are signs. But are they merely? "Image advertising" would signify its sponsor, but does this always tell us more about contemporary image advertising than we learn about the French court ballet from knowing that it glorified Louis XIV? Both may offer semiosis that exceeds and is little explained by reference to their patrons. Part of the essential pedagogy of the humanities (in its traditional form or the modern variant we call "cultural studies") is to repress sign-consciousness: "This is not just a sign—a poem/ movie/show—it is part of your life."

There is a continual ebb and flow in the level of our sign consciousness as we respond to new obstacles and new facilitations within our signifying activities. In this perspective contemporary semiotics, with all its technical elaboration, simply emerges from our spontaneously heightened sign consciousness as an extended and structured occasion for signs to reflect (on) themselves.

3

CONCEPTS OF SIGN

Chapter 1 indicated some of the difficulties of forming a clear concept of the sign. To rehearse this just a moment, what is a dollar? Is the value it represents a distinct physical entity of any sort? The U.S. treasury bill used to be a sign of the gold it could be redeemed for. What did it become when they quit that? What is an astronomical constellation? What do dollars and signs of the Zodiac have in common?

The quick glance at a few strands in the history of the problem that follows is not a "survey of the literature"; it is a very personal sampler that highlights issues related to the theory undertaken farther on. The history of semiotics has itself grown into a special study in the last 30 years, a study I have no pretension to represent in its breath or integrity.[1]

I would like this chapter to introduce a few ideas about signs that are not my own to any reader who doesn't know them. Ideally, I would like to keep my hands off these brief vignettes and let other authors speak for themselves without imposing a personal framework; yet there is one potential source of confusion that is utterly unproductive. To ward it off, I must warn about a problem in terminology. In the words of Ferdinand de Saussure:

> Our definition of the linguistic sign poses an important question of terminology. I call the combination of a concept and a sound-image a *sign*, but in current usage the term generally designates only a sound-image, . . . the sensory part implies the idea of the whole.
>
> Ambiguity would disappear if the three notions involved here were designated by three names, each suggesting and opposing the others. (1915, p. 67)

What Saussure says here about ambiguity in current usage is still true. His solution, to use the word "sign" to indicate a whole that has two parts—the "signifier," and the "signified"—is not adopted in common speech nor in the technical writing of authors who follow other traditions. It is commonplace to say, for example, that while Saussure conceives the sign as having two parts, Charles S. Peirce conceives it as having three parts, Charles Morris gives it five parts, and Roman Jakobson, in his discussion of function, identifies six parts. This is confused. Peirce sometimes takes word "sign" to mean the whole with three parts, but more often he uses it the way Saussure uses "signifier," meaning one item that combines with, in his case, two others. He has no distinctive term for the whole that comprises all three parts.

As long as we know about this ambiguity, it is usually harmless, and where it can do no harm, I perpetuate the ambiguous practice of saying "sign" for "signifier." Where I want precision, "sign" or "sign-complex" is the whole and "sign factors" are the parts. Contrary to his own practice, I keep Peirce's neologism, "representamen," as a near synonym for "signifier." Using "sign" for both whole and part is an example of *markedness,* like using "man" to mean either "males" or "people." (See chapter 13.) It takes a political movement to eradicate such patterns, not just a good theory!

THE LATIN TRADITION

The extensive medieval Latin language development of semiotic concepts, of which I will say little, draws on older Greek philosophy of which I will say almost nothing—just this: The Greeks had one word for verbal signs and another, similar one for natural signs (like symptoms), but no word for both. We ought not suppose that the preparedness for a unified concept that the English language shows is universal; some people think it is a mistake because the physical correlates of the two types of relations are so different. (See chapter 12.)

The student who goes further in medieval semiotics than I do will need to be alert to separate conventional formulas from deliberated ideas and to distinguish by-the-way remarks from more thorough attempts to get at central issues. The mode of writing in this period, which hides disagreements in exfoliating commentaries on commentaries, makes us outsiders very reliant on experts. But here is something that seems nearly plain. From William of Ockham:

Spoken words are used to signify the very things that are signified by concepts of the mind, so that a concept primarily and naturally signifies something and a spoken word signifies the same thing secondarily. . . . Nevertheless, to silence hairsplitters it should be pointed out that the word "sign" has two different senses. In one sense a sign is anything which when apprehended brings something else to mind. Here, a sign need not, as has been shown elsewhere, enable us to grasp the thing signified for the first time, but only after we have some sort of habitual knowledge of the thing. In this sense of "sign" the spoken word is a natural sign of a thing, the effect is a sign of its cause, and the barrel hoop is a sign of wine in the tavern. However, I have not been using the term "sign" in this wide sense. In another sense a sign is anything which (1) brings something to mind and can supposit for that thing; (2) can be added to a sign of this sort in a proposition (e.g., syncategorematic expressions, verbs, and other parts of speech lacking a determinate signification); or (3) can be composed of things that are signs of either sort (e.g., propositions.) Taking the term "sign" in this sense, the spoken word is not the natural sign of anything. *Summa Logicae,* (c.1300/1974, pp. 31–32.)

"Syncategorematic"—words like "the." Syncategorematic terms were understood to have no "meaning" of their own but to determine meanings or relations for other terms. "Supposits"—takes a particular reference. The horticultural and affective references of "rue" are different "suppositions" of the same sign. "Natural"—the opposition of nature and artifice is woven all through the history of semiotics as it is through the whole history of Western thought. Here, concepts which must resemble their objects (cf. images,) are regarded as "natural." Words, which, learned by training, need not resemble their objects, are "artificial."

The apex of Latin semiotics occurs, according to John Deely (1982), in the Iberian Schools that extended the medieval tradition well into the seventeenth century; here he reports we find semiotics integrated with a well-developed theory of relations. Deely makes a compelling case for the continuing relevance of this work. The importance of the Latin tradition to us today depends in part on how we regard the reaction against it that began in the Renaissance and that we may see, for example, in the philosophy of John Locke.

JOHN LOCKE

Locke's work reflects the Newtonian revolution in physics; his aim was to carry its reliance on observation and its tolerance into philosophy. Explaining the actions of signs serves, for him, to show how experience rather than scripture can account for our knowledge.

Locke's summation at the end of *An Essay Concerning Human Understanding* (1690/1964) is frequently cited as the first use in English of the term "semiotics." In this passage he proposes that all human knowledge is of three types. The first is knowledge of things as they are in themselves—physics, in its broadest interpretation. The second is knowledge of what we should do—in a very broad sense, ethics. Semiotics is his third type. (Actually, while the passage is in English, the term, as you see, retains its Greek orthography. I do not have any idea where the English usage first occurs; presumably in a later source than this one.)

> All that can fall within the compass of human understanding, being either, *First,* the nature of things, as they are in themselves, their relations, and their manner of operation; or, *Secondly,* that which man himself ought to do, as a rational and voluntary agent, or, *Thirdly,* the ways and means whereby the knowledge of both the one and the other of these are attained and communicated; I think science may be divided properly into these three sorts: . . . *First, Physica.* . . . *Secondly, Practica.* . . . *Thirdly,* Σημει–ωτιη . . . the third branch may be called Σημειωτιη or the doctrine of signs: the most usual whereof being words. (Book IV: xxi, p. 443)

The word "sign," per se, does not play a very extended role in Locke's inquiry, but the concept is nevertheless pivotal. Although he does mention diagrams and other representations as types of signs occasionally, Locke means chiefly words and ideas when he mentions signs:

> Truth, then, seems to me, in the proper import of the word, to signify nothing but *the joining or separating of Signs, as the Things signified by them do agree or disagree one with another.* The joining or separating of signs here meant is what by another name we call *proposition.* So that truth properly belongs only to propositions; whereof there are two sorts of signs commonly made use of, viz. ideas and words. (Book IV:5, p. 354)

Locke observes that words combined form propositions but that ideas combined without words are so chimerical that we cannot really talk about mental propositions of pure ideas (images). The split between mind and matter suggested here is very prominent in the *Essay.* Locke, writing at the beginning of modern scientific materialism and attempting to find a basis for knowledge that was founded on observation, had to regard the sign as a category that was partly mental and partly nonmental. With words and ideas, his notion of signs is split down the middle. With this split, Locke imposed the Cartesian duality of mind and matter on semiotics. Split this way, semiotics is rather feeble. The scientific outlook that developed after Locke had little use for a unified understanding of signs. To the best of my knowledge, the first author who addressed this is issue tenaciously within semiotics was Charles Peirce, two centuries later. Even Charles Morris, who was greatly inspired by Peirce and among the first to expound and develop Peirce's doctrine, echoes Locke in this respect.

CHARLES MORRIS

Charles Morris provides a formulation of semiotic problems oriented by the positivism of the Vienna School. The following definition, from one of Morris's last books, *Signification and Significance* (1964), is quite close to and consistent with the view he advanced much earlier in his programmatic, "Foundations of the Doctrine of Signs," (1938/1971). In the passage that follows, defining a sign-complex of five factors, the algebraic letters serve only to emphasize that Morris takes the word "relation" in a mathematical sense; the algebraic form is naught but a stylistic ornament.

> Semiosis (or sign process) is regarded as a five-term relation, v, w, x, y, z, in which v [a sign] sets up, in w [an interpreter], a disposition to react in a certain kind of way, x [the interpretant], to a certain kind of object, y [the signification], (not then acting as a stimulus), under certain conditions, z [the context]. (p. 9)

His first example immediately follows:

> Karl von Frisch has shown that a bee which finds nectar is able on returning to the hive, to "dance" in such a way as to direct other bees to the food source. In this case the dance is the sign; the other bees affected by the dance are the interpreters; the disposition to react in a certain kind of way by these bees, because of the dance, is the interpretant; the kind of object [nectar] toward which the bees are prepared to act in this way is the signification of the sign; and the position of the hive is part of the context. (p. 11)

The example makes it clear that the definition of semiosis presented and the definition of sign suggested do not predicate mind. Morris is tenacious in keeping mental entities out of the picture:

> while this formulation is behavioral and such sign behavior is open to objective study, an organism may experience and, in the case of human beings at least, may report on its own sign behavior. Nevertheless, a behavioral formulation is more basic than a self-observational formulation, since semiotic must deal with sign processes in animals, in children prior to the acquisition of language, and in personality disturbances where self-observational reports are absent or unreliable. (p. 3)

Morris's notice of context as a sign factor and his formulation of definitions of syntax (the relations of signs to each other), semantics (the relations of signs to their objects), and pragmatics (the relations of signs to their interpretants—the effects of signs) remain influential.

ARTIFICIAL LANGUAGES—LEIBNITZ AND FREGE

The project of inventing languages to resolve or to investigate the problems inherent in natural language is another source of conceptions of sign.

The earliest elaborate proposal for a formal language was Gottfried Leibnitz's *Characteristic Universalis*. It was to have three divisions, the *ars characteristica*, which would name things and concepts unequivocally, an *ars combinatoria*, which would formulate propositions, and an *ars rationes*, which would calculate new discoveries from these propositions. The project was intended optimistically as a practicable means to improve communication and knowledge. This idea of artificial language as a practical working tool has survivals in Esperanto, in computer languages, and in attempts to purify scientific discourse of vagueness and hidden premises. (Morris's "Foundations for a General Doctrine of Signs" was that sort of project.) There is another use for artificial languages that inverts their function, and that is to take them as an object of study rather than just as a tool. In this role artificial languages provide models for the investigation of logic, thought, natural language, and mathematics.

In contemporary logic, artificial languages descend historically from the algebra of propositions of George Boole, who did not regard the *Laws of Thought* he published in 1854 as a purely abstract adventure but as an in-

Figure 3.1   Frege's manner of graphing logic

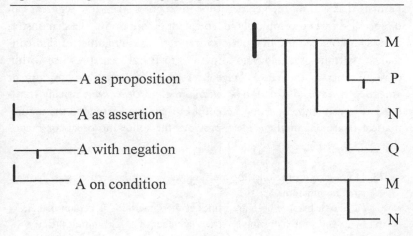

vestigation of the patterns of human reason and, thereby, the logic of divine creation (Gowri, 1991). The decisive intersection with semiotic occurs in the work of Gottlob Frege, the first to analyze subject and predicate as function and argument, whose studies of the logic of arithmetic lead him back to the study of ordinary language. Frege (1879/1969) invented graphic symbols for logical calculation, a sample of which are shown as figure 3.1. (I do not have space to discuss the system, except to remark that each element, that is, the vertical and horizontal line segments, has a precise meaning and that such figures, in combination, permit an exact accounting for the derivations of propositions.) The eighth element that Frege introduces in his system is "identity of content." This occasions his following observation:

> Identity of content differs from conditionality and negation in that it applies to names and not to contents. Whereas in other contexts signs are merely representatives of their content, so that every combination in which they enter expresses only a relation between their respective contents, they suddenly display their own selves when they are combined by means of the sign for identity of content; for it expresses the circumstance that two names have the same content. Hence the introduction of a sign for identity of content necessarily produces a bifurcation in the meaning of all signs; they stand at times for their content, at times for themselves. (pp. 20–21)

Frege provides an example that is a bit too complex to include here. It's point is that within one geometrical construction, the same segment can be specified by two completely independent descriptions. The demonstration is striking because it appears to transfer the ambiguities of sign consciousness from psychology to structure, to reveal their presence within pure, abstract mathematics. Frege later retreated from this position, or amended it via his distinction between *Sinn* and *Bedeutung,* usually translated as "sense" and "meaning." Rudolf Carnap, who extended the mathematical treatment of these ideas provides the following précis of Frege's theory:

28–1. The two expressions "the morning star" and "the evening star" have the same nominatum.
This holds because both are names of the same thing, a certain planet; in other words, the following is a true statement of an astronomical fact:
28–2. The morning star is the same as the evening star.
On the other hand, the following holds:
28–3. The expressions "the morning star" and "the evening star" have not the same sense.
The reason for this is that the two expressions refer to their common nominatum, that planet, in different ways. If we understand the language, then we can grasp the sense of the expressions. . . . The nominatum is not, however, given by the sense but only, as Frege puts it, illuminated from one side. (1958, p. 119)

Frege's conception of the sign-complex is tripartite: signifier, sense, and meaning. Having worked this concept out for mathematical expressions and applied it to words and noun phrases, he extended it to sentences as a whole, concluding that the ordinary "sense" of a declarative sentence is the proposition it asserts; the ordinary "meaning or nominatum" of that sentence is its truth value. (A refutation of this result can be found in an appendix to Bertrand Russell's *Principles of Mathematics,* 1903/1956).

LINGUISTICS—SAUSSURE

Ferdinand de Saussure (1915/1966) formulated a conception of semiotics for the purpose of clarifying the subject and methods of linguistics. The concept of semiotics ("semiology" in his terminology) oriented linguistic study distinctly and separately from physiological phonetics, ethnology, anthropology, philology, and other disciplines that interacted with the study of language but which, from his point of view, did not center on its essence. The results of his analysis, though offered only as a description of language, have, as he predicted, served to clarify the study of a broad range of signs. Saussure's theoretical framework for the sign gave a specific content to two ideas that otherwise might have remained vague, the idea of a sign system and the idea of a social fact.

The fulcrum of his analysis is the distinction between "language" and "speech":

> But what is language [*langue*]? It is not to be confused with human speech [*parole*] of which it is only a definite part, though certainly an essential one. It is both a social product of the faculty of speech and a collection of necessary conventions that have been adopted by a social body to permit individuals to exercise that faculty. Taken as a whole, speech is many-sided and heterogeneous; straddling several areas simultaneously—physical, physiological, and psychological—it belongs both to the individual and to society; we cannot put it into any category of human facts, for we cannot discover its unity.
>
> Language, on the contrary, is a self-contained whole. . . .
>
> In separating language from speaking we are at the same time separating: (1) what is social from what is individual; and (2) what is essential from what is accessory and more or less accidental. . . . [language] is the social side of speech . . . ; it exists only by virtue of a sort of contract signed by the members of a community. (p. 9, 14)

We have already noted that Saussure understood the sign-complex as duple, but his two-part analysis of the sign is only a preamble. The idea that fired the structuralist imagination is that the single sign cannot stand alone. For Saussure, it must be part of a *system*, Neither the signified nor the signifier are independent entities for Saussure.

SEMIOTICS AS A FOUNDATION
FOR PHILOSOPHY—CHARLES PEIRCE

Charles Peirce stands alone in the persistence, scope, and invention that he brought to bear on the problem of constructing the idea of "mind" *within* a theory of signs.

Here, from his later writings, are what we might be tempted to call "subjective" and "objective" definitions of the sign, but the point is that they are interchangeable. Peirce preferred the second, which is more abstract and more readily connected with his own mathematical studies, not because it is more objective but because it is more clearly foundational. "A sign, or *representamen,* is something which stands to somebody for something in some respect or capacity. It addresses somebody, that is, creates in the mind of that person an equivalent sign, or perhaps a more developed sign. That sign which it creates I call the *interpretant* of the first sign." (CP 2.228; 1955 p. 99)[2] The next definition, rather than presuming the idea of person or mind, presents a relational framework from which a concept of mind can be constructed.

> A sign, or Representamen, is a First which stands in such a genuine triadic relation to a Second, called its *Object,* as to be capable of determining a Third, called its *Interpretant,* to assume the same triadic relation to its *Object* in which it stands itself to the same Object. The triadic relation is *genuine,* that is its three members are bound together by it in a way that does not consist in any complexus of dyadic relations. (CP 2.274; 1955 pp. 99–100)

Peirce intended to resolve the duality of mind and matter by according a more foundational role to relations than to mind or matter separately. His notion of triadic relations entails the "interpretant," the third sign factor just mentioned, a word we have already seen adapted by Morris. His early understanding of it is explained in a paper of 1867, "On a New List of Categories":

> The occasion of reference to a correlate is obviously by comparison. . . . Suppose we wish to compare the letters p and b. We may imagine one of them to be turned over on the line of writing as an axis, then laid upon the other, and finally to become transparent so that the other can be seen through it. In this way we will form a new image which mediates between the images of the two letters, inasmuch as it represents one of them to be (when turned over) the likeness of the other. Again, suppose we think of a murderer as being in relation to a murdered person; in this case we conceive the act of the murder . . . and thus we resort again to a mediating representation which represents the relate as standing for a correlate with which the mediating representation is itself in relation. Again, suppose we look . . . [up] the word *homme* in a French . . . [-English] dictionary; we shall find opposite to it the word *man,* which, so placed, represents *homme* as repre-

senting the same two-legged creature which *man* itself represents. By a further accumulation of instances, it would be found that every comparison requires, besides the related thing and the correlate, also a *mediating representation which represents the relate to be a representation of the same correlate which this mediating representation itself represents.* Such a mediating representation may be termed an interpretant, because it fulfills the office of an interpreter, who says that a foreigner says the same thing which he himself says. (p. 291–292).

Some observations on this passage: The first interpretant, a continuous transformation of one letter to coincide with the other, is a mental entity that doesn't duplicate any actual nonmental entity. The second interpretant, the conception of an act (the act of murder) is a mental entity that we believe to correspond to a nonmental entity. The third interpretant, the dictionary's spatial juxtaposition of terms, is not in the first instance a mental entity. The interchangeability of these three cases is characteristic for Peirce, reflecting his sense that understanding the universe as a structure of signs would obviate the division between mind and matter. His investigation of experience includes the real world as perceived in experience, and his investigation of the real world includes experiences as they occur in the real world.

THE SIGN AS A SOCIAL FACT—THE PRAGUE CIRCLE

The Prague Circle, which flourished in the 1930s, adopted the concept of sign as a method of orienting its enormously wide-ranging research, which included all aspects of linguistics as well as artistic and social criticism. Members absorbed and in some measure depended on Saussure's ideas, but their work could hardly seem more distant from his in temper and method. This was a semiotics of altogether new purpose. Geographically and temporally, they labored on a fragile island between Joseph Stalin and Adolph Hitler, and from this island they surveyed the problem of the free unfolding of culture as a matter of universal human urgency. The sign was the concept that gave unity to culture across the boundaries of history, geography, and economy. No social expression could be foreign to their interest. Where detail of structural exegesis is concerned, their greatest theorist was, I believe, Roman Jakobson. In the matter of setting the firmest conceptual arch over the global phenomenon of culture, the most compelling voice is perhaps Jan Mukarovsky's. In his work, in Jakobson's, and in their colleagues' in the circle, art emerges for the first time as a primary subject of semiotic analysis. The concept of the sign permitted them to forge a methodology in art criticism that could synthesize Marxian insights and historical and ethnological relativism with a deeply felt sympathy for diverse human values.

> the basic constitution of the individual consciousness, even at its innermost levels, derives from content belonging to the collective consciousness. . . . any mental content that exceeds the bounds of the individual consciousness acquires the character of a sign by the very fact of its communicability. . . . In fact all sciences known as humanities . . . deal with phenomena that have the more or less pronounced character of signs due to their double existence both in the world of sense perception and in the collective consciousness. (Matejka and Titunik, 1976, p. 9)

The studies of the Prague School, which at their best are profound, are studies of structure and meaning that enormously increase the urgency and import of semiotic studies. A semiotics that omits the notion of structure that emerges with Saussurian linguistics invites vagueness. A semiotics that fails to acknowledge the discrepancy between what signs designate and what they tell about it—designation and meaning, object and interpretant, or what my generation painfully rediscovered as "difference"—courts superficiality. A semiotics that does not take up the challenge of the Prague Circle to reflect on the central issues of culture risks sterility. Does this heritage lend itself to theoretical consolidation? We must narrow our focus in some respects, as the next chapter proposes to do.

4

CRITICAL PHENOMENA OF SEMIOSIS

From this experiment we conclude that the dancing bees tell each other not only about the presence of food but also about the kind of flower in which it can be found. . . . The scout can tell how far its mates will have to fly . . . and which direction . . . the beehive is a most interesting example of a society. . . . The only limitation to our admiration is the fact that this social unit is governed not by an idea consciously pursued but by inborn urges manifesting themselves in rigidly fixed behavior patterns.

—Karl von Frisch, *Man and the Living World*

By way of an introduction, the first three chapters engaged a range of problems linked to semiotics by different authors and by my own musing. This chapter orients the particular tack of the rest of this book and explains what I hope it will gain.

The key question here, for me, is: What sorts of phenomena will we understand better in the perspective of semiotics than we could without it? Karl von Frisch, quoted above, was the discoverer of the bees' "language"; yet his own reflections might give us pause: Is this a "language" that can be better appreciated with semiotic analysis?

Semiotics develops a perspective, that is, a way of regarding or describing things. We need hardly expect that the question What is its proper subject matter? would have a hard and fast answer. I own a pair of binoculars that are just fine for looking at birds. They don't seem to be of much use for stargazing or reading fine print, but who knows what may come into view? The birds do not define the binoculars. For a definition, lenses, focal lengths, magnification, and such do better. But the purpose of looking at birds may well select and determine the binoculars. What do we want to look at in the perspective of semiotics? What are the phenomena about which we will not realize our maximum capacity for insight unless we have recourse to semiotics? Such matters are what I call the critical phenomena of semiotics.

As the criterion of insight does lend itself to logical definition, I can answer the question only in rough terms and with as much reliance on rhetoric as on logic, not pretending that a matter of opinion is a matter of fact. Basically, I will argue that we need not concern ourselves with phenomena that are well accounted for by physics nor with phenomena that seem adequately described by biology. Our business is the conscious mind. Some readers will find this attitude commonsensical, but in fact it is controversial, and other readers will find it superficial. For this reason, the first two of the sections following acknowledge the positions I reject. The remainder of the chapter expresses the position I adopt and defines the tasks of the rest of the book.

PHYSICAL, BIOLOGICAL, AND SEMIOSIC PHENOMENA

Are tides and erosion signs? First, let us ward off the literary ploy that goes like this: "Indeed the tide is a sign! It can be a symbol of inevitability, as in Shakespeare, 'There is a tide in the affairs of men.'" This is not to the point. Anything can be *taken* as a sign, but the question here is not about taking. My question is: Is the tide a sign before we take it one way or another? I say not.

Yet there are two arguments, similar but worth distinguishing, that tides and erosion are semiotic phenomena. The first and more profound construes all phenomena that exhibit continuity or regularity as participating in the principles of sign relations.

This viewpoint is made explicit in John Deely (1990) and has, as he demonstrates, roots in Peirce and in Latin philosophy. A version of the conception that the physical universe has inherent, idealike constituents appears in Henry Stapp's (1993) interpretation of quantum mechanics. I am not at all inclined either to endorse such a conception nor to dismiss the viewpoint that it captures. The impetus behind Stapp's investigations is metaphysical, however. Regarding natural processes as signlike in themselves adds nothing at all to what chemistry and physics tell us about tides or erosion or atomic particles. At best, it gives us another way of visualizing facts we already knew. (Neither is such speculation a way to discover "what signs really are," for what signs really are is up to us to decide.)

The second and more trivial but, alas, more commonplace way to maintain that tides and erosion are semiotic simply recirculates the notion that everything we encounter in our experience is a "representation," an idea constructed by our minds. Although it is salutary to be reminded from time to time that all our notions of the world may be subject to disagreements and changes, this second point of view is otherwise unproductive. It is as if, before each sentence of this chapter, I inserted the words "In English one might say that. . . ." It wouldn't be a lie. It is true, also, that the book would be different if it were not composed in English. But we have little to learn in being continuously reminded of this limitation. It is similarly true that our thoughts might be considered representations (not my position in part III), but that doesn't make it useful to regard the physical world as a sign. Common sense asks: A sign of what? A sign to whom? Common sense is rightly skeptical: Semiotics can leave the subject matter of physics to physicists. (The related problem, how perception and semiosis are related, is addressed in chapter 12.)

Is bee language a sign? Thomas Sebeok, (for example, 1994) has won wide prominence for his principle that life and semiosis mutually entail one another. That is, there can be no life without sign processes and no sign processes without life. The intriguing descriptions of quasi-artistic production among birds and mammals he has compiled and the play activities of social animals that he analyses as equivalent to name making are only the culmination of semiotic functions that he traces back to the transfer of information in DNA. Yet we have ask what, if anything, we learn about these phenomena by attributing semiotic descriptions to them. Has the semiotician any news for the biologist or the ethologist?

It is more convenient and pleasant to describe honeybee communication as a "language" than to describe it in stimulus-response terms, but the facts are such, so far as we know them about honeybees, that the "language" metaphor is simply an ornamentation of the more mechanical description. It adduces no further insight.

So it is generally with semiotic attributions to biological relations. The word "recognize" is another semiotically flavored term that is used as loosely as "language" and seems to promote the same confusion. The strictest interpretation would emphasize the root (cogito, cognize) as embodying an a priori hypothesis of mentality. Yet we speak rather loosely of an enzyme or an antibody "recognizing" its target, which, again, suggests merely a fancy way of talking chemical reactions. The in-between cases are quite a muddle. Take this example, which will be all too familiar to some readers. Cockroaches, one of the most primitive and ancient animals, seem to have a really uncanny ability to "recognize danger" and evade assault. When you try to swat a cockroach with a newspaper, it seems sometimes to catch a telepathic clue. But the roach escape mechanism is known. Its underbelly has tiny hairs that are projections from nerve cells whose dendrites extend directly into the leg muscles. These hairs are sensitive to air pressure waves that are excited along the surface the bug is standing on as soon as the newspaper begins to move, an early response system of the quickest sort—just one nerve cell. Although Charles Morris might insist that the air pressure wave is a vehicle representing the newspaper—its object—and the muscle activation an interpretant; although Peirce might argue that this interpretant represents the newspaper to the roach in the same way the airwaves did, we are still dealing with a phenomenon that seems exhaustively explained by biology. The overcoat of semiotic terminology does not illuminate it any further.

Part of the problem here is the difficulty of saying what life is. There may be some allure in the illusion that we get a better idea what the essence of life is when we describe it semiotically, speaking of the "language" of DNA or the "messages" of the immune system. Not so. The underlying relations fail to identify life. We could say "The swelling river *tells* the ocean that the mountains had heavy snows." This metaphor is available in any situation where A causes B and B causes C. We can then make out B (high river) to be a sign of A (mountain snow) to C (the attentive ocean). Ridiculous, to be sure. But how is the dance "language" of the bees any different?

WHAT ARE THE CRITICAL PHENOMENA

The point of specifying some critical phenomena for semiotics is not to set boundaries. When we want to say where a mountain is, we usually supply the location of its peak, not its perimeter. Our pursuit here is analogous. Such commonalities as "communication," "transmission of information," "recognition," "signification" will not do to point out the peak.

In his treatise *A Theory of Semiotics*, Umberto Eco proposes *lying* as the critical phenomenon of semiotics (though not in those terms. He recalls the term "proprium"—unique property—from medieval logic, 1976, p. 57) In his formulation, wherever there is the possibility of lying, we have a sign. In Eco's analysis, lying is inexplicable without a theory of semiotics. This suggestion is delightful, but the definition works only if we presuppose a mental context.

Otherwise, why should we not regard a vaccination as a lie? The vaccination instructs the body to respond to a disease that is not present. Sometimes we speak of a deceptive person as a chameleon, and why not? Every example of natural camouflage is a form of lying. As before, these cases *can* be described as sign transactions, even the vaccination (vehicle—vaccine, object—pathogen, interpretant—antibody), but again our understanding of the phenomenon is not thereby improved.

The difference is obvious. Eco has deliberate, intentional lying in view. Where the biological and physical explanations prove in principle unsatisfying is where we want a perspective that captures the idea of mental life: consciousness, will, intention, fantasy, understanding and misunderstanding. Our claim to fame in a nutshell will be to deal with mind, not to say what a mind is, but to clarify in some small measure what it means to use one. Our minds are so much dependent on socialization that it may seem hairsplitting to align semiotics with mind rather than, as Eco does, with culture. The difference for me is, first, that I remain open to the possibility that animals, perhaps even very lowly ones, may have a conscious mental life, and it may quite exceed their culture. I don't know how to tell. Second, if we become able to say in a reasonable way what a sign is, we can derive a notion of culture therefrom as a collection of signs. Eco wants the reverse derivation. He defines the object (signified) of a sign as a "cultural unit," but having no prior, independent suggestion what culture is, this seems vaguer to me.

The phenomena I take as truly critical for semiotics all involve conscious mental life and are all complicated. In reviewing some of these I revert now and then, as before, to the comparison of biological and semiotic descriptions as suggestive of a threshold. The comparison brings out the role of mind.

1. Natural language. Natural language is a semiotic phenomenon par excellence, and, indeed, Saussure had to "invent" semiology to make sense of it. As a counterbalance, I am particularly interested in phenomena that are not logically dependent on language. The following seem to me good candidates: radical individuation, hypothesis, and deliberation.

2. Radical individuation. The individuals of a biological species diverge very widely in their genetic makeup and metabolic function, but they have an overall unity of form such that an explanation of the biological processes of one member of the species will apply to the others. In the vast preponderance of sign production one can argue that the same rule applies. For example, sentences in language permit a unity of description in that their references can be deduced, in principle, from a finite vocabulary and syntax. Most conversations are routine. Greek vases vary but perhaps no more than orchid species. However, we do not find within the biological differences of individuals the type of diversity that is exemplified by, for example, the nine symphonies of Beethoven or by nine different interpretations of the French Revolution. These differ radically: in organization, function, and form.

   Despite this, we comprehend them. We make sense of James Joyce and e.e. cummings as well as of Edward Gibbon, and we very insistently differentiate between understanding and misunderstanding them.

   In the aggregate, our production and reception of radically individuated texts or artifacts is a phenomenon that will make more sense when analyzed in terms of semiotics. (See especially chapter 15.)

3. Hypothesis. We should, from semiotics, expect a picture of mental life that integrates knowledge with hypothesis. A hypothesis represents a state of affairs regardless of whether that state of affairs exists or does not exist. ("I won't go to the museum today because if it rains next Sunday we could go to the museum instead of the zoo.") The semiotic pregnance of hypothesis seems self-evident; however, there are some biological structures that could be described in the same terms. Whatever there is in the neurology of a lady toad that prepares her to respond to the song of a gentleman toad exists whether the song does or not get sung, and this preparatory capacity might possibly be said to represent the song and so might be called a hypothesis. To put more distance between ourselves and toads, let us consider more specific manifestations of hypotheses.

   a. Ethical commitments. People bind their behavior by codes of general principles that cannot be described as "conditioned reflexes" because they require continuous interpretation. These principles typically rely on hypotheses. ("If thine eye offend thee. . . .") In ethical principles the situations to which hypotheses apply are only roughly indicated. Their interpretations rest open.

b. Plans. What is the difference between an irrigation ditch and a riverbed? I should say that the first, unlike the second, must have a plan or purpose. I think it is impossible to define "irrigation ditch" in such a way that the definition could serve to distinguish all irrigation ditches from all other natural and man-made riverbeds without using a concept like "purpose." A plan is not a physical object, but, like a moral code, it can constrain physical relations.

c. Fictions. Things that could not exist play a large role in our lives. The distinctive role of representation comes into view with the highly specific yet limitlessly varied character of the fictions we invent. Fictions do not, by the way, presuppose spoken languages.

d. Inference. Here is a hot potato. I can't hold on to it or hold forth on it very long, but we must take a look. Inference is one of the classical problems of philosophy and touches the earliest literature we might call semiotic. Inference is not the same as implication. Given two premises of a syllogism, we can infer what they imply. Peirce offers a much celebrated division of inference into three types (instead of the more usual two): deduction, induction, and his third, abduction. Abduction is the invention of hypotheses from which facts could be accounted for by deduction. Aristotle called this the discovery of the middle term. For example (his), if the earth were round, we could account for the lunar eclipse in terms of its shadow.

4. Deliberation. Deliberation is tied closely to hypothesis and inference but involves distinctive constructions (discussed further in chapter 22). We say we deliberate when we decide among alternatives by thinking about them.

PLAN OF THE WORK

Language, radical individuation (particularly as we see it in art, ritual, and customs), hypothesis, and deliberation are the sorts of phenomena that motivate semiotics. Insight about such phenomena is our goal; those are not, however, the topics that organize the book. The plan derives from the two tasks that these phenomena highlight, to characterize representation as a relation in consciousness and to track the principles which lead from simple to elaborate signs. Elaboration is a theme of part II where ideas that have proven fecund in understanding the structured aspect of signs salient in language and discernible also in mathematics, music, architecture, and elsewhere are reviewed. Part II employs no adequate idea what a sign is. Part III develops a conception of the sign and assumes a stance vis-à-vis mentality. Part IV, returning to the theme of elaboration, can then treat structures as signs. In part V there is a partial turn from theory to analysis. A comparative perspective is developed with emphasis on artistic signs.

Parts II through V together are meant to fill out the ideas announced on page 3 by the definitions in the first paragraph of chapter 1. By way of a conclusion, part VI essays responses to some of the anxieties alluded to in the second paragraph of that same chapter to illustrate the interaction of semiotics with other discourses.

PART II

Sign Systems

Systematic structure is so nearly ubiquitous in signs that it may be more informative to begin with counterexamples: the heart figure, ♥, and the nearly extinct barber pole. In a former time, that red-and-white spiral was part of a loose family of "logos," guild emblems, that identified trades, but each of these signs was utilized independently. They did not combine into larger "sentences" or depend on each other for identity or meaning. Some vocabularies, such as letters or words or notes, build combinations; the units in others function independently.

Our main traffic light signals in Toronto are red, green, yellow, and flashing green, a simple vocabulary. No larger signifying units arise by combining two or more signals. The commands a dog knows might seem to make a system to the trainer, but to the dog, perhaps each one is an independent, self-contained unit, with a few exceptions perhaps for some complex sequences. Similar signs do not necessarily comprise a vocabulary. Beepers, bells, and buzzers, as for example in doorbells, telephone rings, clock alarms, and belt pagers, are similar but do not comprise a systematic vocabulary. In contrast, the meaning of a sentence is not just the sum of the meanings of its words. The meaning of a total position in chess is more than the sum of the meanings of the position of each piece.

To begin the study of semiotics on the side of system rather than on the side of signification, as we do here, is partly arbitrary. To begin the study of semiotic system with linguistics, rather than with Vetruvius's analysis of architecture, axiomatics in math, harmony in music theory, or the instructions of the ten bamboo school of Chinese painting may be arbitrary a second time. Language is the most domineering species in the "semiosphere" (Lotman, 1976) much as *Homo sapiens* is in the biosphere, but biology does not need to start with humans.

But the choice is only partly arbitrary. Before Saussure's systematic account of language we had no practical principles to compare the structures of the other systems with each other. Although semiotics draws on ancient philosophical currents, its twentieth-century flowering was strongly characterized by initiatives in linguistics and literary studies. This is not the historical current of thought that provides the best conception of the sign. In that respect, philosophy offers more than linguistics. But it was ideas of system emerging from linguistics that most dynamically connected the philosophy of signs to the concrete data of culture. Chapter 5 reviews the notion of system that emerges from Saussure's Linguistics. Chapter 6, considering counterproposals aiming at a more comprehensive view of language than Saussure's, argues that these can not supplant his. Chapter 7 enlarges the idea of system to encompass grammar with its psychological entailments. Chapter 8, after reviewing a radical rebuttal of the postulate of systems, provides a framework for crediting their reality.

5

VOCABULARY

Saussure's *Course in General Linguistics* (hereafter *CGL*) (1915/1966), the main matter of this chapter, is a posthumous compilation of his students' notes, with some consequent duplication and disorganization, and is a mere 200 pages, of which the last third seems generally ignored. But it was certainly the right book at the right moment, judging by its influence. The book's main argument is that the essence of language is its systematic character. This is the fundamental perspective of structuralism. Saussure speculates briefly on the possibility of semiotics ("semiology") as an independent discipline, but his analytical purview is really restricted to language.

This chapter joins a chain of précises of and commentaries on the *CGL*. Among several theoretical works that have greater or lesser dependence on his thought, the *Prolegomena to a Theory of Language* (1943/1961) by Louis Hjelmslev stands out for its extraordinary level of abstraction and inner consistency. It is modeled on formal logic and recalls the style of Ludwig Wittgenstein's *Tractatus*. If it had no other merit, it would demand the semiotician's attention on aesthetic grounds as a work of exceptional elegance. Roland Barthes's *Elements of Semiology* (1968) is a commentary on Saussure and Hjelmslev. Barthes's elaborate and probing literary theories and social criticism often are expressed in paradoxes and epigrams, transgressing the border between academic and poetic language in a continuous and extraordinarily forceful assault on the prejudices of conventional knowledge. His *Elements,* approaching the neutrality of a textbook, stands apart from much of his oeuvre. His formulation takes all semiotics to be an extension of linguistics, a view opposite to mine. (References to or citations from Saussure, Hjelmslev, and Barthes in this chapter are to the books just mentioned.)

The chief novelties of the *CGL* were, first, its conception of language as an *autonomous* social system and, second, its elaboration of a theory of language framed strictly in terms of this conception. Saussure's schema is conventionally understood as a series of dichotomies:

Speech/Language
(pronouncing/writing)
Signifier/Signified
Signification/Value
Association/Combination
Diachronic/Synchronic

The schematic character of the project is telegraphed to us by its reliance on polarities. Polarities ward off "gray areas." We can anticipate a problem in the relation of the concept to reality just on this basis. Saussure proposed to resolve this difficulty through his first dichotomy.

SPEECH AND LANGUAGE

Chapter 3 noted this first premise. "Speech" (French, *parole*) is what we actually write or say. "Language" (*langue*) is the underlying social system that determines the identities and meanings of words and their combinations. Language, although more abstract, is as real as concrete speech. Our ability to understand each other despite differences of situation and pronunciation proves the fact of our underlying agreement on ground rules. Every individual has his or her style or quirks, but language is superpersonal and autonomous. No individual can decide its continuously changing course.

It is not that language is immune from external pressures. When social groups merge or when one people conquers another, their languages will influence each other. But, Saussure shows, this influence occurs only between the interior systems of the languages preserving the autonomy of the languages vis-à-vis their external environment; hence the influence is unpredictable. Who would have foreseen that in consequence of the U.S. bombing Baghdad, North Americans would now speak of "The mother of all deficits" and like phrases.[1] Similarly, technological invention alters languages yet does not set the nature of the change. Where one language will devise a compound term from current diction (airplane), another will borrow from its ancient roots (French, *avion,* from Latin, *avis,* bird) and a third import foreign coinage.

Barthes adapts the language-speech dichotomy to economic goods. For useful goods such as clothing and automobiles, he assigns the *signifying* values of all design choices to language (the indicators of class, attitude, style, etc.) while assigning the *utility* values to speech. For example, in *selecting* my clothes I frame or accept a statement of values and attitudes that, depending on my economic position, may be more voluntary or more coerced. The relation of the clothes to the values they express is that of language. In *wearing* these clothes, in using them, I speak their sentences.

SIGNIFIER AND SIGNIFIED—THE WORD AS BASIC

For Saussure the basic unit of language is the single word (i.e., not the syllable, phoneme, or sentence). Words are constituted in and by the fact that they represent the conjunction of two elements, a sound (the *signifier*) and a meaning (the *signified*). Saussure's explanation of the function of words explores the character of verbal *signification* and the basis of *articulation*.

Signification

In language, the primary bond between signifier and signified at the level of the word is arbitrary. "Arbitrary" contrasts with the alternatives "natural" or "motivated," relations of signification founded on resemblance or physical attachment of some sort. (Other terms employed in semiotics besides "arbitrary," not entirely synonymous but capturing this distinction, are "unmotivated," "stipulated," "symbolic," "conventional"). Natural significations have only a very minor role in language. As everyone likes to remark of "natural" expressions, Frenchmen do not say "ouch!" and, as for onomatopoeia, it is only in English that dogs say "bow wow."

Words are not altogether arbitrary. The arbitrary part of words is largely in their roots and in the meaning of inflectional syllables. That the word "book" means what it does is arbitrary. That a suffixed "s" indicates plural is arbitrary. But the word "books" is compounded, and, given the first two data, its meaning is systematically determined. The relationships among "force," "forcibly," and "perforce" are not strictly arbitrary.

Combinations above the word level are not arbitrary either, but this is a topic Saussure hardly touches on. When Wittgenstein in the *Tractatus* (1921) describes sentences as pictures of states of affairs, meaning by "picture" what picture normally means, an arrangement that embodies an analogical relationship between signs and their contents, we know what he is talking about, but the analogical relationships are difficult to analyze.

Outside of language, fixed signs of arbitrary reference seem relatively rare. Perhaps we came close with the heart shape and the barber pole, but their histories of motivation are just below the surface.

Articulation

Given a tape recording of a long monologue in a language we did not know, it would obviously be very difficult or impossible to divide it into its component units, to establish the separations between sentences and words. Saussure argued that sound alone furnishes insufficient data. We must regard (for example) "two," "to," and "too" as different words, despite identity of sound, while understanding that "go" and "goes" are forms of the same word, despite difference of sound. In response, Hjelmslev proposed a very detailed analysis of repetition not just of single sound units but of acoustic contexts. The theory is attractive, but the task of recovering of words from purely acoustical data is really quite forbidding. Silences turn out to occur within words and don't always occur between words. Aside from the vagaries of individual performance, vowels that we think of as being the same are pronounced differently in different contexts. Ethnomusicologists who try to establish scales and meters from melograph recordings face exactly parallel problems.

When we do know the language and depend on the synthesis of sound and meaning that words instantiate, the *form* of linguistic articulation is a hierarchy of a specific sort, which exhibits relatively distinct strata. Phonemes, words, sentences, and sentence groups (paragraphs, stories, arguments) constitute separate levels of organization with different regulating principles and properties. It is the differences of their constitutive principles that permit Saussure to seize on words as his basic units.

Hierarchical structures quite as complex as those of language occur in dance, music, narrative, vision, depiction (which is not the same as vision!), and in hybrid genres like cinema and religious ritual, but the segmental and stratificational characteristics of these hierarchies are strikingly different from those of language and do not encourage us to center on a "basic unit" of any sort.

Music, for example, has systematic vocabularies but no "basic unit" corresponding to words. Here the burden of segmentation falls on the "signifier," and different hierarchical strata can share the same principles of construction. In pictures we frequently find the opposite situation to the general one in music. The signified scene, the objects represented, establish the salient constituent hierarchy. This is variable. Some visual representations are more naturally segmented by signifying elements—lines, color areas, brush strokes, camera angles. Visual signs as a whole are characterized by the fluidity of the articulation structures open to them.

SIGNIFICATION AND VALUE

Saussure's conception of value is the most problematic item in the *CGL*. Followed through, it undermines any possible role for consciousness in a theory of semiotics.

"Signification" is the relation between the signifier and the signified of one word. Saussure contrasts signification to "value," the relations within either a family of signifiers (such as cab, cap, cat, . . . nab, nap, gnat, etc.) or a family of signifieds (such as cap, hat, bonnet, helmet, etc.) Although he does not labor the point (as Hjelmslev does), he treats the two sides of value, values among signifieds and values among signifiers, as essentially equivalent types of structure.

Saussure draws on an economic model for these terms: "even outside language all values are apparently governed by the same paradoxical principle. They are always composed: (1) of a dissimilar thing that can be exchanged for the thing of which the value is to be determined; and (2) of similar things that can be compared with the thing of which the value is to be determined" (p. 115).

Thus the value of a pair of shoes involves both comparisons with other shoes or vestments (similar things) and exchange for money or labor (dissimilar things). More specifically, there are value relations (aesthetic differences, utility differences, etc.) among pairs of shoes and there are value relations between different amounts of money (here, straight quantity). Cutting across the independent domains of value for shoes on one side and amounts of money on the other, the economic relation of price unites the shoes and money, corresponding to the semiotic relation of signification that unites word sound and meaning.

Now we come to the deviltry of the matter. Saussure construes value, and along with value, both signifiers and signifieds as pure difference without any positive substance. Each is a position in a network.

> in language there are only differences. Even more important: a difference generally implies positive terms between which the difference is set up; but in language there are only differences *without positive terms*. Whether we take the signified or the signifier, language has neither ideas nor sounds that existed before the linguistic system, but only conceptual and phonic differences that have issued from the system. The idea or phonic substance that a sign contains is of less importance than the other signs that surround it. (p. 120)

In the context of the academic discourse of the first half of this century, Saussure's insistence on the negative character of linguistic facts had bearing, albeit somewhat ambiguously, on the dialectic of empiricism and rationalism. While still pertinent in this arena, I think we are obliged now, with our current interests in the cognitive sciences, to see its broader implications with respect to the place of *qualia* in cognition.

Qualia (qualities) are the stuff of consciousness, the greenness of green, the sweetness of sugar, the hot and cold of temperature. For Saussure, the opposition between the English "ee" (as in beet) and "i" (bit) has nothing to do with the special sensory quality of each vowel. The qualities are totally incidental to the system of differences. The pregnance of his conception is its capture of the equivalence of regional dialects that preserve the locations of contrasts but express them with different sounds. But since Saussure's idea of value excludes qualia from language both for signifier and signified, it makes consciousness irrelevant to language.

For Saussure extends his analysis in terms of differences to account for the structure of the field of signifieds as well. His examples rest on comparisons between languages. The examples are ingenious, but I don't think he provides us any grounds for generalizing broadly from them. The more forceful part of his argument concerns the signifier.

Poets might object to regarding the signification of words as a pure product of structured differences independent of the actual feel of the sounds; nevertheless, such a view is now familiar in linguistics. As we move away from language to other sign systems, the thought of downplaying conscious qualities is freshly painful. The purely systematic view of language implicit in Saussure's opposition of signification and value can be overlaid on other kinds of signs to only a very limited extent. The most nearly successful example is in music. Music theory includes abstract structural schemata that have as little to do with the sensory enjoyment of sound as Saussurian linguistics has to do with tones of voice, but perhaps we are more conscious of the omissions. It is one thing to throw away tones of voice as nonpertinent to language systems and quite another to purge a Mozart symphonic adagio of the haunting effects of an oboe or to purify a rock song of its physical throb. Here we are more motivated to recognize the qualia as essential to the sign.

For the graphic arts, the denial of material values also seems utterly unthinkable at first encounter. But to protest that the theory is uncomfortable does not constitute either a disproof or an alternative. If the important characteristics of a striking combination of green and blue in a Matisse include the absolute (positive) qualities of that particular green and that particular blue, will semiotics have anything to say about them? Should we be content to be dumbfounded by the painting? The systematic study of differences within any medium is a potent analytical tool whether or not such a perspective can survey the whole territory.

COMBINATION AND ASSOCIATION

The opposition of signification to value, which we just reviewed, is essentially a philosophic formulation. The opposition of syntagm and association, which fleshes it out and partly supplants it, is a practical tool. No other apparatus of the *CGL* is so influential, yet so incompletely developed, as this one.

Association, producing the *paradigm*, belongs primarily to language; combination, producing the *syntagm*, belongs primarily to speech. The *syntagm*, a relation in praesentia, is the chain of units combined into a larger sign. Association, a relation in absentia, links a word to all the others that might have appeared in its place, the group, or "paradigm," from which it was selected. For example, in the speech syntagm "a red house," each of the three words combined takes its value from associations with the alternatives provided in advance (and in absencia) by language: "a" with "the," "any," etc.; "red" with "green," "small," etc.; and "house" with "cottage," etc. The paradigms of language provide the alternatives, and in the context of a given situation, speech makes the particular choices and combines them.[2] Barthes pinpointed the opposition of syntagm and association as the lemma of the Saussurian doctrine that had been most infectious and that still offered a fecund instrument for semiotic research.

He furnishes several examples of the wide applicability of this model: For the garment system selection occurs among blouses, among skirts, among handbags, and so on, to form the syntagm of one outfit. In the culinary system selection occurs among entrees, among desserts, and so on, to form the syntagm of one dinner. For furniture, selection occurs among sofas, among coffee tables, among lamps to form the syntagm of one suite. In architecture, selection occurs among types of roof, types of balcony, types of window, to form the syntagm of one building. Barthes emphasizes that these can be signifying choices. The toque and the bonnet do not convey the same attitude; the entree may be plain or festive; the sofa, traditional (conservative) or modern (adventurous).

The idea that Barthes's examples convey is, as he puts it, the schema of the menu. It has found a wide variety of applications. Among the most striking of these are Claude Levi-Strauss's in anthropology and Roman Jakobson's in poetics. In Jakobson's writings, the terms "selection" and "combination" replace paradigm and syntagm. Jakobson proposed that the poetic function arises when two alternatives within one paradigm, instead of submitting to one selection, co-occur in praesentia.

> What is the empirical linguistic criterion of the poetic function? In particular, what is the indispensable feature inherent in any piece of poetry? To answer this question we recall the two basic modes of arrangement used in verbal behavior, *selection* and *combination*. If "child" is the topic of the message, the speaker selects one among the extant, more or less similar nouns like child, kid, youngster, tot, all of them equivalent in a certain respect, and then, to comment on this topic, he may select one of the semantically cognate verbs—sleeps, dozes, nods, naps. Both chosen words combine in the speech chain. The selection is produced on the base of equivalence, similarity and dissimilarity, synonymity and antonymity, while the combination, the build up of the sequence, is based on contiguity. *The poetic function projects the principle of equivalence from the axis of selection into the axis of combination.* (Jakobson, 1960, pp. 358–359)

Jakobson illustrates the formula underscored above, which became almost a slogan of structuralism, through meticulous and rigorous analyses of phonetic, lexical, grammatical, and rhythmic structures of poetic manifestations ranging from poetry as such to poetic elements in political slogans, novels, and other forms. A brief, classic demonstration takes the simple saying "A man's home is his castle." The equation is understood as poetic because in the paradigm of dwellings, home and castle cannot normally be copresent (unless "king" or "prince" is selected in the paradigm of dwellers, a possibility excluded by the paradigmatic opposition to "man": cf. "The king and all his men").

Selection and combination, reformulated as the opposition of metaphor and metonymy, became for Jakobson and for scholars inspired by his work the superordinate forms of cognitions. In fact, Saussure's opposition of combination and selection (syntagm and paradigm) draws on deep roots. Similarity and contiguity are the relations by which Aristotle accounts for memory. In a striking reprise of this historical psychology, Jakobson (1971), with the Russian neurologist A. R. Lurija, proposed an analysis of traumatic aphasia due to specific brain lesions in terms of the loss of selectional or combinatorial organization in speech. Although the simple schema they proposed has yielded to more richly differentiated theories, the analysis of speech (and other cognitive) disorders in relation to strictly defined grammatical and lexical incapacities remains an area of continuing research interest.

DIACHRONIC AND SYNCHRONIC

Synchronic linguistics studies the state of language as a system at a given moment in time. Diachronic linguistics studies the change in the system through time. Saussure emphasizes this difference with a special intensity of polemic because in asserting this distinction, he was arguing (successfully, as it turned out) for a redirection of scholarly effort within the field of linguistic research.

As he saw it, diachronic linguistics and synchronic linguistics deal with entirely different types of data. In language history, a change is, typically, an inconsequential accident involving no signification and largely isolated. The fact that the English plural form for a group of words evolved from final "i" (fot, foti) to their present pattern (foot, feet) is interesting but signifies nothing. The underlying synchronic fact that is not altered is that there are two numbers, singular and plural, expressed by a single inflection. What changed was merely the material embodiment of this fact. As the language system moves through history, the material permutes in apparently random patterns.

The idea that a system could be isolated from the facts of its historical evolution was a source of inspiration for structural semiotics, but we will note in the following chapter that the program encounters obstacles.

With the preceding emphasis on dichotomies, it is worth noting that Saussure adds a third term to diachronic and synchronic linguistics. In the last section of the *CGL* we learn that geographic linguistics studies the relations between contemporaneous languages or dialects. This study identifies problems and relations that are quite distinct from those of the other two fields. Yet it does seem clear that for Saussure, the contrast between interior structure—synchrony—and external context is all-important, whether that context is historical or geographic.

Any domain of semiosis where we know or sense that variety in expression is supported by a stability in vocabulary may well return us to the conceptual apparatus of the *CGL* or of theories inspired by it, despite any limitations we discover.

Saussure gave us a practical model of signifiers but only a vague conjecture about signifieds. The practical model finds wide application outside of language. Indeed, his main ideas about signifiers are no more linguistic than they are musicological or anthropological. They belong—as he proposed—to semiology or semiotics.

6

FUNCTION

Saussure's systematic linguistics was achieved by defining the problems of linguistics very narrowly. Modern linguistics has progressed since then in continuous tension with the narrow scope of structuralism.

In this chapter we consider some ideas that arose, at least in part, by a critique of Saussure's assumptions, but these ideas do not depart from the most fundamental tenets of structuralism. In chapter 8 we will consider a more radical critique contemporaneous with these.

Under the general heading of "functionalism" I group here a few different efforts to broaden linguistic or semiotics to encompass wider concerns. Here the question of breadth is not about the range of media, although many of Saussure's respondents did indeed take up the challenge he had signaled of studying language and other social systems in the same perspective. Here "breadth" concerns the purposes and effects of signs.

BÜHLER AND THE PRAGUE FUNCTIONALISTS

Saussure defined the sign as the union of signifier and signified. The Prague Circle evolved an alternative or complementary conception, that the sign was characterized by a multiplicity of effects which its members called functions. Karl Bühler who elaborated an extensive philosophy of the sign from the standpoint of psychology, participated in and influenced the work of the Prague Circle in the 1930s. Bühler understood, as few of his contemporaries did, that semiotic phenomena involved processes or relations that could not be captured without a leap into abstractions. We noted in chapter 1 his astute criticism of simple "association" as an account of meaning: "K-L-M" makes us think of "N-O-P," but that is not its meaning. Psychological "association" is one little genie with too many jobs; its fundamental mandate becomes quite confused. A word can have all sorts of associations that are not its meaning.

Bühler's critique of Saussure places the union of signifier and signified in a larger domain. In his formulation, the sign effects a three-way relation encompassing the sign producer or addresser, the sign itself, and the sign receiver or addressee. He identified three functions associated with these factors. The expressive function is associated with the addresser; the sign exercises this function insofar as it reveals the state of the person who produces it. The referential function is the relation Saussure considered and belongs to the sign itself as a part of a language. The appellative function is the effect of the sign on its receiver. Bühler regarded the appellative and expressive functions as psychological. Bühler's examples are very wide-ranging and imaginative, by no means confined to language, but to my knowledge, he does not deal with entire texts (like artworks) as did the scholars he deeply influenced in the Prague Circle.

Prague School semiotics evolved in a situation that demanded engagement. Radical upheaval and experiment within European art in the 1930s—and in the immediately preceding decades was itself but one index of a society in cataclysm. Some members of the circle had emigrated to Prague in the shadow of the Stalinist purges, but they had been deeply involved in the intellectual flowering of the immediate postrevolutionary period in Russia, where they participated in the formalist movement. On one side, then, was Stalin; on the other, the ominous burgeoning of Hitler's nationalism, which would eventually decimate the group.

Prague functionalism was a direct descendant of Russian formalism in literary criticism. In the 1920s the Formalists had rejected the Romantic psychological theory that literature was determined by the spiritual states of its creators and its public in favor of a formal analysis of the material artwork itself. Yet in the same years that saw the Formalists assert autonomous aesthetic structures, the autonomy of art was challenged from a new direction by the aesthetics of dialectical materialism, with its insistence on the social context and economic function of art. Caught between opposed and irreconcilable theories, both attractive for their novelty, consistency, and explanatory depth, Prague theory is remarkable for its refusal to simplify its views for the advantage of a clearer intellectual dogma. The concept of sign that served as a sort of home base did not quickly lead to a consistent system. The notion that the sign served various functions harmonized their several interests.

Prague theory brought considerable discipline and power to the stance of cultural relativism through which these displaced scholars gave voice to just those principles of tolerance that the societies around them were threatening politically.

Exploiting relativism, their work reaches out appreciatively and imaginatively to folk arts, ethnic arts, and discarded periods of art history as well as welcoming and analyzing new styles and new media. Similarly, Saussure's unified notion of language is divided up to allow equal priority to "poetic language," "scientific language," and other socially organized dialects that differ in their communicative functions. (See Garvin [1964]).

We may think of relativism negatively as a refusal to take sides and make judgments, but it allows a constructive aspect. Jan Mukarovsky's doctrine of the "aesthetic norm" is exemplary. His norm is not statistical. He proposes that cultural behavior, including artistic work, is always understood in relation to a norm that is established by its culture; however, movements in art that conform to social norms are relatively short and rare compared to movements that make their mark by violating them in some respect. The norm is known but not necessarily known explicitly.[1] It is communicated among members of a culture by the ways values are assigned to works. Historically, the norm changes continually, and the interaction between the norm and the works that violate or confirm it are factors in its evolution.

Mukarovsky's line of research wreaks havoc on Saussure's argument that historical change is isolated from signification. If, at a certain point in history, a director puts his hero on a dark horse and his villain on a white horse, the values of those signs will have as much to do with historical inversion as with the internal structure of the film. In the arts generally, fine or applied, it is evident that style change can be just as meaningful as the arrangements permitted within the system of a genre at any one moment, and in commercial design, change may be much *more* meaningful than the combinations and selections inside the system. Changes per se must be viewed as signifiers, generally of allegiance or attitude. Style changes may signify such values as rebelliousness, refinement, sensuality, sublimation, progressiveness, or nostalgia. Of course, on reflection, we can say the same of language, even though the agents of its change usually may be anonymous and its rationale more spotty. In our own historical period, the political significance of language change has been explicit in the areas of gender and racial relations. Indeed, we might well doubt whether language is, in the end, immune to the direct influence of individuals when we consider that conscious programs lie behind some of these changes in which we are participating.

Mukarovsky provides a full, formal account of this doctrine in a long essay, *Aesthetic Function, Norm and Value as Social Facts*. A work of art is one in which aesthetic function dominates, but aesthetic function is not limited to art. Any sign takes on an aesthetic function to the extent that it is regarded as an end in itself. Whether this happens or not is again a question of social norms.

JAKOBSON'S SIX FUNCTIONS

With the "aesthetic function," introduced but not defined earlier, our repertoire of functions is increased to four. Roman Jakobson incorporated these in a synthesis intended to draw together European functionalism and Shanon and Weaver's mathematical model of communication. Perhaps the rapprochement is primarily rhetorical. Mathematical communication theory is concerned with quite different issues, but it lent to Jakobson the idea of the "channel" and suggested a broader understanding of "code."

The model posits six possible factors in any semiosic act. There must be an "addresser," the one who utters or writes or otherwise sends the sign; a "receiver"; a "channel," such as live voice, phone, writing; a "message"— what we have called so far the signifier; a "context," which includes the signified; and a "code"—the set of rules that determines the relation between the message and some part of the context.

As with Bühler, each factor is associated with a function. All or any subset of functions may be evident in a sign. Following an idea that the Prague Circle had retained from Russian formalism, the one that predominates is the "dominant."

The functions associated with the addresser and the addressee are like those specified by Bühler. A sign in which the expressive function is dominant indicates the state of the speaker, as in an exclamation or interjection.

The function associated with the receiver is the conative function. When dominant, the sign influences a state of the receiver. This means often, as with a command, a future state. We might say that music, when used to organize and impel marching or dancing, is conative.

The function associated with the channel is the phatic function: contact. "Do you read me?" Or the parent's "There, there, it isn't so bad." Jakobson's examples are hilarious, and it would be cheating to quote them.

The function associated with the message—the vehicle or representamen—is the aesthetic function: the sign taken as an end in itself. All art understood as art is taken to embody this function, and any object valued for its beauty rather than for its ideological value or usefulness—be it a gorgeous car, an elegant teapot or some acreage of untouched real estate—takes on this function. Although Jakobson more precisely, I believe, than anyone who preceded him, showed how the aesthetic function could hinge on structure, he argues (1933/1976) that cultural norms ultimately determine the dominance of this function. As a striking demonstration, he notes that the aesthetic status that one generation accorded only to the poems of Karel Mácha, a subsequent generation accords only to his diaries.

The function associated with the code is the metalinguistic function. When we pause to clarify a term, our discourse is metalinguistic. M. C. Escher's optical illusions might be characterized as metalinguistic; so might a fascinating fugue, when our interest is to see how the form itself works out.

The function associated with the context is the referential function. We don't need to illustrate reference because it is our ubiquitous topic. The idea that is interesting in this scheme is that reference taken to be just one function among equally important others.

This systematic description of six functions, which Jakobson delineated in his best-known paper, the "Closing Statement" of *Style and Language*, has proven one of the most enduring models in semiotics. Yet its exposition by Jakobson draws examples from language only, and its application in other spheres is sometimes difficult to delineate. Although the specific functions can be attributed to expressions in other media, often it is problematic to disengage them, to say which is the dominant.

When a fugue draws attention to its own system by ingenious arrangements, it might as well be called metalinguistic, as I suggested above, or, because the very same structure then turns it back on itself, aesthetic. When Hamlet speaks his soliloquy, who is addressing whom? Is Shakespeare addressing the audience, is Hamlet addressing Hamlet (working himself up?—conative function.) Is it the English Renaissance expressing itself? The phatic function seems often to depend on expressive and conative functions: The lullaby is a contact between Mother and Child (phatic) that has the latter's sleep as its purpose (conative) but that works because it conveys love (expressive). The analysis serves better to inventory the richness of a sign situation than to classify signs or explicate their operations.

SEMIOTICS AND AESTHETICS

As Jakobson pointed out in his address to the inaugural meeting of the International Semiotic Association (1974/1975), it was the work of the Prague School that first brought semiotic theory and aesthetic concerns together. The orientation toward communication is particularly interesting with respect to art precisely because the communicative mission and the communicative accomplishments of art are always in question.

In Mukarovsky's essays, the sign manifesting the aesthetic function is sometimes said to *refer to itself*. The rare cases of genuine self-reference by a sign ("This is a sentence." or Salvador Dalí's self-portrait that shows him painting the picture we are viewing)—not to be confused with self-reference by a person—are not especially characteristic of art. Better to say, perhaps, that the aesthetic function is a *substitute* for reference. The idea that the aesthetic function of a sign is identified with the value a sign acquires for itself seems, on the other hand, quite straightforward. In this frame, the next questions are: Are works of art necessarily signs? And then, if so, how do they differ from others?

A few special cases aside, "self-reference" is oxymoronic, but we may read it as the first notes of the theme that runs through this book, that reference and structure compete. In elaborating on "self-reference," Jakobson and others gave it some real substance. When the vague notion is spelled out by specific analysis, the aesthetic function in Prague School thinking typically involves foregrounding internal structural arrangements within the sign. This focus is achieved, on one hand, through specific structural characteristics, and, on the other, in the positioning of the sign with respect to cultural systems of value.

There may be some contradiction, not fully acknowledged by adherents of functionalism, in their efforts to reduce the aesthetic function alternately to absolute features of structure or to relative processes of culture; however, we may accept both lines of analysis as partial and as complementary. The structural analysis stresses three factors: the heightened artifice of symmetries of all sorts, departures from stylistic norms, and transformation of the sign's logical character. The cultural analysis stresses the relativity of aesthetic valuation. Whereas structural analysis promises to characterize aesthetic objects as specific types of sign, cultural analysis refuses: The precious manuscript becomes a fish wrap or vice versa—depending only on social values.

SOME MORE RECENT VERSIONS

Both Gottlob Frege and Charles Peirce emphasized the distinction between a proposition and the act of uttering it. Insofar as we regard enunciation as the act of a speaker in a specific context, phenomena are foregrounded (phenomena of self-expression, of practical effects, of entailments) that seem, at least at first glance, to be separable from the representation of the proposition itself. The issues that arise sometimes are treated under the heading of "pragmatics," the term Charles Morris used for relations between the sign and its users. The branch of linguistics called the linguistics of enunciation, founded by Emil Bienveniste, offers meticulous analysis and some systematization of the problems where they concern language.

Among the most fascinating and persistently misunderstood contributions to functionalism, we should note John L. Austin's idea of performatives, nondescriptive statements that effect an actual change in some state of affairs: "I dub thee Sir Such-and-Such," "I pronounce you man and wife," "I declare the games open," and so on. In jurisprudence, a verdict is, we hope, descriptive, not performative, that is, it recognizes a circumstance that already exists. On the other hand, pronouncing a sentence is performative.

Michel Foucault's *The Archeology of Knowledge* (1972) considers the functions of enunciation extensively, in a way that has not clarified general theoretical issues for me; however, in the lecture printed with it in the English version, "The Discourse on Language," Foucault provides a superior context for Austin's point, where he discusses notions of truth that do not hinge on the propositional content of utterances. He observes the instance of pre-Sophistic discourse in Greece, but in fact we can observe similar speech activities in many contemporary cultures.

It has proved difficult to isolate phenomena associated with enunciation from those associated with the proposition, and that is why the very brief treatment in chapter 14 attempts to regard enunciation as an additional feature of the sign itself, with minimal reference to the sign user.

NATTIEZ—PATHOLOGICAL SEMIOTICS

Although not the first to deal with the topic, Jean Jacques Nattiez may well be regarded as the founder of musical semiotics, not only because of his own writing but also because he was so active in highlighting the work of other writers and students that a voluminous discourse replete with its own controversies took form rapidly as in few other special fields of semiotics.

Nattiez develops a model reminiscent of functionalism to define semiotics, a model in which the role of reference is secondary, if not incidental. (His immediate source is Jean Molino, not Prague functionalism.) He characterizes the sign as a link between a process of production and a process of reception. The producer and receiver may or may not interpret the sign in ways that correspond and are certainly unlikely to interpret in exactly the same way. Composers, for example, may hear in terms of their theoretical calculations what their audiences hear coloristically. They hear different meanings. This viewpoint produces rich critical insights about historical theories of music, some of which, Nattiez shows, are biased toward the audience and others toward composers.

But is this viewpoint adequate as a general framework for music or any other semiotic domain? The experience of art is very complex. It goes without saying that much of our experience of art is singular, for each of us receives the work of art into an individual history. It also goes without saying, or should, that the receptions of the same work of art into different cultures will be radically different. But what must not pass without notice is that apart from these differences, we feel that we share something, that the work of art *can* bring to everybody else something that it has brought to us. This is the side of the experience of art and of semiosis in general that is mysterious and that cries out for some talk.

We talk about art, philosophy, the news, and other elaborated representations to develop and valorize our sense of sharing and our sense of the community that the sharing of these signs establishes. Our sign repertoires are how we get in touch. It is to this end we talk about them, test them, build on them, and compare notes.

What we share or think we share or wish to share is exactly what we can attribute to the signs themselves. If we take communication seriously, it throws us back upon the sign. Identifying the sign with the differences between the producer (addresser) and the receiver (addressee) misses the point except when we want to know why a sign failed to communicate. A semiotic founded on this interest is thus a sort of pathology. To be sure, signs have no truly "intrinsic" content; that's a dead issue, but semiotics can study them as though they did. There are no pure chemicals. It would be irresponsible for steelmakers or pharmacists to misrepresent the purity of their materials, but we expect chemistry to provide the laws of pure substances as a basis of their work. We are in a similar position when we dispense with production and reception to focus on the sign.

STRUCTURALISM AND FUNCTIONALISM

Functionalism might be said to extend Saussurian structuralism from *langue* to *parole*. For example, we might say that a sign is expressive if the signified of that sign is the state of the person who speaks it. This signification is not established by *langue*, but the word "signification" might apply in the sense Saussure accords it. Following a similar construal, a sign could be called conative if the signified were a state of the receiver. The signified of a metalinguistic sign is then the sign's vocabulary or system. The signified of a phatic sign is the present relation of the addresser and addressee. Perhaps all these references or significations might prove to be strictly systematic if properly investigated. It seems that all the functions we have considered are referential functions. Functionalism contests the division of *langue* from *parole*. What we have gained so far is an ad hoc method (why 6? why not 7 or 9?) of parsing the social situation of the sign, perhaps a broader idea of semiotic phenomena, but not a new conception of the sign itself.

But when we come to the aesthetic sign, paraphrase in this vein runs into a dead end. Either we accept the paradox of "self-reference" or we are stuck. Thus it does not appear that we could entirely reduce the functionalist perspective to the structuralist perspective even by permitting multiple types of signifieds. Where functionalism comes closest to justifying an alternative paradigm is with the aesthetic, but in spelling out how a sign attracts value in itself, we noted that Jakobson turned back again to the question of the structure of the signifier.

7

SYNTAX

It is striking that Saussure says nothing of grammar. For the most part, he relegates word combinations to "speech." In a review of the pertinent historical context, Noam Chomsky (1966) pointed out that the study of grammar had been so strongly attached to pedagogy that Saussure may have regarded it as a rather arbitrary collection of normative (rather than scientific) descriptions of psychological (rather than linguistic) phenomena. The study of grammar readily involves us in psychology, and part of our task will be to discern the difference between semiotic and psychological issues in grammar.

Vocabulary in language is, in the first instance, a matter of words, and words, ephemeral as they are, seem to be right in front of us. "Ideas are as they may be, but the words are out where we can see and hear them" (Quine, 1974; p. 35). Grammar is conceived in terms of parts of speech and rules about parts of speech. Parts of speech emerge in Saussure's course as descriptive categories but not as mechanisms for controlling the order and meaning of sentences. It is the latter function that makes problems. Parts of speech and rules are abstractions. How can such abstractions have any consequences unless they are embodied somewhere in the mind, even the minds of children who have never heard of such things but still follow the rules? It follows that these principles must operate in the unconscious mind.

Chomsky's theory, the theory of transformational grammar, provides as fundamental (at least) a structuralist framework for grammar as does Saussure's work for vocabulary, but unlike the *Course in General Linguistics*, which is one thin book, transformational grammar does not lend itself readily to a précis. It is specialized and as deeply buried in jargon as cosmology or evolutionary biology. Its complex formulations, resting on very delicate evidence, are further complicated by internal controversy and rapid revision. Although no more than a few indications biased toward particular interests are offered here, it is my opinion that a period of reaction against the dominance of Chomsky's work is now encouraging semiotic scholars to neglect somewhat an enormous fund of suggestive models within this theory that could have rich applications elsewhere (to name just one, the precise description of "governance.")

THE SHAPE OF THE PROBLEM

Chomsky distinguishes between linguistic competence and linguistic performance. This distinction effects the same sort of idealization as Saussure's between *langue* and *parole*. However, unlike *langue* and *parole,* which Saussure proposes as social facts, competence and performance are psychological facts, pertinent to individuals. Linguistic competence is the knowledge and computational capacity of the brain that enables it to use language. Chomsky argues that the structure of language, properly analyzed, will reveal what it takes to do this. Performance concerns constraints that are not part of the language mechanism per se, such as limitations of memory. Chomsky's theory is intended to describe competence, including:

1. Creativity. We are able to understand and to create sentences that are substantially different from any we have encountered previously. The capacity of language to "achieve infinite variety with finite means," to use the phrase often cited from Wilhelm von Humbolt, invokes grammar, more variety in speech arises with word combinations than with words.
2. Acquisition. Young children can learn any language they grow up with, despite the fact that they are exposed only to a relatively small and faulty sample of it. Chomsky reasons that they can do this only if the genetically determined physiological substrate for is much more specialized than we had realized.[1]
3. Reference. Reference is achieved by our competence to relate sounds to meaning, considering especially a sentence as a whole.

SOME CHARACTERISTICS OF THE THEORY

Transformational grammar supposes that the unconscious brain, in processing speech, recasts it in forms that are quite different from the ones we are consciously aware of. This hypothesis is required both in order to exhibit unities across different languages and to account for the diversity of forms within any one language.

In Chomsky's writing and in cognitive theory aligned with his views, these different forms are called "representations." It is easy to follow his use of this term, and I shall go along with it, with few quotes, for most of this chapter. Toward the end I will discuss what I take to be a fundamental conceptual flaw behind this word choice—not a flaw in transformational grammar per-se, to be sure, but one that bears centrally on semiotics.

In recent formulations Chomsky identifies four "representations": the surface structure, the S-structure, the D-structure, and the logical form.

Surface Structure

The surface structure—the sound we think we hear—substitutes for ("represents") raw acoustic data. The acoustic signal for speech is subject to many sorts of distortion and idiosyncrasies, but the conscious image we assemble of the sound of speech compensates for these defects and substitutes some structures of understanding for structures of the raw sensation. For example, "cockroach" in American English frequently is pronounced with a slight silence before the *k* (kah'kroch), but I believe the silence is heard as following the *k,* where we understand a logical division between words to occur.

S-Structure and D-Structure

The surface "representation" provides words but not sense. In Chomsky's most famous illustration, there is very little different in sound or in the order of parts of speech between

(1) John is eager to please.
and
(2) John is easy to please.

But to understand the two sentences, we have to regard John as the subject of the infinitive in the first case and as its object in the second. Our ability to understand such sentences implies that we have an image ("representation") of their grammatical structure in mind (not necessarily consciously). Understanding requires the reconstruction of the sentence to show how its parts are coordinated or subordinated. Diagrams somewhat like those of figure 7.1 (my examples are severely simplified) are held to express actual mental data. This means that the diagram shows relations which are not merely a reflective description. This exact analytical understanding must be spontaneously registered in the brain, consciously or not.

Logical Form

The grammatically interpreted string of words must be correlated with concepts; that is, the D-structure and its transformations must be given a semantic interpretation. A mental data structure ("representation") corresponding to a spoken sentence, but embodying its reference in semantic units is a logical form. Chomsky understands these units—concepts—to be themselves systematic in that they are built up from an internal repertoire corresponding to the brain's given equipment for registering its experiences. If the units of this repertoire are genetically determined, they constitute "semantic universals."

The idea of semantic universals is highly conjectural. So far as I am aware, Chomsky has been content to leave a blank page here in his theory, although others have found things to write on it. The analysis of verbs with their complements (Jackendoff 1987) and the analysis of metaphor (Johnson 1987) have both suggested deep, unifying patterns in linguistic meanings beyond those that are obvious. However, in relation to the hypothesis, the evidence is fragmentary.

TOOLS OF THE THEORY

Chomsky was the first researcher in empirical linguistics to take full advantage of the synthesis of mathematics and logic established by Russell and Whitehead. Prior to his work Hjelmslev (as we noted in chapter 5) had cast a theory of linguistics in a strongly logistic mode, and Zellig Harris (1951; 1960) had provided a solid framework for the application of mathematics to linguistics. However, before Chomsky, no mathematician had attempted to account formally for the full variety of grammatically correct forms of sentences, and no linguist had used mathematics to paraphrase the abstract rules of grammar as known intuitively or taught in the schools. A model that attempts all or a section of this task is a formal grammar. Chomsky's conceptual and notational tools and his experimental pro-

Figure 7.1   Representation of mental data required to interpret grammatical structures

a. (Who gets to choose?) *Sue is the one to choose.*
b. (Whom should we choose?) *Sue is the one to choose.*

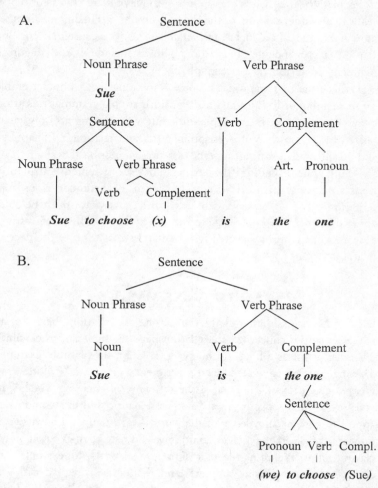

cedures draw prominently on the mathematics of computer science. Rules susceptible to mathematical expression can be incorporated in a computer program that tests them by synthesizing sentences or analyzing them. A generative grammar is a mathematical "machine" that makes a series, or "string," of symbols. The computer has no "instinct" or "feel" for what sounds right or wrong: If the rules permit mistakes, the computer will make them.

Formal grammar lends precision to notions of hierarchy, a concept relevant to an understanding of the elaboration of signs in any medium. The most fundamental are inclusion hierarchies (as where a sentence includes clauses, clauses include phrases, and phrases include words). Figure 7.2 represents inclusion via a tree graph.

Perhaps the tree graph has become something like a popular emblem for formal linguistics, although for transformational grammar it is at most a raw ingredient. Such trees represent context-free grammars only, characterized by the absence of overlapping parts and relations.[2] (Chapters 13 and 18 illustrate a contrasting type of representation.)

The graphs or codings that express analyses of sentence structure in transformational grammar are regarded as part of the unconscious "representation" of it. As we saw with "easy" and "eager," we must be able to conjoin interpretive knowledge to the sentence itself; the brain must employ data structures associated with sentences that capture the necessary relations.

SYNTAX AND SEMANTICS

Charles Morris said that syntax concerned the relations between signs while semantics concerned the relation between signs and their objects. This distinction is difficult in many cases. Chomsky's famous example of a wrong sentence generated by an experimental grammar, "Colorless green ideas sleep furiously," illustrated the difficulty of deciding whether mistakes are due to syntax or to semantics. A semantic solution would need to appeal to general knowledge of the world—for example, knowledge that only animals sleep. A syntactic solution would require rules based on word classifications (extending the logic of parts of speech)—for example, a subclassification of nouns as "animate" and "inanimate" coupled with a rule that "sleep" requires an animate noun as its subject. Chomsky demonstrated here that the division between syntax and semantics is not unambiguously determined by observation.

The syntax/semantics distinction is meaningful only in relation to elaborated signs, for it depends on a hierarchy of wholes and parts. I prefer the

Figure 7.2   Inclusion hierarchy

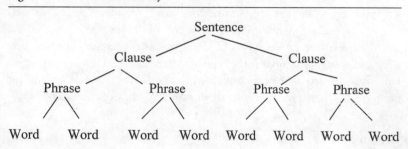

following definition to Morris's because it incorporates that principle: *Syntax* is structure within one factor of one sign (signifier or signified). *Semantic relations* are relations between sign factors. Just as the constituents of a sign may or may not be signs, the syntactic relations that join the constituents may or may not be signs. Word order, for example, can signify an assertion or interrogation. In works of art, syntactic relations can be so invested with feeling that they might be taken as referring to those feelings. The relationship of dissonances to their resolutions in music is probably the sharpest case, but parallel effects occur with color balance in a painting or suspense in drama.

SYNTAX AND TEXT

The ideas summarized in this section concern, in the first instance, the structure of sign factors, particularly the signifier, but because they have implications also for modes of interpretation, most of the topic is deferred to chapter 15.

It seems we never have enough words to go around. The term "text" takes radically different definitions in different semiotic writings. For Hjelmslev, text is the continuous output of *parole;* for Paul Ricoeur, text is a sign which is autonomous in the specific sense that it replaces its own author. For others, text is a sign that bears a rich field of interpretation (i.e., the Holy Grail as a text.) These constructions must not be confounded with each other or with mine, which follows; although appropriating the same term, they are, however, not necessarily competing, not necessarily addressing the same problems. It seems that "text" is a rather busy x in our algebras, an *x* required for different roles in different equations.

In the present theory, a *text* is an elaborated or structured factor (usually signifier)—one that supports analysis into components related to each other in an orderly manner. The components of the text are its vocabulary, and their relations are its syntax. Three types of syntax are *grammar, pattern,* and *idiom.* Grammar is the type of syntax characteristic of languages. Pattern is characteristic of individuated works. Idiom is less dominant but ubiquitous. These types are distinct in principle but occur mixed.

Grammar

A *grammar* is a set of rules governing abstract categories (such as "noun" in language or "diagonals" in chess). *Categories* arise with a distinction between types and tokens. Peirce frequently is credited with this terminology, which captures a logical difference between *langue* and *parole.* The word "Tennessee" occurs at least three times (as *parole*) in every edition of Wallace Stevens's poems but is the same word (in *langue*); those are three tokens of one type. Each copy of this book is also a token of the same type, the "same" book. Categories are instances of types but appear to be distinguished within types generally on psychological, not logical grounds. To our immediate awareness categories are abstractions.

Wonderful complications grow out of the type-token relation, but fortunately, the idea has such strong appeal to common sense that we can cheat, employing the idea as if it were quite solid, and refer those readers who can tolerate some honest confusion to other authors.[3] Categories of grammar are a special case of what Saussure called paradigms. The combinations produced by or governed by grammar are a special case of syntagms, called *forms* in chapter 15 where the theory broached here is developed further.

Pattern

In my view, much confusion and premature impatience with structuralist thought is due to a failure to appreciate the dialectic of grammar and pattern. The opposition of pattern and grammar emerges in the linguistic analysis of poetry and also in music theory. Patterns suggest categories and rules, but these are immediate consequences of the text which exhibits them, without the a priori status they hold in grammar.

Idiom

In *idiom,* coherence is determined by variation on known models. No categories or rules need be presupposed, although they may be adduced. Idioms in language (It's raining/snowing/cool) furnish a first example. Myths as models for plots make another. Teasing out a description of these via categories and combination rules is possible but tendentious. Idioms are grammars in embryo. I do not deal with them further in this book.

GRAMMAR AND CONSCIOUSNESS

Sentence grammar combines words into sentences. Narrative grammars combine categories of events as stories. Grammars of melody combine notes using harmonic or other categories. Meal plans may observe a grammar of food categories (in which ketchup is usually *not* a vegetable). Logic, which combines propositions to form valid arguments, is a kind of grammar. Consciously, grammaticality in all of these is often manifested as a feeling of "correctness" or "wrongness" in context or as coherence or incoherence, or, of course, as somewhere in between. Categories and the rules that refer to them may be just dimly sensed and unnamed in consciousness. On the other hand, the pedagogical tools we master consciously can be fully integrated in our spontaneous use of grammar. If we have had the good fortune to practice with something like tree graphs in an English class, these sentence diagrams may be a factor in our sign use apart from any unconscious "representations." The conscious diagrams and their ilk serve to interpret the feelings associated with grammaticality.

What I want to emphasize is that our immediate conscious experience of grammar—partly quasi-sensory, partly analytical—is usually fragmentary, often vague, and sometimes contradictory, but that for the purposes of semiotics, as understood in this book, what we experience, sometimes called "intuition," is the real thing. The neat and tremendously enticing structures constructed by transformational grammar are hypothetical. Right or wrong, being outside our ken, they are external to semiosis. They may help explain semiosis but they do not describe it or embody it. Two issues emerge here. One concerns the full implications of conceiving representation as a phenomenon of consciousness, the topic adumbrated in the section following. The second concerns the kind of reality asserted for systems given that their presence for us is nebulous. The next chapter addresses this problem.

A QUARREL OVER REPRESENTATION

I state briefly here a claim that is argued in chapter 12 with more bells and whistles. The key point is to distinguish representation from substitution. Does a caterpillar represent the butterfly it will become? To the lepidopterist it may, but it does not to the robin that swallows it nor to itself. Representation is *to* someone or something. Chomsky's research suggests very persuasive models of the data structures that the unconscious brain must form as replacements for the language surface we observe. The S-structures, D-structures, and logical forms of linguistic data don't represent *to* except where they enter consciousness. Each replaces the last. The relation of representation we will isolate in part III hinges on copresence, not replacement.

Confusion between replacement and representation permeates cognitive science. Transformational grammar has gained standing as a preeminent, albeit controversial, model of cognitive processes. However, the directions in cognitive science that it has inspired aim ultimately to take account of the computations effected by the brain in terms of biology. This work does not hinge, as semiotics does, on a conception of the sign. In a sporting spirit, scientists who devise computational models of biological and cognitive processes are quick to seize on flamboyant titles for their delightful inventions: "learning systems," "expert systems," "living systems," "agents," and of course "viruses." We must counter with an equally sporting skepticism. We have not one shred of evidence that any of these simulations brings us one step closer to fathoming or reproducing the mysteries of nature than were the brilliant cave dwellers who devised equally lifelike models of bison, painted on their living-room walls. Among these mysteries is representation in consciousness.

8

THE REALITY OF SYSTEM
IN A UNIVERSE OF CHANGE

Both the Saussurian and the Chomskian ideas of language rest on the fragile postulate of a well-defined kernel of stable structure (language for Saussure, competence for Chomsky) that underlies the chaotic activity of speaking. Functionalism supplements this postulate, taking it as less central and less decisive. This chapter considers a more radical challenge from a theory which denies that language is, at heart, systematic.

In 1929 the brief monograph *Marxism and the Philosophy of Language* (1929/1973) was published under in the name of V. N. Volosinov but is now usually attributed to Mikhail Bakhtin, whose name I use in my references. Political circumstance and personality combined to make Bakhtin an enigmatic figure in literary scholarship; his originality makes him one of the most important. The critical and linguistic circle centered around Bakhtin in Moscow in the 1920s comprised an adventurous group of theorists. This group met a tragic demise in the period of rising repression under Stalin. Since that time the work of that circle has attracted the researches of a growing number of specialists in the East and in the West. Bakhtin's analyses highlight the ambiguity of perspective and plurality of voice conveyed by literary texts.

BAKHTIN'S CRITIQUE OF SAUSSURE IN
MARXISM AND THE PHILOSOPHY OF LANGUAGE

Bakhtin's essay on language appreciates and retains Humbolt's central emphasis on the creative and organic character of language, but he understands this attribute as social, not individual. He associates the idea of an autonomous individual with the self-justificatory mythology of capitalism. Personality follows from social relations. The inner psyche of the individual is essentially inaccessible to analysis.

Bakhtin analyses language as an instrument of communication rather than as the instrument of thought. While accepting Saussure's premise that language is essentially social, he rejects what he calls Saussure's "abstract realism." He regards the abstract concept of system as coercive, implying an authority outside the specific, individual interactions of each person with his society.

Bakhtin discards both the speech/language dichotomy and the related notion that the basic linguistic unit, the word, exists independently of speech. His basic unit is the "particular utterance." The utterance is a sign. What it conjoins is not sound and meaning, as in the Saussurean scheme, but the psychical and social environments. He says: "The processes that basically define the content of the psyche occur not inside but outside the individual organism, although they involve its participation. . . . Psychic experience is the semiotic expression of contact between the organism and the outside environment" (pp. 25–26). The person who undergoes experience is socially organized. An utterance is constructed as a communication between two socially organized persons. Even in inner speech or in the absence of a specific addressee—as in the case of a person writing a diary or painting a picture—the utterance still presupposes and, therefore, indirectly represents a social group.

The continuous implication of social relations in all of speech, public, private, or interior, does not imply a fixed system. Language is essentially fluid. A synchronic system could be said to exist only, at best, from the point of view of one subjective consciousness at a particular moment in time. Two prejudices color Saussure's conception. The synchronic system is manifested only in reflective deliberation that does not play a substantial role in the active life of language. We don't converse with a dictionary and grammar book in hand. Historically the idea of linguistic system is a product of the study of dead languages: "At the basis of modes of linguistic thought that lead to the postulation of language as a system . . . lies a practical and theoretical focus . . . [on] defunct, alien languages preserved in written monuments" (p. 71).

Moreover, the response to a sign is always an actual or potential creative act: "[u]nderstanding is a response to signs with signs. . . . A generative process can only be grasped with the aid of another generative process" (p.25). Bakhtin does not identify the utterance with a fixed system because the utterance is always a creative act and because what supports it "is not the stability but the adaptability of language" (p. 68).

DIALOGUE AND MONOLOGUE

Lurking behind Bakhtin's criticism of the hypostatized linguistic system, but not fully spelled out by him here, is a paradigm for the contrast between dialogue and monologue that has roots in the Middle Ages, if not earlier. An early essay of Roberta Kevelson (1977) surveys the development of European legal disputation from the Middle Ages to the present tracing a larger dialogue that has dialogue proper and monologue as its component factors. The medieval forms for clerical argument about the interpretation of sacred texts lead to our modern courts. The disputation was highly governed and stylized. When both sides have finished their pleading (the dialogical voices) a "sentence" or "verdict" (ver[um]+dicere=true+to say) is pronounced by a higher authority (the monological voice). This latter represented the authoritative monologue of God's word that men dispute. In England another dialogue developed between written law (the sheriff's law) and the oral law (the king's law, which was also the common law and sometimes therefore the refuge of the sheriff's outlaw). The legal courtroom preserves its ties to the medieval tradition of interpretive dialogue in its "terms of law," "terms of contract," and "terms of a sentence."

But even aside from jurisprudence, the model is truly pervasive. Parallel forms were adopted by the early Renaissance royal court when it abandoned jousting contests for the more sublimated competitions of the "art of conversation," which, after stylized dialogical exchanges, accorded the royal hostess the honor of pronouncing the sentence, what we call today the last word.

The voice of authority is monological. Bakhtin associates the history of linguistics with the priesthood, which is coercive and monological. In ascribing the essence of language to a fixed system, linguistics accepts an authoritarian stance that endorses the definition of a "correct" usage. This is hardly a dead issue in our own day. Resistance to linguistic authority or an attempt to capture it figures as a plank in many broad political agendas. For the cultural progress of former colonies asserting national status, it often appears important to promote the recognition of a local dialect or

Creole as a full-status language. A broader view of "correct" English has seemed vital to many who are working for the wider sharing of privilege among racial and economic groups in our society.

Thus social issues are at stake in our concept of language. By taking the individual utterance and the complementary response of understanding as the basic units of linguistics, Bakhtin has proposed to turn attention from the system of monologue to the activity of dialogue.

UNANSWERED QUESTIONS

Bakhtin's salutary criticisms of system illuminate an unease that we face in identifying the complex, heterogeneous activities of communication with the simplified mechanics of an abstract formal model. However, nothing in his polemic answers the questions that motivated the hypothesis of a system in the first place. The miracle of language is that we understand each other fairly well some of the time. How are we to account for this fact? Clearly there is an important measure of agreement that we share in using language. How does this agreement, this social contract, exist? "We want to understand and be understood; and we learn our native tongue from our elders. Even without the pressure of legislation and dictionaries, our vocabularies tend toward uniformity" (Ryle 1949, p. 33). It is obvious that language is systematic *to some extent*. The theoretical problem is not, of course, to figure out how systematic it is at a given time and place but rather to determine the status of the system in relation to the status of our description of it. When we describe a language system, are we describing a statistical average? a hard and fast fact like the facts of arithmetic? a physical (physiological) structure in the nervous system? an authoritative consensus? or something else? Is the description itself part of the reality we mean to apprehend or a structure apart?

Jan Mukarovsky and Noam Chomsky present opposite ways to respond to these questions. Mukarovsky spells out relations between a semiotic system and its social exploitation much more precisely than Ferdinand de Saussure does. In so doing he shows some sensitivity to the endlessly changing variety of use that Mikhail Bakhtin highlights but retains a central place for system. Unfortunately, Mukarovsky's terminology in describing the "social norm" is confusing metaphysically. As we have already seen, Chomsky shows how a language system may be rooted in biology, but the dialectic of systemic stability and social change is not modeled in this theory.

MUKAROVSKY'S "SOCIAL NORM"

Mukarovsky characterizes the norm as a real object of social consciousness. A "social fact" is a fact that results from social relations and that is known as a fact to its society even when its members do not fully submit to it. In this sense, "correct" grammar may be a social fact. (It is a social fact that Santa Claus wears a red suit.) A "norm" is an evolving social fact that is partly independent of the signs that institute it and refer to it. The norm provides a context for the evaluation of signs, both normal and eccentric, but norms other than those that guided their production may also participate in the interpretation. It follows that the norm cannot be reduced to statistical dominance.

Take the infamous cigarette ad, "Winstons taste good / like a cigarette should." The full force of the slogan is available only to those who, at least dimly, retain an ear for "as." "Like" takes its effect from sounding uncultured. The slogan represents the cigarette as a break from pressure, with the pressure to speak grammatically, by school rules, representative of social pressure generally. "Like" relaxes the norm. But it still has to evoke the norm it relaxes, or some of its point is lost. In fact, the point may now be lost. The old "correct" usage has considerably eroded, and this very ad may have made an important contribution to the erosion.

Mukarovsky adds a dimension to the Saussurian concept of a social semiotic system. As Saussure formulated the idea, speech exploits language, but any tension *between* speech and language, any lack of congruence, is neglected as a minor accident. In Mukarovsky's scheme the fit between speech (or literature or artistic works) and the system that they evoke for interpretation may be either more concordant or more discordant. The concord and discord are part of the meaning, as where the slangy quality of the Winstons ad conveys a hint of rebelliousness.

THE ROLE OF RULES: SYSTEMS AS LIMITS

Recall (from chapter 7) that Chomsky argues that children must be born with a predisposition for learning language. Among their innate endowments, as automatic as the sucking reflex, is a propensity to interpret their experience as expressing a rule of one of the types they are genetically equipped to recognize.

What we might highlight for our purposes is the observation, psychologically fundamental and seemingly indubitable, that humans—perhaps some other animals too—have a fascination with rules—finding them, inventing them, representing them, communicating them, testing them, breaking them, changing them—from infancy. Our involvement with rules is creative. The scope of our rule *making* is as impressive as the scope of rule using. Teachers do it. All authorities do it. Kids improvising ball games and tag games do it. Linguists and cognitive psychologists do it. It's both a way of accounting for what we find and for controlling the world. We do not know whether animals a mite simpler than ourselves invent any rules, but reports of animal trainers suggest that animals enjoy using rules. No doubt it broadens their minds.

Note how we often find rigid rules with qualifications more fun and more clear than probabilistic rules. We would never say "Three strikes, more or less, and you're out." But what an elaborate forest of regulations we are ready to invoke, deciding what is a strike and what is not!

Semiotic systems are efficacious factors of social life, not convenient fictions; they realize abstract rules not statistical averages; they emerge from biology and do not require class authority. The *semiotic system* is a limit.

The concept of limits from mathematics is now understood to represent an intrinsic reality of many complex phenomena, but I don't think the role of this idea is appreciated as widely as it might be. The limit of a process is the result toward which it would tend if left alone. A mathematical limit is the final value or range of an infinite series; for example, the limit of $1 + \frac{1}{2} + \frac{1}{4} + \frac{1}{8} + \ldots = 2$. To situate the notion very briefly and indicate its scope, this is first of all the idea that permits a resolution of Zeno's paradoxes. It is inherent in everything the differential and integral calculi accomplish. It is a basic, constitutive idea ("abstractive limit") in Whitehead's *Philosophy of Nature*, which remains an important cornerstone of the attempt to wed modern physics to the phenomenal world of experience. The "attractor," a central conception in the emerging science of chaos is another incarnation of this same idea. We cannot explain the action of a thermostat or the behavior of a healthy organism without entertaining the reality of limits; yet a house with a working thermostat need never maintain precisely the temperature to which it is set, and total health may be an impossible ideal.

A semiotic system is a limit of convergent rule production and rule communication. The concept is *least* problematic with regard to language. It is evident, as soon as we compare language itself with classical music, Noh theater, Renaissance architecture, international diplomacy, holiday rituals, and the like, that systems vary widely in their degrees of systematization and in the ways they are manifest and authorized.

A norm does its job despite being elusive or perhaps even impossible to realize. Its job is regulative. We must not say on that account that the norm is "merely" an intellectual construct. It is a construct, to be sure, but one that groups together real-world elements that interact to develop or sustain a condition. The norm is a goal toward which as system tends to adjust or against which it expresses deviation.

Recognizing limits seems to be part of our basic mental equipment. In normal life no one gets hung up by Zeno's paradoxes, and we do many tasks that require the equivalent of knowing a mathematical limit, such as catch baseballs.

The deeply and universally human activities of rule finding, rule making, rule sharing, rule testing and breaking can be convergent or partly convergent in accord with our desires for social coherence. We have both explicit and intuitive methods of harmonizing our rules. When they are at least partly convergent, we may speak of the agreement they project as their limit, and, if signs are what are regulated, then the rules are a semiotic system.

Within the dominant turbulence of dialogue, systems are real factors. Semiotic systems may crystallize only transiently in *usage*, but as projected limits that are part of a shared apparatus for understanding usage, they have more longevity. We emphasize the following characteristics:

1. A grammar is not to be equated with any average, such as most frequent usage or common speech.
2. Each person participating in a grammar has a picture of it, although not necessarily a clear, consistent, and articulate conception. The status of the description is not the same as the status of the system.
3. Those who at any time wish to gain effect by contradicting the prevailing grammar still depend on and may help define that grammar.
4. Together conscious and/or unconscious thought create the grammar. Given the hunger for rules we observe, there is no reason to think of a dictionary, an etiquette book, a style manual, a regulation

on vocabulary from the Acadamie Française as an unnatural imposition on natural language. Furthermore, the expertise expressed in a dictionary has every reason to play an authoritative role, since that is what society as a whole looks to dictionaries for. The critical disappointment that greeted *Webster's Third International Dictionary* reflected an understandable distress at the publisher's increased reliance on averages (popular usage) where judgment, authentic authority, was desired—a cop-out.

5. Among the fully or partially conscious expressions of grammar, a very special place must be accorded to pedagogy. This principle is widely recognized in anthropological method.

6. None of the foregoing diminishes the observation that the status of grammar in language is volatile.

7. The boundaries of semiotic systems are utterly vague most of the time, and subdivisions into idioms, dialects, and the like, are unreliable and transient. (Saussure's remarks on this point in the final part of the *CGL* are quite interesting.) We can best characterize these regions by archetypal examples. Hence the importance of canonical collections for cohesive societies.

8. We do not abandon the postulate of distinct systems even where the concrete evidence is disparate and intransigent. Semiotic systems and the social effort to harmonize systems are so basic to us that they remain effective factors even in situations of extreme contradiction.

PART III

Analysis of the Sign

We have so far acquired partial ideas of semiotic system and sign system. These ideas will prove essential to understanding signs but do not tell us what signs are. Saussure's conception of the sign as a signifier correlated with a signified is inadequate to give us a handle on the behavior of signs in mental life. What it leaves out is the angles. The sign is biased. Representation is of something *as* something. Turkey and pumpkin pie signify Thanksgiving as festive. The cross and the lamb both refer to Jesus but as a martyr and as a fount of gentle love respectively. When the lamb in the Psalms refers to the Jewish people, it refers to them as vulnerable. Chapter 3 took note of the sign's bias via brief references to Gottlob Frege and Charles Peirce. Even to call an object a "book" is to focus on its potential to be read rather than its weight or color or inflammability. We refer to it, in Peirce's phrase, "in some respect or capacity."

Chapter 9 acknowledges Peirce's schematization of these relations in the context of a comprehensive philosophy. Chapter 10 develops a method of speaking about aspects of mind, a deliberately minimal method, intended to orient semiotics. Chapter 11 employs this method of speaking about mind to construct a schema of the sign derived in its form from Peirce but independent of his philosophical commitments. Chapter 12 considers the place of the sign in mental life, its boundaries, its correlation with consciousness, and its embodiment in the physical world, drawing our study of mental life out of psychology and back into the world of signs.

9

PEIRCE'S PROBLEMATICS FOR THE SIGN

In part II we contrasted an orderly synchronic system (*langue*) to a chaotic diachronic environment (*parole*, dialogue). Peirce's semiotic, oriented as it is by science, rotates the axis of intelligibility by 90 degrees. Concurrent signs represent for him an accidental if not chaotic competition, but over time signs develop in comprehensiveness and converge on truth. Thus— importing Saussure's terms, which Peirce did not use—the synchronic picture is chaotic; the diachronic development shows order.

Peirce originally called his philosophy "pragmatism." By this name he signaled his principle that the meaning of an idea was its intellectual consequences. The word has gotten into a lot of trouble: Using "pragmatism" to mean practical compromise is a later corruption and has nothing to do with us. I would like to retain "pragmatism" as an epithet to identify Peircean semiotics, as a major family of semiotics contrasting with "structuralism" and "functionalism."

Peirce's semiotics is, I think, the most elaborate, audacious, inventive, and grand that we have. When I began my work in semiotics, Peirce was almost an obscure figure. Now there is so large and diverse a literature about his work or deriving from it (and, finally, a biography; see Brent 1992) that I do not think it my responsibility or my special competence to offer a summary. This chapter permits me to acknowledge my debt to Peirce, to indicate my differences from him, and to review some of the ideas that we take from him.

I also cannot take on the task of guiding the reader with respect to the abundant and evolving literature on Peirce. My own understanding of his thought was strongly colored by the interpretations of David Savan, and I regret that his invaluable little handbook remains out of print. The range of orientations of Peirce scholars is itself striking. Savan worked primarily as an analytical philosopher. An author to whom I have a very deep but different debt is Roberta Kevelson, less for detached analysis than for her empathy with Peirce. She knew every inch of his manuscripts and seems able to write of the world through his eyes.

SOME ASPECTS OF PEIRCE'S LIFE AND WORK

Charles Peirce (1839–1914) wrote about semiotic problems throughout his career. From 1861–1890 he worked as a practicing scientist with the U.S. Coastal and Geodetic Survey. His published papers include long and elaborate reports on color measurement, and instrumentation problems. Although he contributed to philosophical journals and spent three years teaching, he was not by employment an academic. A concern with science, understood as an unfinished and rough-and-tumble laboratory activity, permeates his writing.

The imprint of Peirce's understanding of practical science on his semiotics is decisive. The dominant pictures of signs in his imagination are images of *developing* knowledge, of knowledge in progress rather than knowledge as a fixed block of information. Evolving scientific knowledge provides such an image or model on the large scale as does detail of inference on the small scale.

Peirce (whom Bertrand Russell credited with founding the mathematics of relations) also undertook extensive researches in mathematics and constructed a mathematical or quasi-mathematical treatment of some of his fundamental semiotic ideas. The mathematical notion of the matrix (the chief notational device of linear algebra, his father's specialty) seems to have made a special imprint on Peirce's way of picturing signs. In algebra, a matrix is an array of numbers or values, finite or infinite, in two or more dimensions. A key move in their mathematical treatment is to represent a whole matrix, with its myriad entries, by one letter. The idea of one sign that subsumes a host of anterior signs is a recurring figure of thought for Peirce. This is his figure for the "hypothesis," the proposed summary of a multitude of data. He can thus write, "the sensation of a particular kind of sound arises in consequence of impressions upon the various nerves of the ear being combined in a particular way, and following one another with a certain rapidity. . . . a sensation is a simple predicate taken in place of a complex predicate; it fulfills the function of an a hypothesis" (Collected Papers 5.280; 1955 p. 237) Or more dramatically: "A man is a sign." Peirce is quick to switch from part to whole by this same sort of substitution. A syllogism, which a linguistically oriented semiotician will tend to see as at least 12 words in 3 sentences, often is treated as 1 sign by Peirce. Such a conception of wholes and parts posits the idea I attend to further in part IV, "Elaborations of the Sign," but notwithstanding his specific contributions to logic, I don't find any hint in Peirce, as I do in structuralism, of an analytical framework for a *generalized* understanding how parts relate to wholes within sign factors.

Peirce aimed at an all-encompassing philosophic synthesis. Because he incorporated semiotics into his foundation for philosophy, any adaptation of his ideas in the context of a doctrine less philosophically ambitious is likely to emaciate them. Indeed, that is the case for the following chapters of this book. I provide cursory indications of Peirce's doctrine here to clarify this difference.

PHILOSOPHICAL FOUNDATIONS

All Peirce's philosophy develops his doctrine of Categories: "a Category is an element of phenomena of the first rank of generality . . ." (CP.5.43. I use the capital "C" for Peirce's foundational Categories to avoid confusing these with grammatical categories). Peirce's scheme of Categories recalls the Kantian scheme of encounter (or intuition), concept, and judgment, but he calls them simply "Firsts," "Seconds," and "Thirds." I take the nudity of that nomenclature as an emblem of his intention to render a pure analysis, completely independent of the connotative baggage of historic philosophic terms such as "being" and "essence."

Firsts are qualitative possibilities. They may or may not exist and have no relation to time. "Red," "Kafkaesque," "elliptical," are firsts. Seconds are individual facts of existence. A First is solitary, but a Second, for Peirce, requires two elements, one more passive and one more dynamic. There must be a relation of resistance. Instances of Seconds might be a bat striking a ball, a rock occupying a position in space and time, a thought occurring to you, a shoe exhibiting a color, a mark aligning with a clock hand, or, in quantum physics, a value and a measurement.

Thirds are continuities and regularities and are instantiated by, minimally, three elements, one of which connects the other two. Thirds provide the schema for signs.

TWO NOTIONS OF SIGN: DESIGNATE AND SITUATE

"[N]o Representamen actually functions as such until it actually determines an interpretant, yet it becomes a Representamen as soon as it is fully capable of doing this; and its Representative Quality is not necessarily dependent upon its ever actually determining an Interpretant, nor even upon its actually having an Object."

—Charles Peirce, *Philosophical Writings of Peirce.*

The terminology I develop in this section is not Peirce's. A sign is often considered a type of tool, a tool of thought. But taking "tool" as referring just to physical objects, we see two quite different conceptions under this same rubric. On one hand, a tool is an artifact manufactured specifically to serve the manipulation of other materials. On the other hand, a tool is also any object employed for the purpose of manipulating other objects, as were we to say: "Recent ethology shows that several primates other than man use tools" (e.g., chimpanees use twigs to fish for termites).

A similar distinction fits signs. I will refer to the first as a *situate* and the second as *designate.* The *sign-situate* is a sign only when situated as one. The *sign-designate* is understood to be a sign even if idle or misused.

The distinction is fairly obvious, but one sequitur may not be. The *description* of situate tools requires a more abstract method because it cannot begin with the already isolated implement. To describe how an arbitrary object acts as a tool, we need to abstract some essential principle. For example, a branch is a tool because it is used *as* a lever or *as* a floater or *as* a poker. Corresponding to these employments, the branch must have certain qualities or capacities, for example, elasticity, buoyancy, strength. These correspond to what, in the case of signs, Peirce calls the "ground." Talking about tools-designate or signs-designate, we can presume this analysis already accomplished.

A sign-designate in a given situation of use is *also* a sign-situate. An English sentence is a sign whether uttered or not—a designated sign; but a cloth tied to a tree on Sunday to show a later-arriving friend the path to join my picnic—a situated sign—may cease to be a sign on Monday. Peirce is oriented by the sign-situate. What a grammar book lying idle on the shelf represents is not Peirce's primary concern. His distinctive interest in a sentence is what it would accomplish in a actual context of a particular use; his focus, opposite to Saussure, is *parole,* not *langue.* Because his approach is abstract and general, it is not always obvious that he is reasoning about concrete sign occasions, but, as per the preceding argument, it is this very orientation that requires abstraction. His formulations become more transparent when we insist on this point.

For example, Peirce's central notion of the "interpretant" covers so much territory that it is coherent only when it is situated. What, we may want to ask, is the interpretant of a red flag? The answer could only be an endless chain of perhapses and might bes. If we reinstate the red flag into situations, we can specify interpretants: "Seeing the red flag,"

"the engineer slammed the brakes" or
"the bull charged furiously" or
"all the marchers knew where to turn" . . .

Peirce is not unaware of the designated sign, which he addresses via the category of "legisigns," but these are a subgroup in the larger picture.

THE ANALYSIS OF SIGNS INTO FACTORS

Peirce regards the sign as characterized by its relation to an object and an interpretant. As noted in chapter 3, he does not offer a distinct term for the trio of sign, object, and interpretant taken as one whole. His "representamen" is synonymous with "sign" with the same ambiguity of double usage; kidnapping it for the "signifier" exclusively is, so far as I know, my imposition.

Peirce sometimes refers to the representamina, object, and interpretant as a "First," a "Second," and a "Third" respectively. I am not sure I grasp the logic of this elegant economy, however. It is clear in other contexts that the representamen can be a First *or* a Second *or* a Third: His first sign classes (qualisign, sinsign, legisign) divide signs according to the Category of the representamen. Here we see that the representamen may comprise positive qualities and positive facts, not just empty "difference." The breadth of possibilities for representamina contrasts with Saussure's structuralism where all the signifiers are what Peirce calls "legisigns": constructs of rules.

Peirce's notion of the sign's object reflects his preoccupation with scientific knowledge and with truth. He distinguishes a "dynamic object," an independent *Ding-an-sich* that influences semiosis (for example, a natural fact that determines the outcome of an experiment) and an "immediate object" internal to the sign-complex.

Some signs have no dynamic object at all in Peirce's sense. An imaginary landscape, fantastic or realistic, is such. A consistent and logically complete semiotics can be constructed without any notion corresponding to the dynamic object, but such a semiotics (mine is of this type) must be content to put aside questions of factual truth. It is one thing to develop a system that does not assert any view of a reality independent of representation and quite another to deny that such a reality exists.

Peirce's conception of the interpretant is probably his most original contribution, but it is an idea that develops over many years, and I am not yet convinced of its unity. As I understand it, Peirce's idea of the interpretant responds to at least four motivations: to provide a theory of mind, to characterize the bond between the object and representamen, to account for the growth or elaboration of signs, and to integrate semiotics with a theory of inference (especially nondeductive). The conception of the interpretant constructed in chapter 11 is essentially a restricted subset of Peirce's ideas. Here too it is a matter of focusing on a narrower group of problems. The problems of inference and of the growth of thought are largely outside my purview.

TYPOLOGY

Peirce classified signs in several ways. The best-known and most influential is his classification of signs as icons, indices, and symbols.

I caution again that every theory has its own use for the small repertoire of available semiotic terms. Peirce's icon is not Erwin Panofsky's icon (which Peirce would call a symbol), and Peirce's symbol is not Carl Jung's symbol (which Peirce, no doubt in great dismay at the very notion, would probably have to call an index, if he accepted Jung's claim that they were natural).

The trichotomy of icon, index, and symbol considers the *relation* between a representamen and its object. (More strictly: between the ground and the object. The concept of the ground is discussed in chapter 11.) In explaining icons, indices, and symbols Peirce somewhat conflated three types of analysis. One explanation refers to the Categories, the second explanation characterizes dependencies among the sign factors, and the third concerns similarity and contiguity, that is, types of association.

The most popular conception of this trichotomy takes this last tack and is surely inadequate, but let us review it. In this way of thinking, icons are signs by similarity (pictures, diagrams, metaphors, etc.). Indices are signs by cause or contiguity (samples, smoke for fire, proper names, metonyms, etc.). Symbols are signs by arbitrary rules (languages, flower symbols, chess pieces, etc.). The problems arise from the indistinctness of similarity and contiguity.

Similarity and contiguity are results of signs. They are not given a priori; they are interpretations. What are similar flowers to me are not necessarily to the honeybee. The relation of cause represents at best a selection. (Did I catch a cold because of a virus or because I was tired?) More important, most similarities have causes—that is the essence of imitation, deliberate similarity. Most causes induce resemblances if seen from the right vantage: The billiard ball strikes another that then moves with similar speed to the first. It is obvious that a photograph can be understood as similar to its subject or as caused by its subject, but really, the same applies to a painting. The light strikes the lens of the painter's eye, and, if similarity will be a result, it is because patterns will be transmitted through the artist's nervous system and paintbrush to the canvas. In medieval herbology the "Doctrine of Similars" held that leaves worked curatively for organs that they visually resembled, an icon provided to man by God. Or an index? We cannot start out from similarity and cause.

The definitions that seem to me most tenable are those Peirce gives in the synopsis to one section of his article "Sign" in Baldwin's *Dictionary of Philosophy and Psychology* of 1902 (Peirce 1955 p. 104). These definitions are formed in terms of dependencies among the sign factors: "An *icon* is a sign [with a representamen] which would possess the character which renders it significant even though its object had no existence." "An *index* is a sign [of which the representamen] would, at once, lose the character which makes it a sign if its object were removed, but would not lose that character if its interpretant were removed." "A *symbol* is a sign which would lose the character which renders it a sign if there were no interpretant."

In accord with these definitions, we can describe a picture as an icon. A picture has a certain character, which would enable it to represent any scene that shares that character, whether such a scene exists or not. You might run into someone who looked just like a portrait painted 100 years ago. The qualities that enable the painting to resemble this person came into existence without the person's intervention. Peirce's favorite example of a pure icon is the mathematical equation for the ellipse that happens to represent the earth's orbit. (It can be seen that these icons all depend on qualities—Firsts.) Similarly, we may take a photo for an index. A photograph, although it can function simply as a picture, usually is taken as evidence of the appearance of some real person or situation. Its function requires a real connection with its subject—in the form of relative spatial position—and this requirement identifies it as an index. My file dividers are signs only because of their positions relative to my files. Smoke can be a sign of fire only because they are connected. (These actual relations are facts and relate indices to Seconds.) As an example of symbols, take sentences. A sentence is physically independent of its topic in every respect but requires a rule of interpretation (the hallmark of a Third).

In the preceding paragraph the parentheses isolate references to the Categories and show, I think, that the definitions do not depend on the Categories.

A terminal point. Peirce's choice of the word "symbol" comes to seem second nature to Peirceans, but it goes against the grain of dominant usage. We do speak as he does of mathematical or chemical symbols, but elsewhere common usage weights "symbol" and "symbolic" with a quasimagical connotation. Therefore, on this point I break with the Peirceans. The term I will use for an arbitrary, rule-governed sign is *term*. I've been doing it all along, and you didn't mind. The corresponding adjective must be "stipulated," which is a compromise, but "terminal" won't do.

MINDS

It is best to think of icon, index, and term (symbol) as aspects of sign a rather than as types because they co-occur. Figure 9.1 is a reminder of this point.

The whole theory that has been sketched is without *essential* reference to persons or minds. The dividend for Peirce, as a analytically oriented theorist, is that he can hope to say what mentality is in terms of semiosis rather than the reverse: "signs are not to be explained by reference to some occult and intrinsically private power called 'mind,' but mind itself is to be explained in terms of those manifest and inherently intersubjective processes called semioses" (Colapietro, 1989, pp. 9–10). Peirce construes signs as embodying the process of synthesis, which prior philosophical in-

Figure 9.1   Stipulated indexical icon

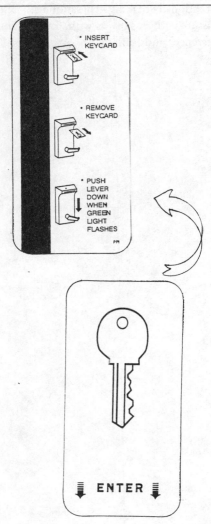

vestigations had seen as essential to knowledge and thinking. The progress of interpretants enriching or approximating an object to which they are never fully equivalent diagrams the movement of ideas. With regard to chronology, we can note that Peirce gave expression to this idea before

Saussure's *Course in General Linguistics* saw the light of day and that he conveys an insight rationally that my generation has wanted to wrest by reaction against Saussure with slogans, as with "Every signified is a signifier" or the play of "diference" and "differance."

10

PSYCHOLOGICAL ASPECTS
OF SIGNIFICATION

In the next chapter, I retain the Peircean form of the sign as instantiating an irreducibly triadic relation among three factors and I retain his terms, representamen, object, and interpretant. However, I propose a basis for this conception which does not depend on his foundational Categories (Firsts, Seconds, and Thirds). I reject Peirce's philosophy not in favor of some other but rather in favor of less philosophy. The result may have no more depth than a street map, but I hope, like a street map, my readers will be able to accommodate it to their own epistemologies and ontologies. To get along without Thirdness, I will have to explain the interpretant in a somewhat different manner from what I have done so far. That task is the main business of chapter 11. I also will have to approach mentality differently, and that task falls to this chapter. I am interested in using the idea of sign to show what is special about mentality, and I find that what I regard as special pertains to consciousness exclusively. The unconscious is a good concept, but we will see that it has no need of semiotics for its development.

Consciousness is a scramble. An idea that obsesses us on Monday may disappear entirely Tuesday and Wednesday only to return on Thursday for no reason apparent. We take "stream of consciousness" almost as a synonym for randomness. We miss the obvious and don't see things right in front our noses. We jump to conclusions. But all this disorder is disorder only with respect to a particular order: the order of physics (including biology). Physics constructs a world where groups of events have groups of consequences or precedents in a dependable manner, where mutually entailed occurrences occur with temporal adjacency, where a law that holds on Monday and Thursday is bound to apply on Tuesday and Wednesday as well. Note that the world of physics is not the world that first presents itself to our sight. That is the whole point of the baby's game of peek-a-boo. A face comes in and out of view, and the baby learns to conjecture that the apparently disappearing face continues to exist in between: The baby begins, quite instinctively, to construct the world of physics. It is an essential construction, a sign, some would say (chapter 12 presents a contrary view), of a world that has no need for signs. The unconscious is a similar conjecture that allows a physical and biological accommodation of the conscious mind. It posits that when an idea appears to vanish and then reoccur, it had not really ceased to exist in the meantime but simply had taken up residence in this other place, the unconscious, just as in peek-a-boo.[1] Physical order thus is maintained in the mind by supplementing the conscious with the unconscious.

There is nothing wrong with this line of thought, but physical explanation (while using signs in its presentation) does not require recourse to the *concept* of semiosis, and semiotics is not properly concerned to establish physical explanations. For our present purposes we have no need of the physical world or the unconscious.

ITEMS AND PROCESSES

Consciousness has no clear boundaries.

Normally, to be conscious means to be conscious of something. (Perhaps this does not hold for all meditative states.) In a given moment we are sharply aware of some things at certain times and dimly aware of others. Consciousness includes a foreground of foci of attention and a general background of feelings—including, as William James emphasized, the feeling or the hum of being alive), beliefs, intentions, and assumptions.

An *item in consciousness,* or *item* for short, is anything we attend to. Items belong to the foreground. A *process* in consciousness is the background. Items and processes in consciousness are generally distinct but not always sharply divided. For simplicity, I will speak as if the division were firmer than it is. The relation of the foreground and background is very fluid with frequent exchange of contents between them. My mood can become an item of attention just as a disturbing bank statement that I put aside can slip into the background and become part of the process of feeling and knowing that surrounds my new thoughts.

An item in consciousness may be anything at all that an individual is conscious of, an object, a memory, a feeling, an idea, a hunch, a condition, an event, and so on. There is no a priori limitation. Items can be simple or complex. Seeing me you might be conscious of my face, my eyes, my tonsils, my bad manners, my history, or whatever. However, there are limitations that are evident empirically. I distinguish between you as the same person I had coffee with yesterday (but haven't seen in between) and the regular cup of coffee, which is a different cup of coffee from the one I drank yesterday even though it may look more similar to yesterday's coffee than you now, newly outfitted, do to you yesterday. Two encounters with one person could easily be two items, but it seems difficult to be conscious of the individual, him- or herself, as consisting of two or more items in the sense suggested by the example. Similarly, coffee is an item, but two successive cups of coffee don't easily make one item. I mention these constraints to show that the notion of an item of consciousness, flexible as it obviously is, is not a wild card. In chapter 11, items are taken to be the normal immediate factors of signs. Chapter 17 proposes that processes take this role in special cases.

ITEMS AS INNER OR OUTER

"Every sane person lives in a double world, the outer and the inner world, the world of percepts and the world of fancies" (Peirce, 1955, p. 283).

Now as I write I see my paper and pen—"percepts." I close my eyes to think and see them still—"fancies." The immediate advantage of dealing with items of consciousness instead of percepts and fancies (or "ideas," "sensation," what-have-you) is to go with the flow. We can say that you close your eyes but still have the same item in consciousness as you did when they were open (although now as a memory instead of a sensation). In taking this stance, we do not deny the possibility of distinguishing imagination from sensation. We just put the problem aside.

John Locke said the two chief species of signs were words and ideas. He meant to separate mental and external signs that way as Petrus Fonseca did, c. 1600, in dividing signs into "formal" and "instrumental." By considering sign factors to be items in consciousness, which may be either of the internal or external world, I propose to devalue this difference.

Examined closely, almost all items in consciousness blend internal and external phases. We divide our awareness with considerable ambiguity. We may discipline ourselves to recognize dreams as internal, but this is a matter of culture: They look and feel as if they include an external world. We cannot shake off the philosophical riddles that frame our split view (for example, the idea that the whole universe is an idea) like water off a duck's back. Rather, depending on temperament, they can substantially enhance our confusion for seconds or days at a time. Sometimes we need to pinch ourselves. "Music is a strange thing," wrote Heinrich Heine, "half way between thought and phenomenon" (from his Letters on the French Stage, cited in Barzun, 1951, p. 306).

The division is neither neat nor logical. Taste is not projected as firmly as vision and may seem more "subjective," but why? Nor is the mind-body split simply binary. (Where do I imagine your thoughts are? In Buddhist psychology the mind's perception of thoughts is held to be fully analogous to its perception of visible objects. Why not?)

How intimately blended our internal and external worlds are, is a point Daniel C. Dennett (1991) emphasizes. When taking in a scene, we can attend only to a tiny fraction of it at any given instant (not more than 15 degrees of arc). Unaware of this, I take the image of one part in memory as a substitute for external perception as my gaze moves to another part, the eye moving several times per second to build up a composite picture.

If for some reason we need to categorize an item as external or internal, I would suggest recourse to the type-token relation. The constellation of images or impressions is stabilized by a unity on one side of the line or the other, which we might call its focus. The idea of bicycles is internal because the focal item, an idea, ties together a disparate group of external experiences. On the other hand, a particular bicycle is external because as a physical object, it ties together and controls the myriad images I may have of it.

CONSCIOUSNESS ITSELF

I have been speaking of consciousness—without saying what it is—simply on the basis of my acquaintance with it. I am not committed to a particular understanding of consciousness and do not believe that the theoretical position established here and in the next chapter depends on one particular conception of consciousness. For example, for present purposes it does not matter whether self-consciousness is entailed in consciousness or not. Our consciousness, bound up with language and other complex systems and texts, is very sophisticated, but it may be, for all I know, that consciousness can be very simple. Peirce asked us to imagine a creature whose entire lifelong consciousness would be the stink of rotten cabbage or a certain shade of crimson. Kalu Rinpoche, in his *Fundamental Instructions in Vajrayana Buddhism,* insists that the lowly leech has a consciousness capable of experiencing pleasure, pain, desire, and frustration. (Personally, I am unable to imagine what Peirce requests although I can extend some empathy toward the leech.) Russell's conclusion in his *Analysis of Mind* (1921) is that the minimum of consciousness is a sensation with a belief.

A dismissive way to think of consciousness is to regard its entire contents simply as the incidental shadow play of brain processes that are complete and self-sufficient without it. This is much how we regard mirror images: It would seem silly to formulate an account of the world in the mirror without taking into account the world on the other side. On this view any rational patterning of consciousness is a by-product either of order in the physical world (which causes orderly sensations) or of order in the unconscious or of a combination of the two. On this view consciousness has no independent organization or function. The assumption there is that the same information that we hold consciously could be held unconsciously, a plausible but arbitrary assumption.

This is a humbling perspective. If it is valid, my efforts to comprehend signs in conscious mental life largely apart from any consideration of underlying biological and physical computations will prove a poor investment in the long run, like an independent description of the world in a mirror; yet the motivation for semiotics is to do this. Semiotics attends to relations in consciousness which, according to the evidence thus far, have no independent isomorph in the physical world.

RELATIONS AMONG ITEMS OF CONSCIOUSNESS

What relations can items of consciousness have with each other aside from those relations we attribute to the external physical world?

"Association" is a concept of relations between items of consciousness, but association is just a blanket term. (To see this, we need only contrast it to "matching," for example, a relation Nelson Goodman describes narrowly and precisely in *The Structure of Appearance* [1951]. His matching is a particular kind of association, not just any old association.) The question then is: What different kinds of associations can items of consciousness enjoin with each other?

Sharing a perspective is a relation peculiar to items in consciousness. Perspective is a hallmark of mentality. A *perspective* is a representation that establishes the unity of its contents. The lens of a camera does unify its content in a trivial sense. For the lens, the notion of "point" of view is completely literal. There is a single point in physical space, the focal point, through which all light striking the lens from a given distance will pass. The unity achieved has nothing to do with the identities of the objects photographed. In contrast, a mental perspective brings impressions together in ways that are independent of physical space, although it may include physical relations as a "raw material," and the unity achieved depends on the content of the material unified. A perspective painting records a unity that belongs to seeing, not to the canvas. The fact that a picture can convey a perspective is exemplary of the principle that mental perspectives can be represented, but the picture does not supplant the mind that makes or reads it. Visual perspective is one special case. The first chapter of *The Portrait of the Artist as a Young Man* by James Joyce represents the perspective of a toddler; the perspective is conveyed by the language of the narrative.

The variability of items points out another group of relations, one with a long pedigree in philosophy: synthesis. The mind zooms into and out of items like a telescopic lens. I think of a tree or look at one, and immediately I am drawn in toward its parts (branches, leaves, bark) or aspects (height, health, color) or out toward its context (scenic, historic, genealogical). Each item seems to arise in an analysis of another or a synthesis of many others.

There are various kinds of synthesis: full integration, as with the shape and color of one object; qualified attribution where a property is not securely integrated with an object, as when you suspect a piece of fruit is not quite ripe; grouping, as when you see a basket of fruit as one item and, I suppose, many others.

I don't propose to analyze these fields of relations among items of consciousness comprehensively. I only want to propose that in the relation of representation or signification, items are brought together in a way that is not adequately characterized as simply association or synthesis. The task of the next chapter is to characterize signification as a particular kind of relation among items.

11

WHAT IS A SIGN?

The definitions of the sign and its factors developed in this chapter are schematically like Peirce's but with the consequential differences that (a) their basis is ad hoc psychological categories rather than Peirce's ontological categories; (b) the interpretant is not taken necessarily to be itself a sign; and (c) the "dynamic object" is considered external to the theory. (Although what I presume about mind is minimal, with point (a) I abandon the priority that Peirce accords semiotics over psychology. I imagine different disciplines growing together and interdependently.)

Situated signs are dealt with first; the term "sign" standing alone is taken here, until I signal otherwise to refer to this type only.

DEFINITION OF SIGN

A *sign-complex* ("*sign*" for short) is a triplet of three distinct factors. The *factors of a sign* are *items in consciousness*. The three factors, the *representamen* (also "sign" for short!), *object,* and *interpretant,* are characterized by their functions with respect to each other in an asymmetrical and irreducibly triadic relationship.

"Distinct"

There is some resistance to the full and permanent synthesis of the items comprising the sign. No one would say of a wisp of smoke that it was a sign of fire unless the fire were hidden from view and perhaps of uncertain location. But there are difficult cases; the factors may not be easily or fully distinct.

"By their Functions"

Whether an item is a representamen, object, or interpretant depends ultimately on relations established in the sign.

"Asymmetrical"

The factors in one sign do not permute. In the rare cases where two items might represent each other, we have two different sign-complexes.

"Irreducibly Triadic"

Parts of a sign relation can no more function independently than a stool can rest on just two legs. This does not mean the sign is insusceptible of analysis. We are not inhibited from describing the components or the component relations, but the roles of the factors can be defined only circularly by reference to each other.

An intellectual difficulty of semiotics is that the factors of a sign situation that can be distinguished theoretically are not always entirely distinct in experience. A sign situation is evanescent. We might compare it to a brief flame in which two readily distinguishable materials (representamen and object) react via an event (interpretant) that transforms and encompasses both. The flame reminds us that an event is an object. (A flame is both a chemical process and a visual object.) A fixed image of the sign suggests the inadequacy of a snapshot of a moving subject but is not, on that account, wrong.

REPRESENTAMEN

The *representamen* is the factor that, by its association with an object, evokes and constrains an interpretant of the object. I follow Peirce in distinguishing in the representamen two phases, its *material* aspect and its *ground*. Whatever is specific in a particular representamen that is not required for its representational capacity is an aspect of its *material*. What is required is the *ground*. For some examples, the color of a paint chip is its ground whereas the material shape of the paint chip is incidental. The shape and proportional relations of a technical drawing are its ground, the color and thickness of the paper being incidents of the material. The aroma of a perfume is its ground, and the material chemical composition of the solvent is incidental. All of these incidental features could have a bearing on the effectiveness of the sign, but they do not determine what it represents.

We cannot on an a priori basis exclude any feature of a representamen as merely material; what the ground is depends on the whole sign situation. If we take an art painting or musical performance as a representamen, every detail may be significant: the thickness of the paint, the frame, the posture of the pianist. But if we hang a painting only to represent the work of a framing shop, the ground will be quite reduced.[1]

The material phase of an external representamen is a *vehicle*. For an internal representamen, the material phase is an *image*. It is sometimes tempting but always false to speak of the vehicle or image as representing the ground. The wood-and-metal stop sign at my corner does not represent a Platonic stop sign, nor does it represent a red octagon; it represents an instruction to brake. The ground and vehicle are alternative construals or alternate descriptions of the same representamen, one concrete, the other abstract.

OBJECT

The *object* of a sign is the factor that the interpretant develops or transforms. All thoroughgoing theories of semiotics confront the apparent multiplicity of the object. Here the object will be identified with what Peirce calls the "immediate object."

Consider an X-ray photograph as a sign. Suppose my arm has been hurt and I have it X-rayed. The film is the representamen; its pattern of darker and lighter patches is the ground. What the X ray looks like depends on the actual condition of my arm. My arm, as the physical entity that influences the X ray, Peirce calls the "dynamic object." I start out with an idea of my arm, a "preunderstanding" that comes from living with it, using it, seeing it close up, and feeling its pains. This prior conception of my arm Peirce calls an "immediate object." It is apparent in this case that the immediate object and the dynamic object are close kin, but this is not always so.

In one of Peirce's examples, a man standing at the shore points to a very distant boat and remarks about its heavy freight to his companion. The companion, who has weaker vision, cannot see the boat. Peirce concludes that the immediate object for the companion can only be the patch of water pointed at (Peirce CP 2.231–232; 1955, p. 101).

Peirce's insistence that the immediate object of a sign be something *already* in mind, something that the sign will *develop,* seems exactly counter to that medieval formula that the sign "brings something to mind." His conception echoes pedagogical common sense. No use to walk in fresh on a class of North American sixth graders and start lecturing on Peruvian agricultural production. They won't be able to bring anything relevant to mind. Much better to ask what they had for breakfast, discuss with them where it came from, and get to your agribusiness by that route.

(Although the dynamic object as Peirce construes it is not an item of consciousness; there is a corresponding class of items of consciousness, the propositional functions: "where the break in my arm really is," "what the average temperature of all matter in the universe is," "how Shakespeare understood Hamlet's motives.")

We sometimes indicate the absence or irrelevance of a dynamic object by referring to an entity as a construct. A *construct* is the object of a sign that is not firmly linked to a distinct and influential dynamic object. The distinction drawn here is outside of semiotics proper, since we have no special tools to say what is real, but we can pursue the idea as a matter of common sense. Examples might be the national debt, the Renaissance, and the Big Dipper. The national debt is entirely dependent on the representamina that signify individual obligations and the interpretants that lenders and borrowers develop of these. It is difficult to say whether there is a corresponding dynamic object distributed in space and time. We might understand "the Renaissance" to have as its dynamic object a class of actual historical events, with "events" taken very comprehensively as including, for example, what individual Italian artisans were thinking in 1411. We can hardly doubt the past physical existence of these items, but nothing aside from our signs of them organize and sort them into a whole that corresponds to "the Renaissance." The case is essentially the same for the Big Dipper. The stars are out there, but they are connected only by our signs.

There is still another way one might conceive the object. We might say that what the photograph in itself was capable of representing was not its subject as such but the subject's appearance. This construal of the object recalls Frege's conception of "sense" (see chapter 3) and also Hjelmslev's notion of the "form" of the "content." However, I don't think the appearance of its object conveyed by the photograph is usually distinct as an item from the total impression that it evokes, and this latter is not the object but the interpretant.

INTERPRETANT

The *interpretant* is the factor of the sign that instantiates, or realizes, the relationship of the representamen to the object.

The X ray invoked earlier will show my arm as whole or fractured. This new, more developed idea of my arm is the interpretant. The interpretant is, from one angle, what actually connects the representamen to its object and, from another angle, what is created as a result of their connection. I develop a model of the interpretant by discussing notations of and exhibitions of relations.

The Function of the Interpretant—Relations

It is crucially important to keep in mind how little we learn about representation simply by calling it a relation. Beyond characterizing this relation as asymmetric (if x represents y, then it does not follow that y represents x) we have said nothing about it in general terms. We have not defined the relation by a rule. Compare: When I say A is taller than B, I have a test in mind. I get them to stand back to back and see whose head is higher. I can do the same test with any old A and B, which establishes that I'm dealing with one and the same relation each time. No similarly precise test will confirm that the relation between the sound "shoe" and the object shoe is the same relation as the one that obtains between the sound "happiness" and the object happiness. Maybe each representamen and its object have a different relationship in the same sense that no two marriages are the same.

In formal logic a two-term relation such as "is older than" takes two relata (*Rupert* is older than *Lucien*). However, any *notation* of that relation has three elements, if we count the indication of the relation itself as one element. If $a = b$, then "a," "$=$," and "b," are the three parts. If we take a class of ordered couples such as (a,b) as relations, then "a," "b," and "$(,)$" are three parts. It may be helpful in this context to recall (as Peirce does) the interchangeability of concrete symbols and spatial arrangements. English almost always requires a copula for simple attributions: "Grandpa *is* quite a gardener!" but the arrangement we exceptionally permit—"Quite a gardener, your grandpa!"—is routine in many languages. Either the "is" or the *form* of the whole can be the syncategorem with "Grandpa" and "a gardener" as the other two terms. In a simple declarative like "Lucien runs," the two words and their schema of ordered contiguity are three elements. In all these forms, it takes three items to state a two-part relation.

What has been said about statements of relations also holds for exhibitions or presentations or instantiations of relations. John is taller than Jack. We have the two relata, John and Jack, and the relation presented summing to three. What does it mean to "present" or "instantiate" a relation? Simply having John and Jack stand in front of me won't do it. I might just notice their socks (which, moreover, may be at the same height). There must be some indication of the relation if it is to be presented, not just to be, and if the instance is to be an instance of taller and not just an instance of socks. To present or instantiate a relation we need a third factor besides the two relata. The interpretant fulfills the function of bringing the representamen and object into relation.

The Forms of the Interpretant

The first form of the interpretant is the image that comes to mind in consequence of encountering a sign. Examples are cited in chapter 3 from Peirce, but Peirce also argues that all responses to a sign are interpretants. If I walk around, not across, a yard that sports a keep-off-the-grass sign, either my thought or my action might be taken as an interpretant. This attribution of equivalence deserves great caution. Ludwig Wittgenstein shows recurrently and conclusively that we cannot determine from behavior that a response is mentally mediated, but mental mediation is something we all experience with fascination and conviction. If there is no mental mediation, we have no reason on earth to invoke interpretants describing responses to information; the concept is just extra baggage. A stimulus-response model or some other mechanical or calculation model will do the whole job.

Principally, the interpretant is our awareness and understanding of the object in the light of its representamen. The *immediate interpretant* is mental and is understanding. The *responsive interpretant* is an expression or other act that incorporates or represents the immediate interpretant. The response may exceed or abbreviate the immediate interpretant, but it is nonetheless a derivative of it. Sometimes we have a response to a sign at a considerable distance of time or logic, like a review of a book or appealing a case to a higher court. Let's call these "seven-league-boot interpretants." Such distant responses are still constrained by the immediate interpretant they embody.

The immediate interpretant is intrinsically tenuous, lacking a firm anchor external to the sign, induced by the representamen and object but not in a fully logical manner. It always involves a supplement or some redundancy. All the analysis that suggests consciousness is inefficacious applies to the interpretant. The interpretant is drawn out in time. Often a sign allows a range of interpretants. Several might come to mind. The response is like a quantum collapse; in responding we select one.

CONTEXTS

Charles Morris proposed to take context as a component of the sign, and David Savan points out the absence of this concept in Peirce.

Each factor of the sign has a context: a germane location, a difference from possible alternatives ("a difference that makes a difference" CP 5.504) or, if the factor is part of a text or functions in a system, then its structural relation to the rest of the text or system.

The pertinence and distinctiveness of signs is always bound up with the biological and cultural contexts in which they work. The oppositions of red and green or hot and cold are a matters of biology and culture. If it is true that music cannot say what words can say and vice versa, that can be only because human brains, ears, and vocal tracts handle them differently.

The *contexts of a representamen* are its medium and its structural environment. Media are what they are both because of their physics and our physiology. The word "medium" is more vague than is generally recognized, as it might be a material or a grammar or a technology. We speak of TV as a medium, of prose as a medium, of oil paint as a medium, as CD as a medium. Perhaps this vagueness is more useful than obstructive. Following a prominent tradition in aesthetics, I take the chief orientation of comparative semiotics to be the comparison of media.

In a text the component elements may or may not be signs, or may have a status that is difficult to pinpoint. If we regard a word as a sign, then a sentence is its structural context. In general, a sign system or a pattern provides the structural contexts of its elements.

The *context of an object* is its *world*. But the object has two worlds, the one from which it is extracted and the one into which the sign inserts it.

If you ask me what I want for dinner, you place dinner in the world of my desires. If you tell me what we will have for dinner, you place dinner in the world of your authority or accomplishments. The context from which the sign was extracted may become extraneous to the sign. Having the X ray, the surgeon probably doesn't care how the arm got broken or even to whom it belongs; the X ray places it in the ahistorical context of her tasks. The capacity of a representamen to extract the object from a context is its power of *designation.* Its capacity to determine a new context for the object is its *modality.* These capacities are explored in chapter 14.

The *context of an interpretant* is a *perspective.* A group of signs may be interpreted in a way that expresses a unity (be it of feeling, of attitude, of situation, of argument, or whatever). These share a perspective. Such a unity often is intuited but difficult to explicate and may be perceived in consciousness as a feeling. Among our most general terms for such unities are "personality" and "style." In the following, personality figures in place of perspective but the issue is identical.

> [P]ersonality is some kind of coordination or connection of ideas. Not much to say, this, perhaps. Yet when we consider that, according to the principle that we are tracing out, a connection between ideas is itself a general idea, and that a general idea is a living feeling, it is plain that we have at least taken an appreciable step toward the understanding of personality. This personality, like any general idea, is not a thing to be apprehended in an instant. It has to be lived in time, nor can any finite time embrace it in all its fullness. Yet in each infinitesimal interval it is present and living, though specially colored by the immediate feelings of that moment. (Peirce, 1972, p. 213)

The bearing of this passage is poetic and intuitively gratifying, especially the thought that we register a personality as a "living feeling." What I cannot transfer from Peirce's standpoint to my own is his assertion that personality is a sign. Personality or style in particular, perspectives in general, are items we perceive. Do they necessarily represent anything else? There are situations in which they well may. But in the first instance, I am inclined to say that Mozart's style is the immediate perception I have of all his work that I know when I stand back far enough from it to perceive it as one whole collection. That I may take this impression to represent his personality or his century or as a clue how to interpret a new score is secondary.

We *perceive* perspectives in much the same way as we perceive visual or auditory objects. The difference between sensory perceptions of things and perceiving perspectives is this: With material objects the individual "sense data" that sum are unconscious. With the perception of a perspective we form an overall impression of details that we also may consciously experience individually. All notions of style or overall character are of this sort—*Weltanschauen, Zeitgeisten,* those qualities Barthes like to indicate with "-ness" ("Frenchness," etc.).

DESIGNATED SIGNS

The third factor of a designated sign may be a rule instead of an interpretant. When the sign is used, that is, situated, we will generally find that the rule is reflected in an item of consciousness which then serves as an interpretant, but perhaps only a rather numb, vague, or automated one.

Take words. When used, which means when situated, words may arouse images as well as achieving references. They then have objects and interpretants. The word sitting idly in the book, which is not an item in consciousness, still has an object to which it is connected by a rule. The rule of the sign designate has a relationship with the interpretant when the same sign is brought to life.

All the plausible interpretants of a designated sign, when it is launched into a sign situation, are governed by its rule, and they form a class. The rule defines the class; the interpretants are the members of the class.

Nevertheless, we note a tendency for consciousness to provide its own supplement to the rule, true interpretants if weak ones. First, the relationship of a designated representamen to its object is felt as "correct," a sensation that can be very powerful and colored with feeling. Second, imagery builds bridges between arbitrary representamina and their objects. I hear the word "flower" as unfolding symmetrically around the center vowel of its triple diphthong, like a flower, but I don't hear "flour" that way. Poetry is our evidence that such arbitrary supplements to hearing words are not purely idiosyncratic.

SOME ENIGMAS OF THE SIGN

The theory of the sign suggests some inherently enigmatic and fascinating characteristics; these are not new discoveries.

The Construction Paradox

Relationships among sign factors are asymmetrical. Beyond their logical asymmetry they suggest an illusory temporal asymmetry. The object, even when analysis tells us that it is a construct, seems to exist prior to the sign complex that refers to it. The apparent precedence of the object is a key factor in rhetoric. If I say "The grumbleberries are nearly ripe," or if I say "The global economy forces us to accept free trade," then I take advantage of a disposition of my auditor to suppose that grumbleberries and the global economy have existence prior to my utterance, that they are not mere rhetorical inventions. I think we are even inclined to regard the mood conveyed by a work of music as existing before the composition. Skepticism is not paralyzed in the face of such abuses, but the disposition (which is not a matter of credulity) will be found very widespread. It is part of what Barthes calls "naturalization" by signs.

The Tenuousness of the Sign

The interpretant is simultaneously essential and superfluous. Whatever rationale an external observer might find for a sign in the relationship of the representamen and object—cause, contiguity, similarity, convention— something more is added in the consciousness of the mind that employs the sign, a something else that makes the sign a sign rather than a reflex, a something else that has no objective justification, a something else that amounts to grasp or understanding.

* It is only the awareness of a sign as a sign that allows for the differentiation of meaning from effect. It is generally held that with the idea of the interpretant, Peirce showed the unity of natural and arbitrary signs; however, as long as the interpretant can be identified with the mere consequence of a sign, as Peirce often seems to allow, we have no passage from physics to semiosis. With the stand taken here, that the interpretant must be conscious, we have a basis for asserting the unity of signs.

In *Kanzi, The Ape at the Brink of the Human Mind*, in which Sue Savage-Rumbaugh reports her brilliant investigations of apes' semiotic competence, she mentions that "Panbanisha . . . liked to pretend that she was taking bites out of pictures of food she saw in magazines" (Savage-Rumbaugh and Roger Lewin 1994, p. 277). Although Savage-Rumbaugh sometimes repeats the common error of supposing that a sign substitutes for its object, what is striking here is the converse: It is clear Panbanisha knows the picture relates to food, for otherwise she wouldn't play-bite. At the same time, it is clear she knows the picture is not food, for otherwise she would show frustration or disappointment instead of amusement. We instantly feel that she is connecting the picture *to an image of food in her consciousness,* to an interpretant. In showing us that the sign does not replace the object, the description nearly compels us to attribute consciousness, even sign consciousness, to Panbanisha.

SIGN ANALYSES—THREE PRELIMINARY EXAMPLES

Judgments and Relations as Signs

Is "Jack is taller than John" a sign? First, the sentence, a judgment represented by a sound and interpreted by (say) an image, certainly is. But relation itself, which we characterized as having three parts (John/Jack/is taller than) may be simply one integrated item. We have no reason to think of it as a sign. As soon as it enters into thinking, as when I choose Jack over John for my basketball team, we have sign: I represent Jack as superior on the ground of his superior height. Here the relation is the syntax of the representamen, which may be entirely nonverbal.

Are Words Signs?

We started out with words as the canonical example of signs, but often they barely qualify. If you ask me to please pass you the butter, I may do it almost mindlessly. I need hardly have any idea of "butter" at all, much less of "the" or of "please." Yet reflexive as the response may be, I think I am likely to act with some image of my compliance with the request *as a whole.* Otherwise, you will be quite right to say my action is robotic and does not really involve semiosis. In the *Blue and Brown Books,* Wittgenstein relieves us of the error of supposing we need interpretants to account for such responsive behavior. True, but we need them still to say whether the behavior is robotic or not. The difference is real and important even if we can't find evidence of it. The difference is clearer if we look for the interpretants of sentences than if we get stuck looking for interpretants of words.

WEST SIDE STORY

A text, as a sign factor, may be a representamen or an object or a responsive interpretant.

A work of musical theater, Stephen Sondheim's and Leonard Bernstein's *West Side Story* is a very complex text, a text of texts. In its mix of dance, action, song, speech, and instrumental music the interweaving of structures is probably beyond mapping, and this web of component texts is strung in a framework of signs already too complex for orderly enumeration, that identify theatrical performance and theatrical works as genres. However, this complexity does not prevent us from grappling with the work as a whole.

Taken as a whole, we get quite a different sense of *West Side Story* if we hold it as a representamen than we do if we hold it as an interpretant. Taking it as a representamen, we are likely to understand it as representing the street gang life of New York City (its object). We are prompted by it to interpret the gang life (that is, to form a conception, an interpretant of it) as glamorous, dangerous, exciting, and ripe for tragedy. This gives us a disappointing view of the work: a musical comedy that exploits gross social distress for the sake of virtuosic theatricality.

Taken as a responsive interpretant, the text is richer. Now we are prompted to see that *West Side Story* is establishing a relationship between a prior text, the *Romeo and Juliet* of Shakespeare (as representamen) and our New York City gangs (as object). The *ground* of this representation is the common element, the tragedy of a love that crosses clan boundaries, the rival families of Verona in one case, the street gangs in the other.

This is what everybody knows about *West Side Story,* but let us test a bit further.

Am I not on a rather shaky ground? Why this quasi-anthropological circumlocution, "clan boundaries," as if I were Scotland or proposing an abstract theory of kinship?

In seizing this "neutral" term equally distant from Verona and New York, I tried to focus on an underlying principle of analogy supporting the interpretant. But what an unprincipled analogy I am whitewashing! Look at the disanalogy that *West Side Story* brushes off as merely comic: "We're not deprived, we're depraved." We have no clans here but *families* in one case, *gangs* in the other. It's Donald Duck and his nephews again; it's Little Orphan Annie: Advanced capitalism devalues the historical family and takes in the orphans as its comic mascots. Where *Romeo and Juliet* displays the conflict between passion and historical role, *West Side Story* displays the chaos of an ahistorical society.

The music suits. In the first work, the unending obligation of heroic pentameter suggests one perspective with origins and destinies under its rule. In the second, the facile heteroglossia of Bernstein's Latin, jazz, and avant garde compositional technologies advertises another: Anything goes if it works.

12

BOUNDARIES OF SEMIOSIS

Semiosis—the use, action, or production of signs—is a component of conscious experience but not the whole of it. The boundary between semiosis and pre- or extrasemiotic experience is vague and complex, as impossible to pinpoint as the shoreline with its tides. This imprecision is not a deficiency of theory. It is an observable fact that our theory should model.

The point that representation is just one part of the larger whole of experience is well illustrated by an example in Dennett, although he gives his example an interpretation opposite to mine. What, he asks, was the taste of beer the first time you tasted it, before you learned to like it (1991, pp. 395–396)? He seems to think that it had no specific taste, no *qualia*. Dennett's understanding seems to be that what we mistook for taste was really a frustrated urge to spit the stuff out. Such a disposition may well have been part of the experience, but I also remember a taste. He provides no reason and I find no reason to be skeptical about the taste. It was, in my case and perhaps in yours, offensive, in part because I had not yet learned to represent it. I had no clear idea of beer. The taste seems quite different now that I know the idea and can match any new brew against it. (I make a sign: new taste as object, beer ideas as representamina, appraisal as interpretant.)

Various examples of mental entities that are not signs are collected here in the hope of making the idea of sign more vivid by contrast but also to show that thought develops signs where there were none. Then two other related problems are considered, whether it makes sense to speak of unconscious signs and how signs are stabilized.

THREE DUALITIES

Everyday knowing must reconcile three dualities that establish relationships resembling representation but that do not consist in irreducibly triadic relations of items of consciousness. By the definitions of chapter 11, the following are not signs.

1. *Abstractive duality: the dual characters of items.* Normally, the token does not represent the type; the vehicle does not represent the ground. These are alternate phases of the same item. We noted that wooden beam sunk into the ground with a piece of sheet metal attached to its top does not "represent" a traffic sign. Nor does it normally represent stop signs as a type. The exception occurs if we use the stop sign as an example. "See, this is what I mean by a stop sign!" Now it represents its type. If I say, while drawing it, "This is the Greek letter mu," then I make the token the sign of the type. Conversely, if I ask you to recommend a good book on the French Revolution, I employ the type as a sign of its token. Outside such moments of reflection, the book represents the French Revolution, not a bibliographic category, and the drawn Greek "mu" represents a sound, not a graphic type.

2. *Epistemic duality: "sensation" and "appearance."* The well-rehearsed opposition between raw sense data and the well-formed impressions we make from them does not entail representation. Perceptions as such are not signs. Every species has its own way of constructing an *objective world.* We make categorical distinctions among trees, lamp posts, and fire hydrants. Dogs apparently don't. Vibrations above 20 kilohertz are not sounds for me. They are for Fido. The species-specific objective world is called an *Umwelt,* following Jacob von Uexkell. (For discussion see Varela, Thompson, and Rosch [1991] and Deely [1982]). For higher life-forms, the *Umwelt* entails a distinction between self and nonself that becomes an elaborate art. Motion of the self becomes perceptually different from motion in the environment: When I move my eyes the picture changes, but I don't see this as motion of the world. A bird on the grass cannot take a step without vigorously bobbing its head. Wouldn't this be visually distracting for the bird? It looks like it, but we really must suppose it all neurologically compensated. The grass probably looks as

stable to the bird as the rug does to me when I walk around. The translations are extraordinary, but we should not consider them "representations" in our technical sense. They are "presentations." What the organism constructs as an object of perception—the stable carpet or stable grass—usually does not represent any *other* item of consciousness. The initial, raw sensations are unconscious and imperceptible. Normally, the resultant object is a true *substitute* for the sensations that it replaces, the output of their input, not their sign. Still, exceptionally, the foregoing does not hold. When I feel something peculiar in my pocket, have trouble placing a voice on the telephone, or look around half blind to find my glasses, I use minimally interpreted sensations as signs of possible objects. The flicker of light (representamen) may be a reflection off the metal frames of my glasses (object), and I consciously interpret representamen and object by envisioning my glasses in such and such a position. The exceptional perceptions in which we are aware of appearances as stand-ins for a physical reality unavailable to us are indeed signs. The doubling of perspective that allows us not to believe what we see occurs with dreams, new bifocals, excesses of philosophy, or the patent illusions of cinema, magic shows, and certain psychology experiments. Otherwise, seeing is believing. Most of the time, appearances are all we have to go on. They make our actual world, not signs of it.

3. *Phenomenal duality: inner and outer.* We divide our experiences in various ways as mental and external. We understand some things, like the images we see with our eyes closed, as being within our minds, while we understand what we see with open eyes as external. Chapter 10 noted the continuity of experience across these domains, and we need only point out that one does not represent the other. In some semiotic theory, a mental image is regarded as a representation of an external fact, but normally it isn't.

Insofar as we are considering experience (and not the world of the "dynamic object" of Peirce), the two are part of a continuum, and the mental image is usually not an item distinct from an object of perception. It is simply a part of seeing; we couldn't see without one. The real room you can see around you is a mental integration of very small bits perceived separately. What is a little harder hold on to, but really implied in the same observation, is that the case is no different for distant objects. What I perceived five seconds ago is, for the most part, incorporated into my notion of now. Memory is the only direct perception I have of what happened five years ago as well, not a sign of it. Imaginary objects and hypothetical situations are not perceptions in the same sense, but they are equally without representation. They *are* possibilities or impossibilities; they do not *represent* possibilities or impossibilities. What is a possibility? Something we imagine that also might occur. No representamen here, as long as we stick to the ill-defined inner world. If we *make* a sign or buy into one (horoscope, soybean futures, speak a wish) that, of course, is another matter and not "inner."

THE EMERGENCE OF SEMIOSIS

Our jungle of signs grows by imperceptible degrees from a soil of autonomic reaction. The objective world, which we seem to experience immediately, arises with the interaction of the physical environment, our perceptual mechanisms, and our sign systems. The green of green grass is an objective fact that cannot be attributed to any one or two of those three factors without the others. It is impossible to say at what point signs intervene. Fifty years ago the weight of anthropological evidence suggested that color systems were largely a matter of social conventions that differed radically between one culture and another. More recent work in neurology and experimental psychology has revealed unities in this diversity that point to a fuller role for biological mechanisms.[1]

It may be the biology of Gestalt grouping that determines whether we see forests or trees, but it is surely the taxonomy of culture that determines whether we see trees or bushes, flowers or weeds. More elaborated perceptions are controlled by signs, but there is no clear threshold. We have no litmus paper for the first occurrence of semiosis.

"Raw" perception constructs a world of shapes apparently independent of our own movement and position, that is, the world that can hold still while we move in it and a world in which the motion of objects does not imply our own displacement. This very complex achievement seems to be essentially autonomic. In a further phase, recognition establishes persistent entities that may come in and out of view. We can see that much of this, too, is autonomic, but certainly not all of it. This level of perception has ambiguities, its "new" moons and "returning" seasons, which suggest that sign systems start to play a role. The balance begins to shift further with categorization: Perceiving X as a type of Y, we lean heavily on culture and language, but there is still an autonomous support.

At some point in this chain of increasing sophistication we can note the emergence of objects that would not exist at all if they were not signified, what we called constructs: the lanes of a street, nations and their debts, and so on. Quick inspection shows us that we live in a constructed universe for which our everyday language provides much of the load-bearing support- ive structure. For the reader who doesn't know this viewpoint, which is cer- tainly a signal accomplishment of semiotics as a praxis, Barthes's *Mythologies* (1972) is a good point of departure. Let us not neglect to un- derstand, however, that we also have access to presemiotic experience. The access is not easy or complete, but with the disciplines of meditation, reli- gion, and art it is not denied. We are at some liberty to *re*construct. We are not permanently consigned to a "prisonhouse of language" or any other semiosic jail.

SHOULD WE ALLOW FOR UNCONSCIOUS REPRESENTATION?

The point of view that it is natural to attribute computation to the un- conscious and representation exclusively to consciousness has directed this study from the outset. This view stands in opposition to the jargon of cog- nitive science and psychoanalysis, although it is perfectly consistent with their theories.

Representation

Representation in our sense requires an interpretant. Representation, in a full-bodied sense of the word, involves a connection between two data for- mations over and above or apart from any that they enjoy as input and output. Such a connection is the interpretant. A computer may, without interpretation, connect "17 + 25" with "42" as input and output, but we represent the relation as a "sum," which is a real idea (item) and quite a different matter. The difference is absolutely fundamental for semiotics.

What is this idea, in this particular case, a "sum"? A mathematician could supply a tidy, formal answer, but most people who think they un- derstand what a sum is have no formalization at the tip of their tongues.

Something is there, an item of consciousness, however diffuse. When I work out my checkbook balances, a little bar graph bobs up and down, mostly down, in a corner of my imagination. Computers have no place for such nonsense. Typically, interpretants are redundant. We might have something in mind like an assortment of archetypal examples that drove the point home in grade school, where it was picked up in a moment of "intuition," a moment of confident but really hasty generalization.

Redundant and tenuous connection is the very stuff of signs. Since tenuous connections are exactly what computation avoids, there is an antithesis between computation and representation. (This is an indirect reason to suspect that the unconscious has no more room for interpretants than computers do.)

Computation

We attach meanings to the inputs and outputs of a computation, but the computation does not include or involve those meanings.

Contemporary linguistics demonstrates that any mind or machine that can deal with language must transform the corresponding data structures in several stages. The question here is whether the intermediate data formations should be called "representations" as they typically are called in the literature of the field. It is awkward to fuss about a word. I would be happy with alternative uses of "representation" if I felt assured the difference of meaning had been acknowledged, but this doesn't seem to be the case. Since the hub of the question here has to do with intermediate data that arises in computation, the point may be clarified if we take specific simple cases.

1. Consider adding 17 apples and 25 oranges to get 42 pieces of fruit. The three numbers of the previous sentence are representations or signs of the numerical size of three sets of fruits. In the course of actually making the calculation, other numbers appear. For example, you might add 7 to 5, making 12, write 2 and carry 1. What does the one you carry represent? There is an answer internal to arithmetic that it represents 10, and, since we are merely adding whole positive numbers, we could even imagine that it represents an unspecified 10 pieces of fruit. (Fully unspecified: We don't know how many of the ten are apples!) But that interpretation is entirely the

province of an external observer doing her own interpreting. It has nothing to do with the computation.

2. The vacuity of the intermediate configuration is patent in the real-world engineering problems that have to be calculated in terms of the imaginary number "*i*." Both the engineer's "*i*" and the "1" we carry are artifacts of computation. Here the input-output description is fully adequate to the activity in question. The notion of representation is extra baggage.

3. A more dramatic example is furnished by the so-called hidden registers of connectionist computing. These are registers that the machine "learns" to use but that neither people nor their computers know how to interpret.

The so-called "representations" of language that are attributed to unconscious intuition in transformational linguistics are like the carried digit, or "*i*," or perhaps even like hidden registers. That complex data formations exist we need not doubt, but there is no basis for attributing representation to them. They are fully described when characterized as inputs and outputs, for one replaces the other.

Replacement

What the word "representation," when used in cognitive science, actually refers to is *replacement*. There is another concept in computer science that we should evoke as an antidote, the notion of "rewriting rules" symbolized

$$X <— Y$$

for Y replaces X. We may state as a principle, that, if Y fully replaces X, then Y does not represent X. The U.S. dollar no longer represents gold because it has fully replaced it. The nerve impulse from the eye fully replaces and does not represent the chemical disturbance in the retinal rod that fully replaces and does not represent the light striking the retina.

Confusion on this point results from mistaking the function of data in its context of use with its function for an external observer. Imagine a neuroscientist with fabulous instruments who is able to view both the nerve impulse and the retinal reaction. She, as an outsider, may ascribe representational status to the former, but it is extra baggage. Neither she nor the retina nor the visual cortex nor any other "subject" is actually using one to *mean* the other.

In these replacements the salient feature is the preservation of structure, or "information." The transfer of information (transformation) preserves quantitative structures but carries no trace of their origin. The optic nerve impulse is properly a *transform* of the retinal data, not a representation.

A seismograph replaces vibrations with a convoluted ink graph on paper. What the seismograph does is not semiosis. What the geologist does with the seismograph is semiosis because the geologist holds together *three* items, graph (R), earthquake (O), and a physical theory relating them (I), all at the same time.

Unconscious Signs in Psychoanalysis

Psychoanalytic doctrine adopts the language of signs and symbols; we speak of Freudian symbols or signs of the unconscious revealed in dreams. This usage obfuscates. Although the boundary of consciousness is variable and hazy, the functions of consciousness and unconsciousness are distinct in psychoanalytic theories, and there is no reason to attribute signs or representations to the unconscious. Quite the contrary. The whole thrust of the theory is to provide a causal link in the unconscious, consonant with physics and biology, for connections that appear in consciousness as arbitrary.

When figures emerge from the unconscious, why, then they are not unconscious. They are conscious. Such are dreams, old memories, slips of the tongue, and the like. It is only when these are brought into a consciousness—either the analyst's or the analysand's—that we can say they *function* as sign factors and are not merely by-products from a computational process. Telltale evidence, but only to the observer.

We have the same relation to the unconscious that we have to external physical reality. It impinges on us, and we come up with theories about it that work. There is no reason to attribute representation to either.

Unity of Signs

If we accept that all semiosis belongs to consciousness and is distinct in that way from simple input-output relations, we display the unity of natural and conventional signs. Dark clouds as "sign" of approaching rain and a blotchy complexion as a "sign" of alcoholism are natural signs. It is reasonable to ask whether the use of the same word, "sign," both for these indexes and for terms such as words and emblems is more than homonymity. Both are the same sort of thing because the causal basis of connection between representamen and object, observation of nature in one case, artificial stipulation in the other, is secondary to the way the connection is instantiated, the tenuous, conscious interpretant that links X to Y.

INVESTMENT

The plan I carry in my head for my day's activities is a representamen that takes those activities as an object (with much supporting imagery to interpret between them). In contrast, my intentions to type each next word of this paragraph need hardly count as anything but a phase of the act itself. They are not signs of the act to follow. Those intentions lack conscious interpretants linking them to the actions, which follow on them automatically. Yet the difference between the advance plan, which is clearly a sign, and the immediate intention, which is not one, is not obvious. The critical difference between the two cases is that I *could* speak or write out the day's plan. This is not incidental.

Semiotics is not a part of psychology. The simmering soup of thought, with its chunks of sign and other stuff, some half dissolved and all aswirl, is somewhat recalcitrant and not wholly inviting to semiotic analysis. It is our privilege to study signs invested in the more stable vehicles. It is the mind's intercourse with physical media that allows us to speak of artifacts of mental life. In saying what a sign is, we noted but gave no heed to the difference between image and vehicle or between immediate and responsive interpretants. For identifying the sign these are essentially interchangeable. For studying particular signs they are not.

Humberto Maturana's biology (1971, in Maturana and Varela, 1980) describes cognition as internal adjustment within the closed system of an organism. Organic systems and especially nervous systems are able to retain patterns of the deformations they undergo; these retentions constitute learning. On this basis, Maturana is able to build up a picture of cognition based on fundamental biological principles that extends to interactions between organisms and even to language itself (which he calls an "orienting behavior"). But one question strikes him as inadequately answered in this framework: It is evident in the case of higher organisms, especially people, that they are able to manipulate traces of their experience, their retentions of deformations, without fully responding to them. He asks: "How does the nervous system interact with its own states and how is it modified by them as if they were independent entities?" (p. 23).

The question, in my view, attributes a capacity to the nervous system that it in fact does not have. The nervous system is quite limited in its capacity to cordon off particular states as separate entities. Chapter 3 cited Locke's observation that ideas combined without words are so chimerical that we cannot really talk about mental propositions of pure ideas (images). This seems nearer to the mark. To use our own thoughts as independent entities, we must couple them with more stable vehicles. We *invest* them in external representamina. When these investments are well established, they serve us even in their physical absence. By themselves, images are chimerical. An image tied to an external vehicle allows sets of otherwise chimerical patterns to reinforce each other. A group of musical notes or a word links together muscle patterns (for writing or dancing), visual and/or aural patterns, and concepts. Through investment in materials, signs are stabilized. They are also made available to share.

But having defined items as we did, with one foot in memory, another in perception, are we identifying anything new here? Our items would seem already partially invested in the material world. This is indeed the case, and we can identify only a relative difference. Three factors contribute to the security of these semiotic investments. First is social sanction. The material investment of a representamen is more secure when a group of people recognize it as such. (Two as a minimum: "They're playing our song.") Second is intended physical modification. I take the idea represented by a painting or even one stone placed on another to be more securely invested in material than an animal discovered in a cloud or a natural rock formation. Third is endurance. A tune memorized is an expression more securely invested in its material than one improvised and immediately forgotten.

We backed into the driveway of psychology to check the map; here we can regain the main road. We will rarely need to speak of items, for our most interesting signs are invested in the shared materials of our objective worlds.

PART IV

Elaborations of the Sign

The elaboration of signs is fundamentally paradoxical. As signs become more elaborate, they tend to lose or loosen their hold on their objects. It is tempting to say of a particular fugue or a particular algebra, "This is not a sign; it does not refer to anything. It is only significant in itself for what it is." But that is not the whole truth of algebras or fugues. First, on study, we would find that these elaborate things arise out of simpler ones that were more clearly referential. Algebra arose from the same arithmetic that recorded commodities, and music appears in its oldest genres to be implicated in referential contexts of poetry, religion, or work. Second, the ties are not severed. When I say "arises," I don't have in mind either the history of those arts per se, nor their current forms of production per se, but something in the history of which we still find a living trace in current production. Third, and very important, the initial objection has no bounds. Can't we say that a thorough philosophy defines all its own terms, making a closed system that doesn't really refer to anything outside itself? Can't we say language is closed the same way? Don't we like to say "Nature follows art," to point out how we see the world in terms that artists have taught us, closing off the visual world as tightly as algebras and fugues? Is not every culture a closed system of representation, representing nothing outside itself except as a negation (an "other")?

Closure approaches in all these cases because elaborated semiosis manifests a competition between structure and reference. This competition, or dialectic, has its moments of truce and synthesis, most obvious in language and perhaps also in visual depiction, allowing the elaboration of structure, if it is sufficiently constrained by rules, to subserve reference. Competition is the general rule.

STRUCTURALISM

Alert to this dialect, we can return to structuralist semiotics not as an alternative to pragmatism but as its supplement. Sense is not the whole of meaning, but we do make sense of signs by grasping their structure.

Frederick Jameson's study, *The Prison House of Language,* regards structuralism as any thought that takes as its model Saussure's linguistics or the new sciences of Sigmund Freud, Karl Marx, and Emile Durkheim. His deconstructions reveal problematic consequences of the premises of these authors.

We have already sampled (in chapters 6 and 8) the dialogue that Jameson's study and the "poststructural" critique generally extend. To study structure is to examine an abstraction. When you make an abstraction, something is left behind. That neglected something is likely to turn out to be significant in another context. We are exploring worlds in which abstraction is of limited efficacy; yet abstraction remains an essential bootstrap. There can be no final verdict in the contest between studies of structure and studies of context. Structuralism is attractive when it makes progress in its own task. Structuralism has attracted exaggerated criticism in recent decades not because its task, like all good tasks, is limited but because structuralism got stuck.

What is the task? Let us compare a mathematical and a semiotic perspective of what structure is.

Whitehead and Russell defined "having the same structure" through the arithmetic of relational numbers in their *Principia Mathematica.* As Russell himself describes it in the retrospection of *My Philosophical Development* (1959), the key idea here is correspondence or *mapping.* Imagine a cloud of helium gas with its molecules randomly arranged, and imagine another cloud of hydrogen gas with the same number of molecules identically arranged or perhaps identically except upside down and with all the distances halved. The one-to-one correspondence, not just between the molecules of the two clouds but between all their relationships, is identity of structure. Russell's favorite examples of structure include the analogical relation between a sound and the phonograph record that plays it. The first is a dynamic, temporal arrangement—in air; the second, static and spatial—in vinyl. There is a sense in which they have the *same* structure.

In this mathematical view, structure is a domain of similarity and difference, which, like color for the blind, has no substance of its own.

Structure for semiotics is both more concrete and more elusive. It has to do with our consciousness of order and organization. We tend to reify structure, speaking not of "x and y having the same structure" but of "the structure of x." In structuralism we attempt to objectify an aspect in perception and thought that gains its salience for psychological, cultural, and/or logical reasons. No holds barred. We cannot expect a quest for the essence of structure to lead to a tidy, homogeneous formula. So far we have some clear ideas about certain types of structure and some vaguer ideas that there must be others. "Structuralism" has now become a battle cry in semiotics. To be "poststructuralist" is rather like having the head of a moose over your fireplace. Well and good, but structuralism should not be sealed and posted before its letter is finished.

In my view, structuralism got stuck in the hypnotic spell of some brilliant but excessively simple reductions, particularly a narrow construction of articulation and combinatory relations, a false lure that promised a closer approximation to the world of mathematics than we should hope to realize. Of necessity, what follows is still abstractive and reductive. I hope the pieces and angles in my Lego kit will not discourage extension or reconstruction. Structuralism is an unfinished project.

Chapter 13 concerns variety in the way wholes are divided into parts. Chapter 14 concerns referential functions of syntactic hierarchy. Chapter 15 contrasts two types of textual coherence. Chapter 16 regards the coherent text in the constellation of other texts with which it interacts. Chapter 17 picks up a cue that was dropped in chapter 10, the possibility of taking a sign factor to be a process of consciousness rather than an item.

13

COMPARATIVE ARTICULATION

Under the heading of articulation I bring together some observations on the division of wholes into parts, a matter foundational for the structures that arise in vocabularies and texts.

Articulation structures may be attributed to representamina or objects, depending on the case. Consider clock time. Clock time has a particular articulation structure regardless of which factor of the sign it functions as. Clock time is a sign system in which units of measure and quantities are the vocabulary categories. Insofar as either an analog clock or a digital clock can represent the "same time" (or represent each other), we might take a time so represented as an *object*. But a particular time is the *representamen* of a moment of the day. The interpretant of an articulated representamen imposes an articulation on its object. Thus the hour constructed by the sands of the hourglass is plastic and evanescent while the same hour constructed by a clock is rigid and articulated.

By convention, *articulation* refers either to an articulatory structure as a whole or to a single point of division established by the whole. Saussure noted that "articulation," referring to a division, derives from the Latin *articulus,* for joint, but he did not comment on the ambiguity of dividing and joining. As we situate linguistic articulation in a wider perspective, this ambiguity will be prominent.

DIVISIONS

Articulation divides wholes into parts. This is our starting point, and right here we find variety. We distinguish parts from aspects, groups from classes, bounded units from contours. Parts may be distinct or indistinct, separated, conjunct, overlapping fully or partly, or included one in another. Articulation is quantitatively variable: Some wholes are highly articulated; some are more continuous.

Any part we consider as a product of articulation for the purposes of semiotics must be an item in consciousness. Normally the dots which make up the TV picture and the separate frames of a cinematic film would not count for us as articulations. Certainly some kinds of brushstrokes in painting do. They hold attention.

The quickest and most lively display of the varieties in divisions of whole appears when we contemplate pictures. A nose remains a definite part of the face even when so painted that we cannot detect its boundaries. A looped line in two dimensions must have at least three articulated parts, as two segments and one circle (or deformed circle) join at the loop's point of intersection. Now change that line to a very loosely configured rope, depicted in perspective as in figure 13.1. The three parts are barely articulated, but a new division appears where one strand passes behind the other, cutting the representamina, not the rope.

Dividing and grouping are converse. Dividing a collection forms subgroups; grouping within a collection divides it. *Groups* within a structured object associate parts without changing their arrangement; *classes* are abstract subcollections of parts that do not retain the arrangement of the whole. Classification is a product of at least two articulations; one yields parts and the other divides objects into *aspects*, such as color and shape or weight. *Aspects* are subdivisions coextensive with the whole. Parts that include parts form a *hierarchy*. Hierarchy is taken up separately later.

Figure 13.1   Articulation of representamen and articulation of object

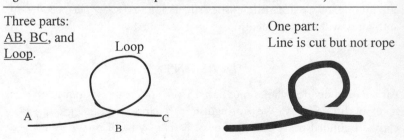

Three parts:
AB, BC, and
Loop.

Loop

One part:
Line is cut but not rope

A   C
              B

Contours or Inflections

Contours or *inflections* are parts or units established by continuous defor-mation or change. Paradoxically, there is a kind of articulation structure that we incline to characterize as inarticulate, because it occurs within con-tinuous change. Waves do divide a surface, making crests and troughs, but we cannot, by normal perception, pinpoint the divisions. Mathematically we might do so via the theory of derivatives, which locates specific points where the direction of change or the speed of change reverses, but bare-handed, so to speak, these are articulations that elude our grasp even when we can reproduce them precisely. Nevertheless, distinct shapes and distinct relations of similarity arise through undulations, modulations, and defor-mations, and these too can divide wholes into parts.

DIFFERENCES

Both Saussure's structuralism and its critique in the poststructuralist literature view semiotics as a map of differences. The optimistic version of this concep-tion is Saussure's tenet that a sign is fully accounted for as linking a network of differences among signifiers with a network of differences among signi-fieds. The pessimistic version envisions the sign as different from its object in a way that makes the exact linkage impossible. Either way, "difference" squeaks by. The notion that raw difference is an atomic constituent of our semiotic universe also arises in perspectives that have no conscious intersec-tion with continental linguistics, for example, Wolfgang Köhler's Gestalt psy-chology (1969) and G. Spencer-Brown's calculus of distinctions (1973).

But "difference" is a stop-gap idea. It makes an attractive emblem, per-haps, for the semiotic alienation we considered in chapter 2, but there is no such thing as pure difference. *In situ,* difference is always positive. It is bound up in some physical or logical material. Things differ *in some tan-gible way:* color, shape, the presence or absence of some sensible feature, position or other attribute. The alternative to reified "difference" is a more particular conception of articulation.

FEATURES

Hjelmslev (1943/1961) uses the term "figurae" for vocabulary elements that do not function as signs. A more common term is "feature." A *feature* is a sign factor component that is atomic in a given perspective; that is, it is an element that we do not want to regard as a combination of subelements. The vocabularies that some combinatorial systems depend on in turn depend on a combinatorial vocabulary of features.

The traffic lights mentioned in the introduction to part II combine red, yellow, or green with flashing or steady. (And we do also use flashing yellow or red lights.) In a vocabulary of bells and buzzers, such features high or low pitch, sounding rough or smooth, sounding continuously or in some pattern of intermittence, identifies each one.

Features may or may not be signs in themselves. In the traffic lights, red is and flashing isn't. The final consonants of "flood" and "fled" are the same, and both are features of the words in quotes, but in the second case it is also natural to consider the last "d" as the representamen for past tense. Whether we call the "d" of "fled" a feature or a sign depends on our interest at the moment. Clocks again: A watch face has little lines and dots as features. Each individual dot represents a minute (or second), though it can do so only by virtue of its incorporation into the whole pattern.

Features are perceived as single parts that confirm the identity of the whole; therefore, a feature also can be understood as a representamen in another (and *usually* trivial) sense in that it determines or identifies the articulated complex. (The systematic phonological theory of "distinctive features" [see below], though it concerns identity, is certainly not trivial.)

Realms of sensation and imagination are attributed different structures according to the sorts of feature systems that articulate them. History is variously articulated as periods or epochs, just as a single day is divided into dawn, morning, afternoon, and evening. The feature system as a whole taken to represent the space as a whole gives it a particular character.

BINARY OPPOSITIONS

Oppositions align features in pairs, either by regarding two features as opposed (like "singular" and "plural") or by opposing the presence and absence of one feature (like the "*s*" or its absence to mark singular and plural). This type of articulation is particularly characteristic of language and of social objects supported primarily by language. Logical systems, formal and informal, are primarily systems of two values (true/false). Opposition is an old topic in philosophy; Aristotle identifies seven types.

Figure 13.2   Color oppositions

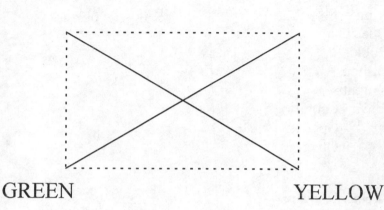

BLUE   RED

GREEN   YELLOW

Binary opposition, as the articulatory type par excellence, demands a lion's share of attention. Color offers an intriguing case. Physiological and some anthropological evidence suggests that color classifications in all cultures build on a neural foundation of two opposed binary opposites, which we can call red vs. green and yellow vs. blue. Intermediate colors, are possible on any of the dotted lines in figure 13.2 but not on the solid lines.

The linguistic theories of distinctive features and markedness depend on binary opposition. Although these are entwined, I discuss the first here and the second later.

Distinctive Features

The theory of distinctive features specifies the sound elements of language as complexes of binary values all of which indicate the presence or absence of one of a small number of characteristics, such as voicing or nasalizing. Descriptions with a similar structure, sometimes invoking contraries rather than simple presence or absence, are possible for a wide range of structures.

Table 13.1 is a distinctive feature description of chess moves; as long as we can keep the moves straight, it doesn't have to matter what the pieces look like. Here Saussure wins: the differences of moves *are* the pieces.

Table 13.1 Chess pieces as complexes of distinctive features

	Diagonal	Horizontal	Vertical	Only 1 Square
King	+	+	+	+
Queen	+	+	+	-
Rook	-	+	+	-
Bishop	+	-	-	-
Knight	-	-	-	+
Pawn - Capturing	+	-	-	+
- Opening	-	-	+	-
- Other	-	-	+	+

Greimas's Square

Figure 13.2, combining two oppositions, recalls Aristotle's scheme of opposites and contraries. The theories of Algirdas Julian Greimas (1983, 1987) highly influential in European semiotic scholarship, develop this pattern; he takes the square formed by a term and its contrary and their two negations as the basis of all sense and intelligibility. Figure 13.3 is his foundational diagram and, in parentheses, an example of its application. To instance the lower contraries, I might take a zombie (for not alive) and Sleeping Beauty (for not dead).

Greimas does not heed the normal and useful distinction in logic between negations and contraries—that the negation of a contrary does not imply its opposite. Drinking and driving are contrary, but not driving does not imply drinking.

Binarism

I mention Greimasian theory because of its influence and suggestiveness, but I have not been able to discover any grounds for believing it. It is tempting to see the seed and essence of all thought in the first acts of binary distinction—background and foreground, up and down, us and them, life and death. . . . Yet we must be wary. Perhaps binary oppositions are merely the easiest distinctions to handle. The binary opposition of Yin and Yang in Chinese metaphysics was absorbed by the later, more sophisticated five-element

Figure 13.3   Greimassian square

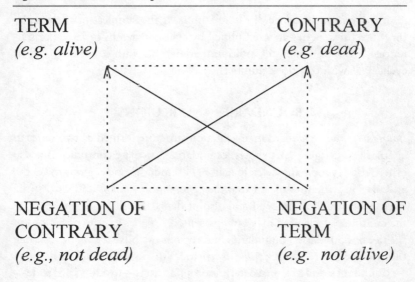

TERM   CONTRARY
(e.g. alive)   *(e.g. dead)*

NEGATION OF   NEGATION OF
CONTRARY   TERM
(e.g., not dead)   *(e.g. not alive)*

theory. Peirce argued that the whole history of science was a progress from oppositions to continuities. Even if binary oppositions are foundational, every caution must be exercised in attributing such structure to higher-level constructs. We can build round walls with square bricks.

Reliance on opposites is a hallmark of Levi-Strauss's structural anthropology, as the title of his magnum opus, *The Raw and the Cooked* (1964/1969), advertises. Whatever final verdict is drawn on this controversial work, it must be acknowledged that the method of binary feature opposition it pursues succeeds in communicating a kind of sense. The problem here, as with Greimas, is to judge whether the oppositions ascribed to various texts really inhere in them or are "fools' gold" reflecting back features of a particular linguistic description.

Although early twentieth-century phonology provided a model for this modern passion for pairs, subsequent phonology has not found the scheme entirely adequate. Noam Chomsky and Morris Halle argued in *The Sound Patterns of English* (1968) that the phonemic scheme of oppositions was realized phonetically and acoustically inside a more universal framework of three-valued scales, from which each language selects two.

SERIES

A single *series*, a sequence of discrete units, is the simplest of all articulatory structures. Series are exemplified by chains of words or letters or sentences. Series also may be multidimentional, as with a chess board, or cyclical, as with our clock numbers.

BOUNDARIES AND REGIONS

Boundaries and regions are an articulation structure formed of two series in alternation, as figure 13.4 shows. Boundaries articulate continua (and also other series), producing discrete regions. Boundaries and regions make the articulation structures of, for example, geographical maps and clocks (the circle, not just the numbers) and also of dance, music, and narrative. As the continua supplanted may be represented *either* as a series of regions *or* a series of boundaries, boundaries and regions establish a *dual articulation* (not to be confused with *double articulation,* discussed further on).

Boundaries and regions determine oppositions—inside vs. outside—but this is not a main point of interest here.

A single feature system may determine boundaries *and* regions, but it tends to represent one or the other, not both. The surface of the earth is articulated by lines of latitude and longitude, a schema of boundaries. These represent lines of division, not the regions that result. In the case of

Figure 13.4   Dual Articulation

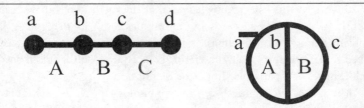

A, B, C   --regions
a, b, c, d   --boundaries

latitudes, the complementary schema (the "dual") is that of climatic zones. These represent regions, not boundaries. For longitude, the complementary system is time zones, which also represent regions. Politically, landmasses are divided into regions. Normally political boundaries are not named except secondarily, as a product of the representamina of the regions, (e.g., the "U.S.-Canadian" border). A football field is articulated primarily by boundaries (the yard lines). For baseball, infield and outfield represent regions; foul lines and bases, boundaries.

A story is a sequence of situations and actions, with every action beginning and terminating in a situation. Situations are then boundaries and actions, regions. Narrative has the option of emphasizing the one or the other. The terminology has a metaphoric flavor here as situations may endure much longer than actions; nevertheless, the logical relation of "regions" and "boundaries" here is much the same as with maps and clocks. Similarly dance enchains positions and motions, which sometimes appear redundant: Knowing all the motions, you might deduce the dual, the positions. But we dare not take the redundancy for granted: Stories may have gaps. Music exhibits the same duality. A melody is a chain of notes or its dual, a chain of intervals. Media that exhibit boundary and region articulation have more complex hierarchies than simple series do.

REPRESENTATIVES

A *system of representatives* is a vocabulary of discrete signs or features that supplants a continuum—a box of crayons instead of the full range of possible colors.

Musical scales are systems of representatives. Pitch is a continuously variable value. If a violinist slides a finger slowly on the fingerboard while bowing, you will hear the pitches between the notes we normally use (as well as the scale notes). Such sliding is part of the art but only exceptionally; pianos can't do it at all. When we listen to scales, the absence of the pitches that would be heard if a violinist slid from one note to the next is not felt as a skipped space. We hear each note as the "next" pitch without any awareness that some in-between pitches are missing.

A box of crayons or a pallet of paints may well appear, if used skillfully, to represent the entire continuum of color, although this illusion is not always achieved or always intended.

The dots of the TV screen, which are not articulations in our sense, do not comprise systems of representatives. Graininess of the image is certainly an aspect that can enter into semiosis but only as an overall quality, not grain by grain. The case of a mosaic is not at all the same. Although the individual tiles may not sustain our interest, they are available to perception and compete for our attention, establishing an aesthetic tension between medium and imagination. The vocabulary of tiles for a mosaic is a schema of representatives.

A more complex example than any of these is the meanings of words. Sets of words readily supplant continua, sometimes blatantly: Are you a "socialist" or a "capitalist"? It can be a tough job to win back the middle ground elided by the system.

VECTORS

Any system reduced to oppositions of positive and negative terms leaves as its residue or kernel another articulatory system. The distinctive feature description of chess moves yields horizontal, vertical, diagonal as features, a positive kernel of spatial perceptions. Similarly, in the home territory of phonemics itself, having boiled down the sap of allophones into the thick syrup of phonemes and crystallized out the pure sugar of distinctive features, we still have "nasal," "dental," "labial," and so on as positive regions of the human vocal tract that do not reduce to binary opposites in relation to each other.

Vectors are articulations whose origins we must attribute to the physical world, including our sensory capacities. The boiling and freezing points of water are vectors. Vectors establish distinct aspects of the texts or vocabularies that exploit them.

Articulation emerges in the negotiation of structural with biological and physical factors. In language the capacity of the vocal tract and the auditory pathway are determinants. Vision can not possibly make use of "octave equivalence" (the identification of a frequency with its double) in the electromagnetic spectrum, as hearing does in the audio spectrum, because the eye's color range is just under an octave while the ear takes in about ten octaves. For purely neurological reasons, odors may have immediately perceptible beginnings but not endings.

Vectors are subject to further articulation, or "scaling," by *scalars*. For example, vectors of tongue taste—salty, acidic, bitter, and sweet are scaled—

as "not," "slightly," "distinctly," "rather," "quite," "very," "extremely," and so on. Binary scaling (present/absent) is a limiting case.

HIERARCHY

Articulation is hierarchical. It establishes inclusion relations of wholes and parts. Language and visual perception theory draw our attention to hierarchies of articulation based on inclusion. The most salient seem to be hierarchies over series in which parts do not overlap, such as the language hierarchy illustrated in chapter 7 by tree graphs. Visual images are similar, except that the order of constituents of a region is not uniquely determined. For example, Leonardo da Vinci's painting *The Last Supper* is a whole that has (speaking roughly) a background and a seated group at table as its most inclusive parts. The seated group includes Christ, the 12 apostles, and the table. To continue involves listing the 12 apostles, which I might do from right to left or from left to right or some other way. The order is at most suggested.

Hierarchies of boundaries, which may occur in narrative, dance, and music, are a second, very different type. Chapter 18 introduces a notation that conveys the difference. If we picture ocean waves hierarchically (the saying goes that the ninth wave is longest), should we connect crests or troughs? Hierarchy may be ambiguous with regard to dominance and/or stratification and/or inclusion.

MARKEDNESS

The theory of marking, due to Nicolaj Troubetzkoy and Roman Jakobson, emerged within and complements distinctive feature theory.[1] This theory considers a single binary opposition as a hierarchy. Binary oppositions in semiotic structures tend to be asymmetric functionally and psychologically. In such opposed pairs, one representamen often has a double function, signifying either a sub-class or the whole class. Figure 13.5 shows this schema. The other term, called the *marked term,* is specialized. The plural form of a noun, usually marked by "*s*" in English, is unique in its sense. The singular form, which has no mark, stands *either* for the individual *or* the whole class. (Here and typically, but not always, the marked representamina is the unmarked plus one additional feature, the mark.)

My dog is friendly.
The dog is a domestic animal.

The second sentence can be paraphrased with the plural "Dogs are domestic animals," but this usage does not give "dogs" a second sense such as "dog" has in the examples. Unless qualified, "dogs" always means "all dogs." Another standard example is tense. The present tense of verbs, which carries no special mark, is used for general, time-independent statements ("Semiotics is ridiculous") as well as for actual present ("I feel ridiculous"). The past tense, distinctively marked, is always time bound. Our favorite example, another noun, is, of course, "sign," which is unmarked both in relation to "object" and "interpretant" and which represents, as an unmarked term easily can, either the part (one factor) or the whole complex.

Michael Shapiro (1983), drawing on Jakobson, has employed the theory of marking to establish a fundamental link between syntactic and semantic

Figure 13.5   Varieties of markedness

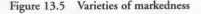

Marked term/Unmarked term

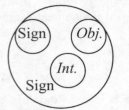
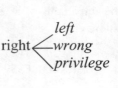
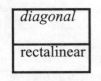

a. Unmarked is part and whole   b. Unmarked takes more antonyms   c. Unmarked finds neutral usage

d. Unmarked bears less interpretation.   e. Unmarked perceptually less salient

relations through the principle that marked representamina align with marked objects. Shapiro exploits this principle to account for linguistic change.

Although originally conceived as a tool to explain details of phonology and syntax, the concept of marking continues to find broader application. Mary Salus and Peter Salus (1978) demonstrate psychological entailments; Robert Hatten (1993) develops a methodology for musical interpretation.

We are currently living through a social experiment with markedness. The feminist movement presses us to revise English with respect to the deeply engrained marking of "man" and "woman" where the zero sense of "man" included everybody. The effort for reform has had considerable impact, but it is hard to assess the effect because markedness is very deeply engrained. We should be encouraged by the largely successful campaign to erase linguistic prejudice from "left" and "right." Vestiges are evident. We still speak left-handed complements and the right thing to do. Although the Salus and Salus association tests show "left" still to be a marked term in relation to "right," the sinister associations have been largely rectified.

Marking is reversible. The shorthand rule is: Marking reverses in a marked context. In ballet after the middle of the nineteenth century, the ballerina normally danced on toe while the chorus remained flat. Dancing on toe is marked for the context of the whole company. If the ballerina comes off toe, however, that gesture is marked with respect to her context. The marked term, whichever it is, is the one that will seem "to mean something" and that we will try to interpret.

Derrida's *Of Grammatology* (1967/1976) uses a further rhetorical twist in the reversal of marking. A marked term is reversed to become a "zero sign" for a new, broader category of which the formerly unmarked term now becomes a marked subcategory. Traditionally "writing" is understood as a marked category within language. Derrida's re-marking makes "writing" mean any kind of conceptual noting and language a marked, subordinate part of writing.

DOUBLE ARTICULATION

André Martinet (1960) claimed that double articulation is a distinguishing characteristic of language. His first articulation is the division of speech into meaningful units—words (signs). The second articulation is the further division of words into meaningless units—phonemes (features). The two characteristics of double articulation he emphasizes are the multiplication of the vocabulary and the complete structural independence of the two articulations. His mode of describing linguistic articulation has the advantage over Saussure's in that it makes no separate or duplicate claim about the structure of meanings.

To claim that double articulation is unique to language merely begs the question. We can already see that every medium has distinctive articulatory characteristics. One of our tasks in part V is to consider some of these characteristics further one by one so we can learn just how media differ and how they are comparable.

ARTICULATION AND REFERENCE: ARE THERE SEMANTIC UNIVERSALS?

Levi-Strauss continually emphasizes that our semiotic repertoire has the overall consequence of articulating a world of experience that is given to us as a continuum. This is not quite correct. Vectors do not originate in signs. But allowing this qualification and discounting the exaggerations of binarism, our world of experience is, to a very large extent, an articulated world, and its articulations arise in semiosis, where the interpretant imposes the articulation of the representamen on its object.

We have glimpsed repeatedly, first in Saussure, then in Hjelmslev, and later as an interpretation of Chomsky's logical form, the hypothesis that the signified of language, perhaps of signs generally, has its own vocabulary and grammar independent of but comparable to the vocabulary and grammar of the signifier. Saussure holds this structure to be determined differently by different languages. The hypothesis of semantic universals is that (all or some) cultural differences in representation are a superstructure over a more basic vocabulary of experience common to all of us.

Taste provides an illustration of the conception aimed at with semantic universals. It is known empirically that tongue taste alone, without olfactory assistance, is limited to sweet, sour, bitter, and salty. These four categories are then innate, born with the nervous system. Chemically, the taste sensitivity for sweet responds to certain sugars, but not to all, and also to at least one amino acid pair (aspartame). On this evidence, sweet is not an obvious chemical category, but it suffices to establish a semantic universal. If the word "sweet" occurs in a sentence, there is clearly a precise class of experiences, genetically determined, to which it can be linked.

But most of the flavor we encounter in eating is due to olfaction, not tongue taste. If we look for semantic universals in conjunction with olfaction rather than tongue taste, the prospect is dimmer. Olfactory capacity differs enormously among individuals and owes as much to nurture as nature. We don't seem to share much of a conceptual framework for smell. The hypothesis of semantic universals loses its force when it cannot appeal to a circumscribed vocabulary. "Cinnamon" is a weaker candidate as a semantic universal than "sweet." How about the visual world? Despite rapidly accumulating research results in this area, the overall balance remains anybody's guess.

Since we can think of sweetness without imagining it, at least not vividly, we distinguish between the experience and the concept. If there are semantic universals, then there must be a further phase of understanding that relates these concepts to individual, actual experiences.

Martin Minsky (1986), beginning at the other end of this latter problem, formulates an alternative to semantic universals. It pictures concepts as bundles of connections among experiences—or rather among the traces of experience that persist in memory. This formulation does not entail a universal, finite vocabulary of building blocks for concepts. While it leaves us to imagine a brain that has a limited start-up set of capacities to articulate experience, it shows how these could diversify without limitation.

The articulation of time by tense seems to grow out of language alone like Athena from the head of Zeus, an articulation very different in different languages. If an underlying vocabulary of distinctions were discovered that supported all tense systems, its vocabulary would be a good candidate for a semantic universal. Even so, its domain of application would be circumscribed. To discover semantic universals for time would be no evidence that they exist for, say, sounds.

Since it goes without saying that our thought has to be built up from a fund biologically supplied and in some measure genetically determined, we can assume that, in some sense, there must be semantic universals. But in what sense? The principles of thought that are truly atomic and universal may turn out to be trivial. Once again, knowing the exact shapes of bricks does not unlock the mysteries of architecture.

Instead of universals, the variability of articulation suggests we look for *semantic resultants*—the products of the independent or partly independent articulations of a field of representamina and a field of objects. Imagine a slide projector without a proper screen. The projector casts a highly patterned image (perhaps a chess-board pattern) on a rough surface, say an irregular stone wall. The resultant image will be very complex, partly orderly and partly disorderly. Articulation seems to me to be like that in its relation to reference. We may share an articulatory system (the projection) and build up our experience of the world from physiologically similar building stones, but our experience is disorderly. The intersecting pattern does not have an independent system; it is a resultant of two or more schemas in negotiation.

To offer one illustration, it appears to me, despite the genesis of much verbal metaphor in proprioception, that the predominant correlates of simple terms in English are visual objects (including motions). Language and vision influence each other, but each has schemata of its own, for example, verb and complement relations in language, *Gestalt* perception rules in vision. Do we have any reason to suppose that negotiation between these is worked out ahead of time in our genes?

Only signs that are not projected on the rough surfaces of nature are really free to give shape to their content. Such are the chess board itself or pure Euclidean geometry held aloof from coarse applications. When signs refer to the world, there is always a gap between the patterns they capture and the shape of experience. All modern semiotic theories recognize this, accepting the principle, *inter alia,* as limiting their own prowess.

14

THE ELABORATION OF REFERENCE

Suppose that, arriving at a dinner, I find a table set for 12. The plates are china, glazed with a bird motif. There is good silver. The tablecloth is embroidered with a floral pattern. Considering these parts, it probably makes sense to say that the plates represent birds and the tablecloth represents flowers. We also might speak of these parts as representing wealth or class. The setting as a whole invites a much more elaborate interpretation; its representation is of a different order. The setting as a whole—a text—does not represent birds or flowers, but rather the character of the occasion at which it will be enjoyed, represents the occasion as formal or informal, festive or severe, and so on. The setting as a whole conveys representations that are a bit surprising, considering its parts, for verbless as it is, it seems to partake of something that we would express in language with future imperative—how I should feel, how I should act. This will be most evident if the invitation has *mis*represented the dinner, and I have arrived inappropriately dressed.

Judy Chicago, with coworkers, made a monumental sculpture some years ago of a table setting. The square of the table became a triangle, a gender motif worked out further in handwoven cloths and individually glazed ceramics. Here the "tense" would be past imperfect indicative, a contemplation of what has been going on for women through the centuries.

Such references are contingent on hierarchies that allow a text to constrain or direct the interpretant of its components. Hierarchies organize inclusion (utensils, place setting, table setting) and possibly importance (plate as the center of the place setting, centerpiece or head of table as the focus of table setting). The setting also has a grammatical syntax that depends on categories (Cloth/tablecloth, napkins; Dishes/dinner plate, bowls . . . ; Flatware/forks, spoons, knives.) There is additionally a semantic hierarchy of dependence among the referents. Chicago's sculpture depends on the reference to and referentiality of a functional dinner setting. The functional dinner setting depends on the referentiality of the stylistically expressive utensils from which it is composed.

Elaboration of the representamen eventually can supplant reference, but before considering that possibility we must understand how it develops reference. In the development of reference, reference by the part is subordinated to the reference by the whole, developing possibilities of meaning we could not predict by considering the parts of a text out of their structural context.

THREE ASPECTS OF REFERENCE IN LANGUAGE: DESIGNATION, ANALYSIS, AND MODALITY

In establishing reference, hierarchical structure plays with or against the constraints of its medium. Sentences are so different from other semiotic hierarchies that we are inclined to abandon the comparison. A picture of a white rabbit might be a picture of some specific rabbit, of rabbits in general (especially in a biology text), or of an imaginary rabbit. A sentence like "John's pet rabbit is white" fixes that variable.

Language appears unique in its capacity to define its own terms. It is special in its facility of naming relations. (But not unique: Mathematics names relations. Uniforms show membership and dominance.) Above all, sentences seem unique in their capacity to designate *aspects* of a situation and combine them.

The following discussion is meant to render sentences and other types of texts more extensively comparable. My aim is not to deny or obscure the special powers and characteristics of language but to show that these are not all of a piece and that the differences between language and other media are not all black and white.[1]

Designation

The indexical component of a sentence refers its other terms to specific situations. There are several sorts. The quantifiers—"all," "some," "any," "a"—limit reference within a named class. Deictic words "this," "that," "now," "then," "I," and "you,"—indicate temporal and spatial positions. Proper names indicate individuals.

Some sentences have no explicit indexes: "It has started to rain." Traffic is at a standstill." To show these sentences are not assertions about the world because of a magic property of language, we must account systematically for their indexical function. In such cases designation is established systematically by markedness. The explicit index is the marked case. If there is no explicit index, the zero sign, the situation of the enunciation— that is, the speaker's present world—is indicated as the unmarked referent (unless there are other clues). When I say to you on the phone, long distance, "It's raining," then in normal contexts you understand the remark to apply to my environment, not yours.

Analysis

A sentence articulates a unitary situation as a compound of agent, object, and action and correlates each with semantic categories. (This is not to say that this analysis originates in language rather than in, perhaps, the visual system, nor to deny that animals might make such analyses.) This analytical capacity of sentences is their most distinctive characteristic in comparison with other signs. A painting of Ralph hitting the ball will obviously use different portions of its total surface to represent Ralph and the ball, but it also will use different portions of its surface to represent Ralph's pants and Ralph's shirt. The viewer must attribute some analysis to the scene. The sentence "Ralph hits the ball" conveys an analysis. The analysis of a story into distinct events usually requires that the story be represented by sentences. In mime or silent film some events merge into a continuity. To "predicate" something of something is to associate with that object an analysis of it or its situation.

Modality

Modality—a term with a very complex history—frequently is described psychologically as the positioning of a proposition with regard to belief or doubt, knowledge, desire, obligation, and so on. "We wish that . . ." "We have reason to hope that . . ." "We believe that . . ." "We fear that. . . ." Languages express these relations with special forms and vocabulary. Rather than invoke psychology, I define modality as an internal function of the sign: *Modality* is an interpretant that assigns the object to a world. For a sentence, the object is the proposition it expresses and its context is a world: a world of existing fact, a world of desiderata, a world of obligations, a world of necessities, a world of hypothesis, and so on. An expressive gesture in response to a sentence (a sigh, shrug, or shudder) can invert modality, assigning the sentence to hope or doubt.[2]

I do not deny, of course, that these different worlds entail different psychological bents. To speak of worlds rather than feelings is a formality. "The world of the unhappy is quite another than that of the happy" (Wittgenstein, *Tractatus* 6.43). There is no universal vocabulary for modes as Greimas seems to imply. Every language, every culture has its own modal system.

Modality is also encoded by markedness. First, mention is marked with respect to assertion. If I wish to utter (or write) a proposition without asserting it, I must mark it in some way, neutralize it with quotation marks or with tags such as "suppose," or "if." "Suppose it rains tomorrow" does not assert that it rains tomorrow. When there are no such marks—the zero sign—then the proposition is assigned to our world. Similarly, pretense (assignment to the world of falsity in the perspective of the enunciator) is marked with respect to belief. That is why any voluntary sign of sincerity is a target of suspicion: The truth needs no special mark.

We have been considering the property of language to "assert" signs "about" situations, a mysterious property on first view, but one that admits analysis. Aboutness and assertion are default positions in a matrix of marked binary oppositions that associate the content of a sentence with objects in a world. Our disposition to understand objects and actions under human control (such as sentences) as signs and our disposition to correlate binary alternatives according to the markedness values we assign them makes a system of stunning economy, but it is not magic.

The capacity to encode designation, modality, and semantic analysis with precision is *sui generis* for verbal signs. No exact equivalents to these appear outside of language. No other medium sustains the contrast of designation with *denotation* (the indication of a class rather than an individual). However, once teased apart, these ingredients of verbal reference turn out to play roles, albeit often more vague, in nonverbal semiosis. This chapter continues with a preliminary consideration of gesture. Chapter 21 studies two works, one visual, one musical, that cannot be understood without attributions of modality.

EXPRESSION

Expressions are signs that take inflection as a ground. Under the heading of expressions I assimilate expressive bodily gestures in the usual sense and representations of these by inflections or contours as defined in chapter 13.

Imagine an expression made by a group of gestures: Jack comes in at two in the afternoon. Jill is already drunk. Spinning around on his heel, he stomps out of the room and slams the door behind him.

The gestures of spinning around, stomping, and slamming make a kind of discourse that is nonpredicative but in its own way structurally elaborate. This is a *transformative expression* that changes the energy level and rhythm of the turning around, the walking, and the door shutting, which are not in themselves expressive. Here they all go . . . *Pow!* The neutral overall action of looking at a scene and walking away is transformed into a gesture expressive of angry rejection.

Unmarked Expressions

Guiding our interpretation of the imaginary scene just presented is again an invisible substructure in the form of a matrix of marked oppositions, parallel to the relations that interpret sentences. Here too markedness relations hinge on the situation of the enunciation. (The rules that follow do not necessarily hold for gestures that accompany speaking. Language may assimilate gesture as punctuation and illustration and/or gesture may assimilate language as self-expression.)

1. *Designation.* The expression, if unmarked otherwise, is "about" (refers to) the state of the enunciator (actor, gesturer). In Jakobson's sense, in the unmarked gesture the expressive function is dominant. In language, the first function of an index is to designate the semiotic object (generally grammatical subject) of the thought expressed. Because the semiotic object is automatically determined by an unmarked gesture (the object is the person who makes the gesture), the usual interpretation of a further index is that it shows a cause or target. Jack's gaze toward Jill indicates her as the stimulus and target of his anger.

2. *Modality.* Again, sincerity is unmarked with respect to pretense. We suppose Jack really means it. The world of the feeling or attitude expressed is the present world of fact.

3. *Analysis.* We wouldn't usually say that Jack's expression is "about" how he feels; rather that we would say it "shows" how he feels. But the only difference is that Jack's relation to his own anger is not named. In "Jack feels angry," "feels" names a relation between Jack and anger. This is not a minor difference, but it is not highly consequential in every case.

Marked Expressions

The foregoing deals with the *unmarked* case. This comes to nothing unless we can discover *marked* cases. How do you mark a gesture as not being true? How do you mark a gesture as not being about the person who makes the gesture? To put it figuratively, what are the quotation marks for gesture? How do we form the gestural subjunctive?

Although we do not literally have quotation marks to mark gestures, we have signs that identify certain objects and performances rich in gestural content as fictive, imaginary, hypothetical, as like "mentions."

Threatening, teasing, and flirtatious gestures are quasihypothetical. These are marked by self-restraint. The self-restraint is codified. (See Bateson [1972] on play in animals.) An expression can be demonstrated without being asserted, that is, it can be "mentioned." If the president of the United States makes the gesture of sending ships into the Mediterranean, he expresses a threat. In peacetime, a military parade is a mere mention, a hypothesis. (Almost. Perhaps we needn't mention that a mere mention can be a reminder.) Mimicry in its most casual and aesthetically least elaborate forms requires that gesture be marked as not referring primarily to the condition of the actor. Both sarcasm and sympathy may be conveyed in part through mimicry. For the former, enough hesitation to show deliberate intention, exaggeration of all sorts, and stylization serve as marks canceling our reflex to understand the expression as representing the performer. Mimicry expressive of sympathy is marked in the opposite fashion, by a spontaneous, diminutive, gentle echoing. In general, the contexts and frames of the plastic and performance arts mark their gestures and expressions, decontextualizing them with respect to author and object.

15

DOUBLE STRUCTURE—
GRAMMAR AND PATTERN IN TEXTS

This chapter compares the two principal types of syntax proposed in chapter 7. Occurring together, grammar and pattern can be supplementary, with structure on each level complete, or compensatory, with violations of grammar balanced by pattern or sketchiness of pattern balanced by grammar. I imagine that our conscious impression of coherence when we make sense of a text reflects our construction of mental diagrams, not necessarily conscious, that embody the logic of these structures. It may occur to the reader that there are many mediating instances combining these two types; I strive to contrast them starkly merely for clarity of exposition.[1]

The view of text structures developed here descends from Jakobson's method of poetic analysis but is meant to rectify or clarify the underlying theory. Both Paul Garvin (1981) and I (Lidov 1979) complained around the same time about a fundamental muddle. Structural analysis in the mode instigated by Jakobson failed to differentiate adequately the structure of language as a system from the structure of particular works. The linguist (and musicologist) Nicolas Ruwet, in a brilliant series of articles (Ruwet 1972–89 inclusive), resolves the dilemma of indicating a double structure by identifying what I call grammar with deep structure and what I call pattern with surface structure. General semiotics requires a different tack, first, because the notion of deep structure is uncertain outside of language, and second, so that we can better understand the modal orientations of the two types of structure. Very, very generally, the modal prejudice of grammar is attachment to society; that of pattern, the converse.

ELEMENTS IN GRAMMATICAL ANALYSIS: *CATEGORIES* AND *FORMS*

A *grammar* for assembling texts is a set of rules than governs the text's constituents and their relations by reference to *categories*. A text pertains to a grammar as an instance conforming to rule. Grammar is abstract. The "paradigms" of grammar are abstract *categories,* such as parts of speech in language, types of steps in dance, or classes of chords in music. Constituents of the text instance these categories. The competent recipient knows these categories *a priori* relative to the text. These categories provide paradigmatic relations *in absentia.* Combinatorial relations between constituents of the text are governed by rules, which, like the categories, are also known *a priori* in relation to the text.

A combination—a "syntagm"—that realizes a grammatical rule is a *form.* Examples of forms: the sentence, the syllogism, the still-life, the musical sonata, standard types of plot, and perhaps the standard press conference.

Grammatical explication is essentially deductive because the specific syntactic and categorical relations of a form are examples of preestablished general types.

ELEMENTS IN PATTERN ANALYSIS: UNITS AND SETS

Pattern pertains to one particular text, a "work," as an independent individual. A *pattern* is a concrete ad hoc arrangement of constituents that establishes relations of similarity and contrast. "Paradigms" determined by similarity and contrast are *sets.* "Syntagms" determined by similarity and contrast are *units.* (Patterns may exploit grammatical similarities, but similarity as such has no role in grammar.) Patterns are discovered by induction or abduction. Pattern is known only *a posteriori* in relation to the text and develops from perceptions of symmetries of all kinds: repetitions, variations, and transformations and contrasts. Examples of pattern: the rhyming words of a lyric poem or the thematic motifs of a symphony. These suggest categories within the poem or the symphony itself that are not manifest (except accidentally) outside the particular work. I call these "sets" instead of "categories" to emphasize this difference. In principle, we do not need to know about a set before we encounter and recognize it as such, whereas we would need to know, for example, what a sentence is to recognize one. Notice that the same structure can function both ways:

"Whose woods these are I think I know" is a grammatical form twice, once as a clause and once as an instance of iambic tetrameter. It is also a unit of pattern which enters into myriad relations of similarity and difference with other verses of that poem, relations for which there is no prior blueprint.

All the arts utilize pattern, sometimes within grammatical constraints and sometimes as a means of contradicting or escaping grammar. The obvious preponderant contribution of repetition and variation within works of music, dance, and architecture, and rhythmic and phonetic repetitions in poetry suggest the wide scope of pattern in those areas. When Ludwig van Beethoven's Fifth Symphony was still revolutionary, E. T. A. Hoffman defended it against contemporary criticisms of its grammar by pointing out the consistency of its patterns.

PRELIMINARY EXAMPLES

Slogans give us a quick view of double structure:

Read my lips:
No new taxes.

Some of us will remember U.S. presidential candidate George Bush's tough talk: The gangster imperative is followed by a noun phrase stripped of its verbal complement ("There will be"). The abuse of grammar—elision of verb—is compensated by perfection of pattern: two units of three words both ending with plural nouns. All words but the last are monosyllabic; this last also is the only one with an initial plosive consonant. The two unvoiced "*ss*" ("*ps*" and "*x*" = "*ks*") hold parallel positions. No vowels repeat. But (read your tongue instead of your lips) they alternate between an anterior set (read, lips, new) and a posterior set (my, no, tax). Regarding accent, we must note the *expressive* performance. Six stresses add rhythm and accentual equivalence to units at the word level and phrase level. (Gesturally, as a transformative expression, the slogan lands five punches and then spits—in all, a better phonetic plan than financial.)

Because grammar is synchronic and social, the replacement of grammatical coherence by coherence of pattern is frequently a mark of a social stance. Chapter 8 noted this regarding the Winstons slogan. The same holds for Bush, talking like a bully, and also for:

A diamond is forever.

Gentler, for sure, but there is still a violation where the adverb complements the copula. Pattern is established by rhythm—weak-strong-weak on
both sides of "*is*" with a set of "*d*s" matching a set of "*r*s." The replacement
of grammar is homologous here with the suggestion of a more permanent
truth. Diamonds transcend the merely synchronic social systems of economic exchange, both of jewels and women.

The role of grammar and pattern in the plastic arts is more fragmentary
because visual articulation structure is so widely various. In representational painting, inclusion hierarchies of constituents usually are established
by the objects represented with or without the inclusion hierarchies established by nonmimetic elements of shape and color. The *Last Supper* of
Leonardo has a background and a foreground, the latter the group at table.
This in turn divides into groups of three. *Last Suppers* are a form in a rudi-
mentary grammar that call for the realization and combination of types,
those types or categories being, of course, those of apostles, Jesus, and the
table. Beyond that the arrangement is a question of pattern, the groupings,
the similarities and contrasts of posture, and so on.

Pattern and grammar need not duplicate each other in painting.
Poussin's *Penitence,* in his second series of the *Seven Sacraments,* shows
Mary Magdalen washing the feet of Jesus. Two sets of figures embellish the
narrative form. Her posture is mirrored by one servant who washes Simon
the Pharisee's feet and another who pours wine, innocuous echoes, but in
addition, Jesus' gesture accepting Mary Magdalen is nearly repeated by a
man across the table who condemns her, thus dramatizing conflict.

Although patterns achieve coherence by display of similarity and contrast ad hoc without appeal to a priori system, the interpretation of pattern
may be enriched by precedent. Our appreciation of rhyme in Frost's "Stop-
ping by Woods . . ." is richer if we know *terza rima,* but the rhyme pattern
can be discovered even if we know no other poem. We could not "discover" that a certain collection of words were a sentence or that a certain
collection of sentences made a syllogism or a story without a prior idea of
syllogisms or of stories.

Pattern has a special effect when its units lie within ranges of temporal
or spatial extent that allow a ready grasp of them as wholes. In these cases,
the similarities in pattern establish sensual continuity and/or emphasis
and/or rhythm. The effect of pattern is then hypnotic and inductive, fa-

cilitating emotional arousal and heightening the power of suggestion. These psychological effects contribute to the association of pattern with the aesthetic.

The examples of analysis that follow are texts from music and prose. I have endeavored, in the case of music, to provide the most elementary example I could, and hence one where grammar and pattern are nearly congruent. For those who can read musical scores, other published examples illustrate a compensatory or contradictory relation between grammar and pattern.[2]

PATTERN AND GRAMMAR IN RHETORIC: JEFFERSON'S DECLARATION OF INDEPENDENCE

I mean to be as indifferent as any doctor, not to suggest whether history has justified this rebellion, whether King George wisely bowed to inevitable destiny or foolishly abdicated his political responsibilities. We will consider only the relation between patterns of rhythm and the grammar of logic.

Before memory was bytes, schoolchildren in the United States often were obliged to memorize the opening of the Declaration of Independence. The preamble has acquired a mythic function. Gary Wills (1978), on whom I much rely, shows how radically the import of the document changed in its first century, as the details of its grievances were forgotten and the preamble took on a quasi-religious mystique. Wills quotes G. K. Chesterton: "the Declaration of Independence, perhaps the only piece of practical politics that is also theoretical politics and also great literature" (p. xxi).

Regarding the sign as a whole, the text represents rebellion by the colonies (its overall object) modally as a necessary and reasonable action (the interpretant). Its preamble is a somewhat autonomous part of the text that represents fundamental laws of government (object) as natural (modal interpretant—belonging to the natural world.) These interpretants are determined by a quasi-logical *quality* established by relations of coherence in the text and not just by logical relations in the content! The logic, per se, is insufficient and is strongly supplemented by relations of pattern.

The science of rhetoric merges grammar and pattern; its tradition furnishes us the figures of the *syllogism, climax,* and *enthymeme,* to which we must add, in the ordinary sense, the figure of the list.

1. The *syllogism* includes: the major premise (MP), minor premise (mp), and inference (Inf).
2. The *enthymeme* is an abbreviated syllogism. One or two of the propositions are elided because they are evident in the situation. Aristotle takes this as the characteristic figure of rhetoric.
3. The *climax:* "a figure in which a number of ideas or propositions are so arranged that each succeeding one rises above its predecessor in impression or force" (*Webster's International,* 2nd edition). Most typically there are three units, but there is no set form.

The syllogism and enthymemes are grammatical forms built on the abstract category or proposition, and its propositions are linked by a rule. The climax refers to no component category; it is a type of pattern as is a list. (Recognizing the "type" is not needed for comprehension of a pattern—an extraneous conception here.)

A syllogism can display a climax: All men are mortal; Socrates is a man; Therefore, Socrates is mortal. Jefferson exploits the possibility that, due to this coincidence, a climax may *sound* like a syllogism.

Turning to the logic-grammar of the Declaration, a single syllogism gives it form as a whole:

(MP) It is right for people to throw off bad governments.
(mp) Our government is bad.
(I) Therefore, it is right for us to throw it off.

The first three paragraphs of the Declaration are concerned, principally, to establish the first premise. Abbreviations are handy to get an overview of the preamble. Let us take

"K (not) = C" for "The King is (not) Cruel or abusive."
"S (not) = P" for "The Subjects are (not) Patient."
"(not) R" for "The subjects are (not) right to rebel."

Then, with Roman numerals for paragraphs, Arabic numerals for sentences, the opening paragraphs of the Declaration argue:

O. Title
   I. If a people rebels, it should give reason. (enthymeme)
   II. Major (1–3) and minor (4–6) premises
      (1) Self-evident truths including,

    If K = C and S = P then R   (MP)
(2) If K not = C or if S not = P then not R
(3) But if K = C and S = P then R   (MP)
(4) S = P   (mp)
(5–6) K = C   (mp)

There follows the list of grievances and, more briefly, a history of loyal patience and then the paragraph with its double conclusion that the colonies "are and of right ought to be" free.

"Ought to be" is a descriptive, logical conclusion. "Are," which enacts what the argument describes (i.e., it is performative, declares something new to be) is of a different modality from the rest. The transformation of modality (from the valorized to the actual) may be viewed as motion rather than as predication; its effect is energetic.

However attractive or natural the major premise may appear now, it was not consensual when it was penned. And of course, as a First Principle, it cannot be justified by logic. What Jefferson claimed to be self-evident is exactly what was *not* evident, but it is proffered in a persuasive pattern. The pattern has much to do with rhythm.

There is no consensus how to scan English prose. Stress varies with intended emphasis of reference. I will indicate a personal reading without providing a rationale. I allow any number of weak syllables between strong, intending to show accents only where they could be realized in a plausible pronunciation. My parentheses confess doubts.

I depart from conventional poetic scansion in allowing and highlighting a stress pattern to which I attribute hierarchy and elision, indicated by the following notation and obvious variants:

1   2   3
       [1   2   3]

As an example, Jefferson redrafted the phrase "Life, liberty and property," making a stronger rhythmic climax by lengthening the last unit:

Life, liberty and the pursuit of happiness.

I am inclined to hear the elaboration as:

```
1      2                              3
Life, liberty
       [(1)      2              3]
       and the pursuit of      happiness
```

(The climatic effect is more salient in that "happiness" was a philosophic buzz word at the time of the composition, a heretical and quasi-mathematical concept with public happiness implicitly opposed to celestial bliss and the "pursuit of happiness" explicitly modeled on the "attraction of gravity" [Wills 1978, 151, 252].

Given its context, the highlighted pattern suggests an affective allusion—a relation of idiom (to invoke the third syntax mentioned in chapter 7)—parasitic on the conventions of school logic. In spoken English, every clause normally has a single primary stress, but it seems in the nature of the third clause of a verbal syllogism to conjoin the stressed terms of the preceding premises, often in an emphatic, three-stress sentence that maintains the accent on those terms while also accenting a mark of derivation:

```
             1
All men are mortal.
   2
Socrates is a man
[1]        [2]         3
Therefore, Socrates is mortal
```

This stress pattern is one we know as a didactic rhythm and associate with logic and one able, on this ground, to allude to logic.

Here is a set of pattern units from the second paragraph, the paragraph which is most critically lacking in a logical basis.

```
             1          2                        3
{1}       Prudence   indeed              will dictate
             1          2                        3
{2}   that government long               established
             1          2                        3
{3} should not     be changed
                                [1          2          3   ]
                                for light and transient   reasons
```

Or again:

```
           1              2             3
{1} laying its foundation on such principles and
           1            2              3
{2} organizing its powers in such form/ as to
           1                    2         3
{3} them shall seem most likely
                      [1         2        3]
              to effect their safety and happiness.
```

Here the switch from surprisingly regular four-syllable feet to three-syllable feet is critical in grouping the last three accents. A more tentative reading:

```
                      1          2                  3
{1} That whenever any       form              of government
                      1          2                  3
{2}            becomes destructive       of these ends,
                      1          2                  3
{3}      it is the right of the people
                                  [1         2       3
                            to alter or abolish it
                                        (1        2       3)]
                                  and to institute new government
```

Again:

```
           1          2        3
{1} that all men   are created   equal
           1              2
{2} that they are    endowed with
                                  [1         2]        3
                                  certain, inalienable rights.
{3} that among these are . . . (as above).
```

Finally:

```
           1              2
We hold    these truths
                      [  (1)   2]    3
                      to be    self-evident
```

The units of pattern shown above as single lines correlate with sentence grammar. There are no grammatical boundaries within them that are stronger than the grammatical boundaries between them (exception marked: "/").

Each of these citations may be understood as comprising a rhythmic climax that alludes to a "rhythm of logic" of which the syllogism is emblematic. There are, besides these, various passages that suggest many other forms of rhythmic regularity. As a supplement, a rough visual arrangement can bring out the pervasiveness of pattern in the first paragraph, which is nearly metrical. Vertically aligned lines are rhythmically similar.

> When
> in the course of human events
>   it becomes necessary
>   for one people
> to dissolve the political bands
>   which have connected them with another
> and to assume among the powers of the earth
> the separate and equal station
> to which the laws of nature and
> of nature's god entitle them
>   a decent respect
>   to the opinions of mankind
> requires that they should declare
>   the causes which impel them to the separation

The list of grievances—alleged actions and negligences—are particular cases, and we need hardly inspect their rhythm. When you have reason (grammar) you don't need rhyme (pattern). Nevertheless, the 19 clauses beginning "He has . . ." certainly make a pattern. The association of a list with the second premise of a deductive syllogism offers another link of idiom between Jefferson's pattern and his grammar; that is, it is an independent pattern but has a place set out for it in the archetypes of argument. We expect the major premise to be a general, established principle. The minor premise, touching specific fact, needs its chain of evidence.

But this is not the first list; there were two others. The major premise of the primary syllogism is a patterned list of self-evident truths, each beginning with "that." This first list includes another subordinate list, a list of rights in the infinitive: "to alter," "to abolish," "to effect," "to throw off." A list within a *major* premise is not archetypal. In fact, it might seem diffuse, hardly the effect here. This configuration is the hub of the action.

Framing the whole Declaration, we have the enthymeme of the first paragraph: (MP) If a people must separate, they should give reasons. The minor premise (we are separating) is *not* stated—following the rule of enthymemes. Just in the place where it *would* be stated, we find the major premise of that principle syllogism with its list. Although no list is called for logically, the syntagmic position of this list, following a major premise and following the plural word "causes," duplicates in the small the pattern of the Declaration as a whole. (MP—List (mp)—Inference.) Not only that, but the modality change at the end of the Declaration is prepared here. The enthymeme is in indicative mood, but what it speaks of—a people should give reasons—then happens. This, too, in the small is the pattern of the whole, which moves from observation to performance.

The Declaration realizes the fundamental modal function of pattern, for its whole point is to effect a social disjunction, a break with grammar writ large. It is typical of pattern to appeal to history ("When in the course of Human Events") to justify a break with convention.

PATTERN AND GRAMMAR IN A SONG

Not to give Jefferson the last word, let us consider the song "God Save the King." Percy Scholes, in the *Oxford Companion to Music* (1938/1975); quotes Beethoven, one of many composers who have written variations on this tune: "I must show the English what a blessing they have in 'God Save the King'" (p. 409). The tune is known throughout all the former British Empire and in all the nations that had intercourse with it.

What melody alone might represent, without a text or context, is considered in chapter 20. Here we have melody and words and may speak of the song as a whole, as representing loyalty to the monarch (object) and representing this loyalty as serene, voluntary, happy, orderly, and natural (the interpretant). Some of the ground of this representation is in the sensory character of the melody as bright, smooth, and slow; and some of it is in the simple coordination of melodic pattern and melodic grammar that makes both seem natural and comfortable.

The tune is a small thing, but the discussion here, despite my best efforts, is the most specialized in the book with respect to music theory (more so than the larger example of chapter 21). Some readers may not wish to suffer all of it; the chapters following do not depend on its details.

The grammar of the melody must be considered with regard to two systems, meter, which structures the time *in abstracto,* and tonality, which structures the scale as a vocabulary and regulates combinations of its elements. The two are coordinated by rules of phrasing. It is very hard to discern a border between the biology of aural perception and the conventions of meter and tonality. The natural quality of simple melodic grammaticality serves here, by association, to link loyalty to the monarch with "nature's law." We can be certain, however, that the musical *nature* of the tune is a very specialized second nature. The scale of the tune, so easy for everyone in the world today who has a Walkman, has not always been easy for the more distant subjects of this crown, some of whom divided their octaves into five roughly equal steps instead of seven contrasting intervals.

The meter is nearly as straightforward as could be. The principal metrical categories are beats, downbeats, and measures (groups of beats). The beats are grouped into measures of three, and the measures are paired. The constituents realizing these categories are the individual notes. Our musical notation shows the first note as the first beat (or downbeat) of the measure. (This is not arbitrary; the downbeats are emphasized notes. In this melody, all the notes longer than one beat begin on downbeats; all groups of repeated notes [which are like long notes] begin on downbeats; the last note is a downbeat; and two of the only three notes approached by a leap are downbeats.)

Yet there is one complication. Hemiola is an old grammatical form (or perhaps idiom) that may be ascribed to this tune. A hemiola typically occurs in the penultimate two measures of slow melodies in triple measure, such as this song. A hemiola recasts these as shown in figure 15.1. Two groups of three become three of two or, what amounts to the same thing, a half-speed group of three. The quick, galliard style to which Scholes traces the tune may not confirm this reading, but it is supported by the third verse and is also compatible with the words used in the United States, where "God Save the King" was borrowed as "My Country 'tis of thee." (Also, "God save" may be iambic or trochaic.)

Figure 15.2 shows a temporal hierarchy articulating the tune and assuming the hemiola, to which we will presently return.

Figure 15.1 Hemiola

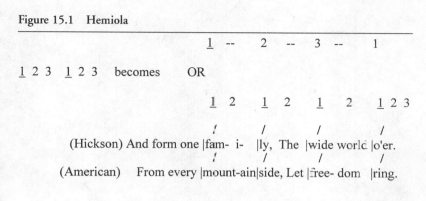

Figure 15.2 Grammatical hierarchy of meter (tree graph)

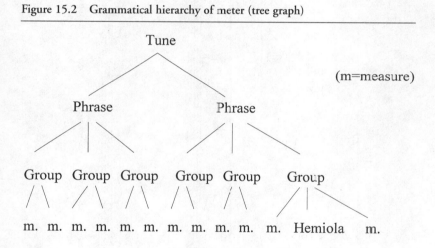

I will characterize the tonal grammar of the melody informally, drawing on a music theory tradition that emphasizes the dependent relationship of ornamental tones to tones that precede and follow them. The categories in this grammar are scale tones and chords; the most elementary forms are (approximately) motions that begin and end on tones of the same chord: passing tones, neighbor notes, and arpeggios, as shown in figure 15.3.[3] The grammar is hierarchic; ornaments have ornaments that are ornamented in turn. Since the last note of one ornamental figure typically can be the first of the next, this grammar generates (in the first instance)

Figure 15.3 Grammatical hierarchy of tonality (net graph)

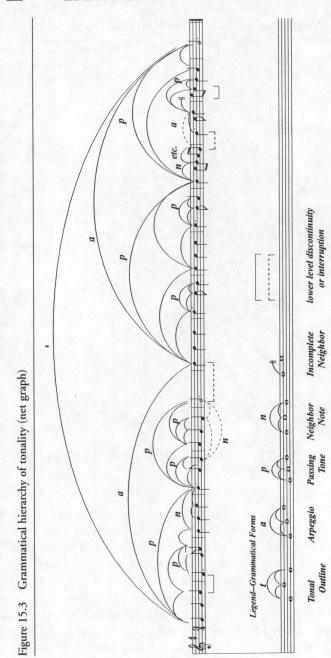

melodies composed of *conjunct* parts. Melody, so understood, exemplifies *boundary and region articulation.*

In figure 15.3, arcs are used to connect the notes of the tune that combine as tonally grammatical forms. A framework of arpeggiation is filled in by motion up and down the scale. The articulatory surface of the music owes much of its aural quality to the fact that most of its notes have grammatical connections both to the note that immediately precedes them and to the note that immediately follows. As exceptions, four disjunctions punctuate the flow; these are highlighted in the figure by brackets. These interruptions—marked in relation to their context—beg attention and interpretation. (The motions shown with dotted brackets are chordal leaps, more grammatically complete in themselves than those shown with solid brackets.)

At the first point of disjunction, the note that is leapt to stands out and adds emphasis to the meter, establishing a rhythmic regularity that sustains momentum. At the second point of disjunction, the note that is leapt *to* is the first high point; the note initiates the climax. The third disjunction is a leap *to* the first note of our possible hemiola. At the fourth disjunction, the note leapt *to* is an offbeat passing note and carries less emphasis than the note leapt *from*. The note leapt from, a short note, is the very highest note of all. By the visual notation, this high note appears to be on a downbeat; however, by the interpretation of hemiola (hemiolas generally are not notated as such), that note is a weak beat. Despite the fact that this note is the highest note, the chart shows it as part of an incomplete ornament deeply embedded at a low level of the hierarchy. In the grammar of tonality, the tone in question does not hold a polar role. To appreciate the function of the note, we must now move from grammar to pattern.

With pattern we see another side of the tune, its *disjunct* units.

Figure 15.4 demonstrates pattern via a notation discussed by Nicolas Ruwet (1972) and elaborated by Jeans-Jacques Nattiez (1975). Reading the array from left to right, the tune is preserved. Except for a phrase division between x_2 and b_1 each single left-to-right series represents a syntagmic *unit* within the higher of two hierarchical levels illustrated by the figure. Reading by column, each column represents a paradigmatic *set,* and each fragment within the column is a *unit* at the lower of the two hierarchical levels illustrated.

The concluding units are difficult to classify. Figure 15.5 shows how, reading them in the light of the hemiola and discounting the ornamental

Figure 15.4   Pattern in the tune (array)

high note, we can discern three elided figures, taking the last note of the first to serve also as the first note of the second, and so on. Such an elision complicates the disjunct articulation of the pattern but coordinates with a disjunction that complicates the conjunctions of the grammar. Elision of this sort is not available to speech (compare: "John caught the ball was rolling off the court"), but it is natural in music, where the disjunct series play against conjunct regions.

It is striking that both the pattern analysis and the grammatical analysis single out the highest note of the tune as an exception to their syntactic

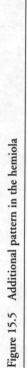

Figure 15.5 Additional pattern in the hemiola

a_3

$m_3 = m_2$

$n_4 = n_2$

diagrams. The highest note is an excess. It transforms the structural schema expressively. We hear it representing a final welling of energy that, in the context of the melody's gracious courtesy, we take as a feeling and show of enthusiasm.

The feeling framed by a melody can be marked by its structural elaboration as "art," that is, as not to be attributed to the performer. The conventional stipulation of the song as a national anthem marks the converse.

This study of structure in signs directly addresses one of the critical phenomena of semiosis identified in chapter 4, the comprehensibility of signs despite their radical individuation. The interaction of pattern and grammar is a source of radical individuality. At any point in the elaboration of a text, grammar may be suspended, taking advantage of pattern, or pattern may be suspended, taking advantage of grammar.

16

THE TEXT IN CONTEXT

A satellite view might encompass: (1) Text in relation to the grammar(s) it employs (issues of agrammaticality, dialect), in relation to other texts that employ its grammar(s) (issues of tradition), in relation to other texts it resembles or alludes to; (2) the text as object of reference in another sign or the text as object of interpretation in another sign; and (3) theories in which meaning depends on intertextual relations—thus "intertextuality" as an antidote to the effacement of references by structural elaboration.

No comprehensive schema for such heterogeneous problems is essayed here. The following commentaries address only a few topics that have—deservedly—a recent or continuing vogue in semiotic conversations: closure and autonomy, dialogue and monologue, discourse, and tropes.

THE FIGURES OF CLOSURE AND AUTONOMY

Signaled by Umberto Eco's early title, *The Open Work* (1962/1980), the idea that texts may be open or closed (cf. "readerly" or "writerly" in Barthes), is pivotal for contemporary semiotics and tied to fundamental question in epistemology: Is our own experience, as a whole, open or closed?

Our objective worlds are plural, contradictory, interpenetrating, and in part unstable. When I sit at the piano playing a Partita of Bach, it becomes a whole world. When I read a novel by Tolstoy, it becomes a whole world. Were I engaged with securities, I imagine the stock market might become a whole world. The English language captures the whole world when I am not listening to music or struggling to speak French or trying to recapture a geometric proof with an indulgent youngster.

The worlds engendered by immersion in texts and grammars control our perception of experiences external to them. In a sense, texts act like theories. Just as we might understand a recession in terms the theories of Marx, under the influence of particular stories and paintings we will see a bureaucracy as Kafkaesque or see a sunset as an impressionistic. These worlds are in constant collision, testing each others wholeness and closure.

A text is *complete* insofar as the whole is sufficient to characterize the parts. The text appears *autonomous* insofar as the relations among its parts (their syntax) seem to displace reference to an external context. The very same elaborations of structure that suggest closure and autonomy, resisting the function of representation, propel the text-representamen into another sign, now as a text-object, inviting interpretation by further representation.

To say that texts and systems make whole worlds would seem to have something to do with closure and autonomy; yet the idea reads two ways. On one interpretation, which descends from structuralism, signs make a world through autonomy. The signs of a closed system interpret each other or refer to each other but are trapped and isolated, like the words in a dictionary taken as defining each other but never touching "reality."

The opposite sense (which might claim parentage both in structuralism and pragmatism) suggests that signs make whole worlds when their closure prevents any limitation on their powers of reference, when their meaning is open to a constant reshaping and regeneration: Whatever happens, whatever we invent, we can extend language to talk about it.

The figure of autonomy recurring in aesthetics and in the semiotics of art suggests that the closure of a text or system renders any apparent references to the world outside irrelevant or illusory. Nobody can say what the 50 codified movements of tap dance or the 5 orders of architecture "mean" outside their respective systems. Sometimes we perceive autonomous sign constructions as having a special aura of emotion or feeling that is specific to them and that is very difficult to refer to the rest of the world.

Two of our familiar semiotic systems that have the strongest claims to autonomy are ordinary arithmetic and Euclidean geometry. It is possible to work in and with the worlds of arithmetic or geometry without reference to any external reality. Each has a vocabulary of elements and relations that combine in certain ways, not in others. Both make sense on their own terms or in their own terms without any recourse to external reference.

We have good grounds then to regard them as autonomous. However, we must not say that these systems are *incapable* of representation or that their capacity for representation is a secondary matter. Russell makes much of this point in his introduction to *Principles of Mathematics* (1903). Arithmetic ought to be set up, he argues, in such a way that it is good for counting things. We could add that we use geometry to represent real space and that Euclidean and non-Euclidean geometries are oriented for us by what real phenomenon they can and can not represent.

There is no shortage of closed sign systems: religious systems that determine thought and conduct, medical systems that cure all diseases or else blame them on the patient, political theories that never encounter negative evidence. The devout will be horrified by the epithet of autonomy, for they know they grasp reality. If they say they grasp the world and I say they grasp only an invented system, our difference is in our point of observation.

THE POSITION OF THE OBSERVER— VARELA, THOMPSON, AND ROSCH

The duality of autonomy and reference is reconciled in the concept of organisms constructed in Varelian biology. Varela, Thompson, and Rosch (1991) define life as the activity of an autopoetic system.

An autopoetic system is one that produces its own components and maintains their interrelationships. Every organism maintains its unity and specificity across a domain of interactions with the external world. These subject the subsystems of an organism, such as its nervous system, to perturbations. An outside observer may understand these deformations as indexes of the environment and may regard the organism as "perceiving" or "representing" the environment by its changes. From an "internal" point of view, that is, one limited strictly to the organism itself, its states comprise a finite range of possibilities that define each other as disturbances and compensations. Each state of the system can be accounted for without reference to an external world.

In the internal perspective that ignores environment, the life of the organism is a closed system. Language is a closed subsystem of the human nervous system. Our minds are like dictionaries in consisting of a closed and autonomous collection of interpretations.

But if the difference between a referential system and an autonomous system is a function of the point of observation, then with texts and with semiotic systems that we understand as complete, *both* positions are available to us. We can immerse ourselves in a film or a novel or a philosophy and then stand back from it. We can see things its way and then see them our way.

But we cannot see our own minds from the outside. Varela and coauthors conclude that we are imprisoned by the autonomy of our ideas as a closed subsystem of our nervous system. I think not; this question returns in chapter 22.

THE FIGURE OF DISCOURSE

Semiotic closure is tenuous. The notion of text I have attempted to develop to this point, as a structure that we understand by attributing a syntactic diagram to it, is idealized. Complex texts do not fully yield to neat diagrams, and this is critical.

A text that establishes grounds for competing interpretants establishes a discourse. We see it as lively because our images of it fluctuate. The text becomes an image of think*ing*. Discourse embodies the movement of thought.

A text offers us a world when three conditions are met: (1) it must capture attention but be too complex to be comprehended readily in its detail and organization; (2) It must *suggest* closure—the associations among its parts must suggest that they belong to a consistent scheme in which they define each other by similarity and difference or by grammatical relations; and (3) the text or grammar must *not* actually yield to the unitary diagram that it seems to promise. These three characteristics are also characteristics of the "real" or "everyday" world to which we are referring our comparison: The world is complex and absorbing; it seems to have unity or at least continuity (which is close to unity); yet we can't quite make out what the unity and articulations are. The loose ends and leftovers create conceptual instabilities that are the representamina of the life of thought, the buzz of unprocessed experiences around the edges of our articulated objective world.

Lively texts do not fully resolve into unambiguous diagrams. An analysis, if sufficiently rigorous and extended, will discover ambiguities. The holes and excesses and contradictions keep it alive. The diagram typically fails for logical reasons, but alternatively, it may fail because of sensory overloading, as with mandalas, op art, or "pattern music." A text that stays alive or one into which, we might say, we project the liveliness of thought is open in some measure. There are corridors in and out. The not-quite-closed texts enter into conversations.

Following Levi-Strauss, we may associate the function of *mediation* with ambiguities in categorization. (The idea is extensively developed but not systematically defined in *The Raw and the Cooked* [1964/1969] and elsewhere.) A simple illustration: If the now-plasticized fable of Santa Claus retains any resonance at all, surely we owe it to the reindeer. The story articulates two oppositions: first, exterior/interior (the harsh and deadly winter vs. the home and hearth); and second, good behavior/bad behavior. St. Nicholas who can brave fireplaces to bring gifts (a jolly Prometheus with the gift of fire) looks after us if we are good (we get the gift of fire); has nothing for us if we are bad (we are out in the cold). All the elements of the story fit the alignment of categories—fiery-suited Santa with his pearly, Teflon locks keeps it all in place—except the reindeer. They are alive and comfortable in the harsh cold, offering at least a faint comfort for those of us who may not have been perfectly good, who may not have fully tamed our animality, who may doubt the categorical integrity of the system. The reindeer are a mediating element, without which the story would be static. The mediation opens the world of the fable and makes the text discursive.

THE FIGURE OF DIALOGUE

Chapter 8 cited Kevelson's reconstruction of the tradition that takes the dialogical exchange of question and answer or of sign and response as the fundamental unit of semiosis. I argued that dialogue does not provide an alternative to system but rather a complement. The governance of dialogue establishes coherence in collections of texts not comprehensively related to each other by pattern or grammar.

Literally, a dialogue is an exchange between persons who hear each other out. Figuratively, Hegel "answers" Kant and Stravinsky "argues" with Wagner. We have dialogues inside our heads and inside one speech when one speech compresses many voices. Hamlet's soliloquy begins with a question and continues dialogically. (But the Nordic Santa Claus story did not respond to the Greek Prometheus myth. There may be a generic or thematic parallelism, but if they are now in dialogue, that is our later arrangement.)

In dialogue a sign from one perspective responds to a sign in another. Sometimes we identify the perspectives with persons, sometimes as "voices" (as in "the voice of conscience" or "the voice of reason"), sometimes as corporate bodies ("the media response"). The dialogue of perspectives is instantiated when a performance interprets a play, an answer interprets a question, an objection interprets a proposal, or a critique interprets a concert.

The Governance of Dialogue

In law, the regulation of discourse by rulings on definition and interpretation is explicit, and its forms of discourse are thoroughly formalized (pleading, interrogation, cross-examination, rendering opinions, sentencing). One orienting problem for research in semiotics is to outline the governance of dialogue in various domains: science, scholarship, small talk, parliaments, classroom, jazz combo, psychoanalytic session, church council, marketplace and so on. All these domains have their rules, rules about for example: diction, who may speak, when, expectations of honesty or interest, tones of voice, topics, degrees of confrontation and deference. They use different signs to assert authority and control: dictionaries, oaths, applause, dirty looks, deprecating remarks, votes, precedents. The rules of discourse, in difference with those of grammars, do not refer exclusively to categories of elements of the signs produced. Michel Foucault's oeuvre provides great studies in the governance of dialogue and shows, *inter alia,* that there are very few domains of discourse in which language furnishes all the signs in play.

Thinking and the Reciprocation of Image and Predication

Mikhail Bakhtin wrote that to understand a sign means to answer it with another sign that could be mental.

Thinking embodies dialogue in two ways. The first, referred to earlier and widely observed, concerns the confluence of contradictory ideas and perspectives in our inner thoughts. The second has, I believe, often been glimpsed but rarely held out for full contemplation in semiotic studies, although we found it among our oldest sources (Panini's concept of "sphota"; see chapter 3). This dialogue comprises the reciprocal production of images and predications, ubiquitous in private mental life but also manifest in pub-

lic semiosis. Speech, the primary domain of predication, unfolds in continuous interaction with sources of imagery. As I understand him, this phenomenon is alluded to by Wilham Lawvere (1969), who finds a parallel
reciprocity intrinsic to mathematics itself. The reciprocation of image and
predication is the dialogue engaged when I get a picture (or feeling) of what
you describe and then find words for what I have in mind.

Monologue

The figure of monologue suggests as generous a range of phenomena. For
the voice of monologue we again count perspectives, not persons. Just as one
person may be at odds with herself, a chorus may speak with one voice. A
sycophant with a circle of "yes men" is monological. Insofar as it is effective,
any totalitarian regime is monological. So, however, is any one logic. Logic
represents, par excellence, interpretation that preserves one perspective.

Dialogue within the Structured Text

Earlier our focus of attention was the dialogues into which structured texts
are inserted. Open dialogue and acts of interpretation also are represented
inside structured texts.

Of course, the openness of dialogue represented within a structured
text is an illusion. Yet modeling dialogue is fundamental to the life of
thought within texts.

In Barthes's *S/Z* (1970/1974), the bases of these illusions are pinned
down with precision. Barthes shows how the fragments that make up the
closed patterns within a novella (Honoré de Balzac's *Sarasin*) attach to external systems in the culture of reference. The collision of these systems inside the novella lends it its lifelike, "discursive" character. Where semiotic
worlds collide, they enjoin dialogues.

Musical theorists from the early Baroque to J. S. Bach himself recommend that the instruments playing a fugue should proceed as voices in a
refined conversation; aimless chitchat is not their model. Indeed, the governance of monologue and dialogue is as deep a theme in regulated musical composition as in the freest improvisation. Myriad socialities are
established and reflected in the governance of dialogue for Dixieland, the
classical string quartets and concertos of Europe, the gong ensembles of
east Asia, the accompanied recitals of classical Indian music, audience and

singer interactions in Arabic musical traditions, and in other traditions. Bach's two great passion oratorios face each other across this axis: One has two choirs but is predominantly monological; the other has one choir but is more dramatic and dialogical.

FIGURES OF RHETORIC

The figures of speech are exceptions or supplements to its grammar, bifurcations in the stream of reference and problematic with regard to the closure of texts. The tropes are classified various ways. Without any intent to supplant more specialized theories, it is pertinent for general semiotic theory to try to ascertain on which sign factor the bifurcation centers: at the representamen or the object, or conversion of the interpretant.

Figure 16.1 is a diagram of these possibilities.

Bifurcation at the Representamen

A formalism worked out by Hjelmslev in *Language* (1944/1970) (and adapted by Barthes in his *Mythologies* [1972]) regards connotation as invoking a relation of alternatives among representamina from differing contexts. To refer to a party as a "soiree" entrains the prejudice, in the context of English-language culture, that French represents elegance. To refer to a party as a "bash" attributes excitement to it by borrowing the slang of sports. Choosing an oboe or a violin to present a melody may be connotative. Choosing Clint Eastwood or Kirk Douglas for a part is connotative because in the "star system," an actor star brings his or her own history and

Figure 16.1 Rhetorical figures

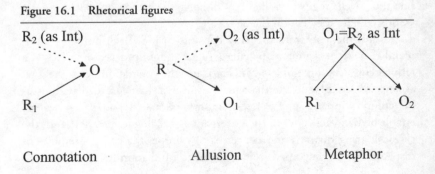

R_2 (as Int)　　　　　O_2 (as Int)　　$O_1 = R_2$ as Int

O　　　　　R

R_1　　　　　　　O_1　　R_1　　　　　O_2

Connotation　　　　　Allusion　　　　Metaphor

public persona to the representation. Picasso painted an ironic *Still-Life* (*Nature morte*) just after World War II; it shows, instead of fruit and flowers, an empty pitcher and burned-out candle. By borrowing the system of the still-life, the representation of want is placed in immediate opposition to the representation of plenty.

Bifurcation at the Object

Allusion invokes a relation among alternative objects of one sign. The title of my book indicates this book, but it also indicates other books: Barthes's *Elements of Semiology* with his allusion to Euclid's *Elements* and also, since Peirce is so strongly associated with semiotics, Peirce's *New Elements of Mathematics*.

Conversion of the Interpretant

Both metaphor and simile take the object of one sign as the representamina of another. The medial factor connecting the first representamen to the second object is thus like an interpretant. In either

(1) Achilles fights like a lion.
   or
(2) Achilles is a lion in battle.

or any other arrangement of this metaphor, and also with big metaphors (a poem is an organism, the universe is a clock, etc.) the underlying formula is: X represents Y, Y represents Z. In distinction to connotation and allusion as defined earlier, the literal representation (X represents Y) is blocked. It is blocked either by presupposition (Achilles isn't really a lion) or by a code word ("like"), so that the first object becomes a mediating representation. Sometimes we don't see the block and use metaphors as if they were literally true, but the difference between metaphoric and literal intention, although not always patent, must not be ignored. Literalness is in large part a matter of intention, a refusal to deviate from the path stipulated between representamen and object, the assertion of a world in which that connection is real. When colleagues comment that all our language is metaphorical, I can only wonder (even if I dare not ask) whether they mean it literally.

17

PROCESSIVE SIGNS—
RITUAL, SYMBOL, AND ART

The axis of opacity and transparency doubles back on itself in the signs we consider here, for these may be so opaque as to seem beyond interpretation and at the same time so involving as not to call for any. Our everyday notion of signs is associated with another idea of more a restricted, perhaps marked, class: difficult or magical or weighty or mysterious indications: signs from heaven, lost lore, secret codes, and the like. Sometimes the word "symbolic" comes up where this emphasis is wanted. The concept of processive signs developed in this chapter responds to the intuitive sense of a category of signs with a special aura, signs that are absorbing, salient, and problematic. In relation to the phenomena that motivate it, the theory is very schematic, but to be of any use, a map has to be simpler than its territory. We could say that at any point, but here especially I hope my selection of certain landmarks will not be read as failure of appreciation for others.

As a neighboring though independent topic, we will consider signs that seem to be incomplete in having no object. To suggest that a sign might have no object broaches a paradox; yet once we embody the representamina of an elaborate sign in a physical medium, producing what doubtless appears a sign designate, this possibility ensues. The elaboration designates a sign. A nonsense poem is more like a poem than like anything else. Anything we put inside a picture frame will suggest a picture. Coming across something made of polished steel with some moving parts, you might well take it for a tool even without having any notion what it was used for. (Peirce would employ a term like "quasi-sign" or, alluding to the mathematical sense, a degenerate-sign.) We shall find in practice that the place of the object is still marked out, its seat warm, so to speak, and that it attracts occupants. The nonsense poem, by default, refers to poetry in general.

Chapter 10 distinguishes items in consciousness from processes in consciousness, cautioning that the boundary is fluid. Chapter 11 construes the sign as an association of three factors, taken there to be items. Here we explore the possibility, reserved then, that a sign factor might be instead a process. Recall that the distinction between items and processes is not simply between things and feelings. A feeling can be taken as an item. Whereas an item is determined by attention, even fleeting, a process involves an sustained engagement in environment, orientation, feeling, and/or disposition. In a processive sign that engagement is a sign factor: A *processive sign* is a sign in which the representamen, the object, or the interpretant is a process.

A processive sign imposes on us. It commands our involvement or it captures our attention by sensory enticement and/or by engaging us in problems of perception, comprehension, or interpretation.

Taking the representamen, object, and interpretant in turn as processes determines three categories of processive signs that suggest a rough fit with notions of "ritual," "symbol," and "art."

PROCESS AS REPRESENTAMEN—RITUAL

Ritual is characterized by the sign user's participation in an event either as an actor or as a witness who identifies with the action. Participation establishes a situation, an orientation, and a feeling, which is to say that it induces a process in consciousness proper to the ritual. This process serves to represent the occasion for the ritual or to represent some characteristic of the participants themselves. It is not simply the lighting of the candles, the sweet food after fasting, or the confession per se that represents me as a Jew, Moslem, or Christian but the fact that I *do* or *experience* it. There is a wide gap between what the lit candles mean and what the lighting of them or the witnessing of the lighting means. There is a wide gap between what the mass means and what going to it or saying it means.

The principle is as readily embodied in secular rituals, such as singing the national anthem before baseball games and taking an oath before testifying in court. For American fans, participating in the first is an experience that represents the game as a quasi-mythic, national event. The oath taking represents the witness as trustworthy. We believe that the oath will orient the modality of witnesses' testimony just insofar as we believe that the witnesses undergo a compelling experience. Either of these signs, the anthem or the oath, may be genuinely coercive—coercive of feeling in the first case, of behavior in the second. The power of the sign depends in part on the participants' actual beliefs—belief in the flag the one honors or belief in the Bible the other swears on. However, beyond the leverage afforded by belief, the rituals have a certain force even for the anarchists or atheists who submit to them or by instinct avoid them. This force resides in the representamina, which are not simply the song or the oath as autonomous entities but the fact of an experiential immersion in them. Participation itself is a part of the representamina in question. One is there, standing for the anthem, or one is there, hand on the Bible, swearing the oath. In ritual, there is no substitute for personal presence. Presence permits a process to be engaged, and that process represents whatever the ritual represents.

We are inclined to characterize certain works of art as ritualistic. Ritualistic art requires some slacking of pace so that, besides noting the work, we note as such the process of perceiving it. This mechanism is manifest in, for example, prolonged postures in the dancing of Martha Graham and the stark repetitiousness of the opening phrases of the *Symphony of Psalms* of Igor Stravinsky. Op art and pattern music are recent movements that capture the opportunity to ritualize perception.

PROCESS AS OBJECT—SYMBOLS

Popular usage of the word "symbol" is my guide here. A "symbol" is a sign that does not merely indicate or designate its object but also involves us in a feeling or disposition affiliated with its object. The flag, the tombstone, and the word "moon" taken fully as symbols represent not simply a nation, a grave, or a satellite but a set of feelings and attitudes we have learned to let these objects evoke, such as a sense of belonging and loyalty, of death and horror, and of romance or madness. The symbol specifies a whole field of experience as its object. In symbolist poetry, some item is fastened on— the rose, moonlight, blood—that entrains a dense penumbra of associations and dispositions. The symbol does not merely designate these, it engages them. The symbol actually provokes a sample of the experience it refers to.

PROCESS AS INTERPRETANT—WORKS OF ART

With works of art we do not merely know that x represents y as z; x induces us to sustain a perspective in which we see, hear, or understand y as z. When engaged with art, we are cast into its perspective. The perspective sustained is an interpretant-process.

To see this, we must distinguish three kinds of excitement that merge: heightened perception of the work as a structured sensuous material, our imagination of its object, and the viewpoint toward the object induced by the work.

For example, a novel offers the tone of its language, the titillations of its romance and suspense, and the excitement of emotions provoked by plot and scene. These are all excitements of perception that happen in step with progress through the book. Blending with this but not the same, the novel offers an imaginary view of its object, the lives and the social world it represents. These are given to us not neutrally but from a particular point of view that we also experience or even inhabit. This perspective— an aggregation of attitudes, sympathies, sensitivities, and dispositions—is the interpretant that connects the novel as a work of writing with what it represents. This process inhabits the reader's mind while the reader inhabits the book. The interpretant-process is attached to the narration as a whole, not to narrative time moment for moment.

The same three dimensions of experience are discernible in painting. The canvas is thrilling to see in its own right. We also view the scene the painting represents, its object. Linking picture and scene is an idea of what it would be like to see that scene without the mediation of the picture, that is, a sense—very much determined by style—of the situation, dispositions, and feelings we would experience were we able to "see it live." The painting sustains that imaginal experience as an interpretant-process.

This scheme is easiest to adapt when we can identify an object of representation, which is not always the case.

SUPPRESSION OF THE OBJECT

Pablo Picasso's *Mother and Child* of 1936 shows a woman seated on a beach with her young child held in her lap; the child is reaching upward. Originally Picasso painted a family group on a wider canvas. On the left, the father stood holding a fish in his outstretched hand just above the child's reach. The child was grasping for the fish. Then Picasso revised the painting by cutting the canvas, which eliminated most of the father's image, and painting over what remained of him and the fish. (The Chicago Art Institute, where the final version hangs, also exhibits the strip Picasso cut off and framed separately.) In the final version, where the child's action has no object, the import of the grasping gesture seems transformed. It addresses something ineffable.

Expressive art is often like this child's outstretched arm, particularly shaped as if to grasp some object but with its object out of view. Commenting on the programmatic titles for his *Five Orchestral Pieces,* Arnold Schoenberg said an advantage of music was that one could confess all without actually revealing anything. Clearly a sign from which the object is deleted is another sort of animal from the complete one; yet common sense begs us not to exaggerate the difference. It seems obvious despite their signal difference, that figurative and nonfigurative art are two species of one genus, that both may belong in the same museum and that operas with stories and sonatas with none should share honors in the same music history text.

As the example from Picasso suggests, the referential object of the artwork when absent is not simply nonexistent: It has been removed by a positive act of abstraction. This is not to say that the individual nonfigurative work must have once had an object that was erased but rather that the genre of the work links it with a prior representational form. Abstract painting was weaned from representational painting with the appreciation of the play of colors, forms, and textures initially used to reconstruct appearances. Instrumental music that is not subservient to dance or ritual derives historically from texted vocal music or from dance. (So far as I know this principle is applicable cross-culturally.) Ballet seems to derive from the redeployment of the gestures of combat to make sport and ritual homage to royalty, the latter eventually transformed by an ideal of transcendence. The eradication of reference with the elaboration of structure is not a development extraneous to semiosis but one of its constitutive principles.[1] Even the phonemes of speech would be gesturally referential if they had not been neutralized by their syntax. This is one lesson from "sound poetry" that liberates the gesture of the syllable, only to transcend it with new patterns.

The work that deletes its object, whether for transcendence, abstraction, or to comply with religious prohibition, retains its parentage with signs and its sign-character. It may still suggest *how* it would relate to an object if there were one. The work has a style, and the style itself is the index of a perspective, a point of view. Viewing the world under the influence of Jackson Pollack's canvases or under the influence of Mark Rothko's we adopt different sensibilities.

CONDITIONS THAT INDUCE THE PROCESSES OF THE PROCESSIVE SIGN

How is it that a sign comes to engage us in such a way that it provokes and sustains a continuous experience? Characteristically, the processive sign imposes on us by its enticements or by problematizing perception or interpretation.

In the case of ritual, engagement depends primarily on the controls of perception entailed by the conditions of presence at the sign situation. Rituals are compelling even when we are ignorant of them, as we may know from seeing "exotic" ritual on film or as guests. Ritual behaviors, although they are irrational and frequently tedious if we insist on a external viewpoint, compel a structured conscious experience when we participate or observe empathetically.

In the case of a symbol, engagement depends primarily on the base of knowledge with which the sign interacts. A symbol is, typically, a relatively simple, unified vehicle attached to a rich network of cultural lore. We are predisposed by training to allow the first to immerse us in the second.

In the case of art, the two preceding conditions play a role, but the distinctive engine of engagement lies in the opacity of the vehicle itself. Often an intensive elaboration and problematization of pattern and grammar directs attention to the vehicle rather than to what it might represent. The progression of thought is obstructed, made, as it were, to detour. The "detours" lead in two directions, both toward the reconstruction of structural coherence and toward immersion in sensation. Thus the capacity of artistic structure to draw attention to itself and to its material embodiment involves us in a process. Prague theory was mistaken to call this detour "self-reference," for in no sense is it a reference. It is a further consequence of the fundamental antithesis of structure and reference.

Russian Formalism studied this antithesis under the rubric of "defamiliarization," a wonderfully rich topic. I'd like to quote all their examples. (See, for example, Welleck and Shklovsky [1917].) The theme, developed mainly for verbal art, shows how changes of context or nuance at any level—semantic, syntactic, narrative—give familiar words, ideas, and images a renewed presence that fastens our attention.

As with the symbol, a further factor determining how liable we are to accept a process induced by art is social bias. One society will learn to look at driftwood as "found sculpture" while another sees only fuel for the fireplace.

Defamiliarization, structural elaboration, and social norms together still give an incomplete account of the condition of our entrancement. The continuous process also depends on a continuous material surface.

Whatever the foreground articulation may be in an artwork or a performance, a background of sensorial continuity is the normal prerequisite condition and the unmarked state for aesthetic engagement. It is this enticing, potentially hypnotic condition that permits our access to sensory qualities. The ability to create continuity is a central focus in the artist's craft and craft training: the steady tone of the musician, the relaxed flow of the drafter's hand, the implacable poise and balance of the dancer, the persuasive unrolling of sound and image in poetry. Behind the rich articulations of an oil painting we can sometimes sense the unity of the undercoat that it modulates like a tonality. The continuous flow of music is particularly palpable and penetrating, even in languagelike styles of music that do chop it up. Is this not the reason why the combination of music with poetry or cinema so deeply transforms their appearance, and why both song and cinema favor less sharply articulated styles as their accompaniment except when they need to depict special stress?

FURTHER EXAMPLES

Ritual

It is logical to extend the concept of ritual to places as well as times, but here we depart from everyday language. A monument does in space what a performance ritual does in time, so that we might speak of monuments as "spatial rituals."

The Washington Monument in Washington, D.C., is abstract: a simple, giant obelisk dominating a large but plain park. Its reference to the founding president of the United States is stipulated; no one could possibly know what it stands for without being told. Knowing the mythology,

George Washington as Cincinnatus, the hero who was willing to efface himself for the sake of higher principles, we can supply a motive for the manner of representation. Hence, an interpretant: George Washington (object) is represented *as* highly principled, absolutely straightforward, and faceless (interpretant). What is the representamen? The sign is invested in a towering granite obelisk, but its ground only emerges on our walking across the park toward it, preferably with the foreknowledge that it is famous. The structure engages a process focused on *encountering*. That process is the representamen. The significance of the monument melds with the (ritual) significance of *visiting* the monument.

Symbol

After the Flood, the Lord stipulated the rainbow as a sign of His a Covenant with the Israelites. The rainbow is not like a receipt stuck away in a shoe box till tax time. The delicacy and beauty and mystery of the representamen corresponds to the complexity of an object-process. The object is the covenant. At a distance, the object, the covenant might be merely an item of consciousness. Up close, one who is engaged by it and brings to its perception a real belief must surely entertain a process in consciousness wherein the Lord's protection and a sense of obligations to Him become a living background of thought. That whole field of knowledge, feeling, and disposition is the process that the rainbow, as symbol, takes as its object.

Some Songs We All Know

At the risk of injustice to the art, let us say for a first approximation that the object of a song, taken as a sign, may be what its title or words have as their object. Later we shall explore a more sophisticated view; this naive one will do for the moment. The Christmas carol "O Little Town of Bethlehem" has, then, that town as a possible object. "God Save the King" expresses loyalty to the monarch. "Happy Birthday" offers birthday wishes. As these are all songs of special occasions, they have a ritual dimension. As the objects we have indicated are all rich imaginal constructs, the songs have a symbolic dimension too. In addition, each song casts its object in a perspective that we are induced to entertain. In the carol we view Bethlehem with nostalgia and tenderness. In "God Save" we view the monarch as dignified, solemn, and beneficent. "Happy Birthday" is actually a waltz (or a waltz precursor, a *landler*), a nouveau riche genre that accompanied the bourgeois invasion of aristocratic sociality with a ferocity of physical impulse that transgressed previous requirements of formal dance for sublimation of the body. The song retains a subtext of carnival that out-of-tune singing does not erase. Since it is so rarely sung well, we are better off as participants than audience, but the idea, if it works, is to engage us in its perspective, a celebratory feeling, as the interpretant.[2]

PART V

Topics in Comparative Semiotics

We gradually shift our course here, attending less to what signs share and more to how they differ. The topics are merely examples, arbitrary ones from the standpoint of theory. I emphasize the arts with the conviction that they are the true laboratories of the great human project of sign making. The verbal arts have provided a field of analysis within semiotics so weighty and specialized that I wished to put my baggage at the other end of the boat. After chapter 18 regards the supportive relation between formalization and play via quick glances at several semiotic media, the discussion settles on music and visual art. This is an ancient and loaded pairing, which had much to do with the development of the concept of "absolute music," the chief locus of controversy in nineteenth- and twentieth-century musical aesthetics. I make no excursion into the history of this problem nor any effort to relate my results to the ancient quarrel. (See Dahlhaus 1978.) Nevertheless, I hope the analyses offered will suggest how inadequate and uninformative a simple polarity of "musical" and "plastic" appears when we can acknowledge hierarchy of content, perspective, and suggestions of designation and modality in both.

As our focus turns more and more intently to the representamen and object, with what may seem just a pedantic obligation of rather stiff and formal courtesy calls on the interpretant, the reader may be tempted to revisit the question whether a theory of signs is needed propose the analyses offered here. If so, note that our discussion of the representamen now turns on two questions inherited from our theory of the sign: How is the signifying structure equipped to entrain, designate, or generalize various objects? How does it constrain and elaborate their interpretation?

18

ARTFUL AND ARTIFICIAL LANGUAGES

Musica est exercitium arithmeticae occultam necientis se numerare animi. (Music is a veiled exercise in arithmetic by the soul unaware of its counting.)

—Gottfried Wilhelm Leibnitz in a letter to Goldbach, 1712.

My hope in adjoining art and formal language is to improve our understanding of two notions I cannot define satisfactorily, "concept" and "play." As we heighten artifice, we may heighten engagement. The "languages" of art seem the most free, most expressive, and most spontaneous. It will serve our studies to place them in contrast with the most strictly regulated.

The terms "natural language" and "artificial language" generally are regarded as self-explanatory, but like many divisions of nature from culture, they form a problematic opposition. A straightforward interpretation might be this: The rules of a "natural language" are intuitive or instinctive and unconscious. An artificial language is one formed and controlled by deliberated, explicit, conscious rules.

Certainly some languages meet this criterion for artificiality, but it is not clear that any entirely satisfy the criterion for naturalness. In many cultures, children's speech is "corrected" by their elders as consciously and as early as any of their instruction in good manners. In North America, we relegated the task to *Sesame Street,* but it still went on. When, as an adolescent, I informed my father that it was no longer "cool" to say "groovy," he and I had clearly accepted the propriety of giving nature a hand with our natural language. We have no reason to believe, so far as I know, that any language in the world is immune from the influence of conscious stylization—artifice. Most people appear to disregard their language most of the time. We must not, on that account underestimate the effect of the few craftsmen who make the models others unknowingly imitate: Shakespeare's English, the king's English, or the American of television shows *L. A. Law* or *Miami Vice*. None of those is a particularly natural language.

It is possible for a purely artificial language to be meaningless—to have no semantic dimension—in the limited sense that it generates propositions that do not predicate anything about anything; however, the most prominent artificial languages do represent something in that they are constructed as models of thought. Chomsky's mathematical models of language are in themselves artificial languages that play a like role.

Similarly, games straddle the division, and their rules, spontaneously invented, are free from the obligation of reference yet capable of interpretation. Seen from the inside, a game constructs a closed vocabulary of activities. Syntactic implication entirely supplants semantic interpretation except that the final state of the game may represent a win or a loss or a success or a failure.

Seen from the outside, games are more referential. The ancient Greek Olympics inherited and transformed the emotional legacy of intercity warfare. But games survive the loss of original meanings. The derivations of chess from military strategy and of ballet from fencing leave only the merest aura. A substitution is not a representation. Games displace real fighting, and game is a real contest, not (in the first instance) a sign of one.

Once we demarcate the playing field and articulate the moves, we have an artificial language, a game.

NOTATIONS

Nelson Goodman constructs *notational systems* formally as a class of maximally articulate artificial languages with explicit rules. The following summary translation of his central conception into the terminology of the previous chapters, including "type" and "token," is rude and crude, for the point of Goodman's formulation is to avoid just these terms, which he finds unclear in Peirce and to construct better tools. But a brief discussion does not provide me the option of a critical review, and other problems would ensue if I retained Goodman's own language, which preserves a conventional but misguided usage of "semantic" and "syntactic."[1]

The chief principles are these:

A. Concerning notational representamina:
A notational vocabulary is a finite vocabulary of types
Each type can be invested in tokens
Given any one token, there must be no ambiguity which type it corre-
sponds to, even if extracted from its context. For example, this require-
ment is met by printed letters (tokens) with respect to their alphabet
(26 types); however, handwritten letters cannot be guaranteed to qual-
ify. It may be unclear whether my handwritten mark is an "a" or a "d."
B. Concerning notational objects
The objects notated must constitute nonoverlapping classes; given any
object, there must be no ambiguity concerning which class it belongs to
C. Concerning notational representation
Each type must represent a class of objects
It follows from (4) and (5): Given any object, there must be no ambiguity which character can represent it. "No ambiguity" means, for
Goodman, that a finite calculation settles the question. To continue the
same example, the normal English alphabet represents sounds, but the
classes of sounds represented do overlap, disqualifying the alphabet as a
notation for sound. The *o* in "got" and the *a* in "father" are not clearly
distinct. The phonetic alphabet, which is designed to avoid such ambiguity, is intended as a notation in Goodman's sense.

Goodman's definition constructs an ideal. There are not many pure
cases.

I believe digits taken as a notation for integers fit the bill.[2] Integers can
be notated; they form distinct and nonoverlapping one-member classes.
The digits are also distinct, and they are of finite types. Given an expression
in digits in a particular system, there is no ambiguity about which integer
it represents. Decimal 17, binary 10001, and Hex 11 are either representations of the *same* number by different forms in different digital notation
systems (a "realist" view) or they represent each other (a "nominalist" view).

Goodman's paradigm case is musical notation. Musical notation is explicit regarding pitches and rhythms. When a note on paper is properly
drawn, there is no ambiguity concerning which pitch it represents. Assuming the instrument that plays the note is roughly in tune, there is no
ambiguity as to whether the note played is a note represented by the note
on paper.

Only the pitches and durational relations of music allow strict notation, for these, subsumed by systems of representatives, have a fully articulated vocabulary. Loudness does not. There are written terms for loudness (*pp, p, f, ff*). Those terms meet the criteria for notational representamina—we can tell them apart—but they do not meet the criteria for notational representation—their objects are not distinctly articulated. (Musical *notation* is as true an example of artificial language as FORTRAN, Basic, or CPlus. Music, per se, is mixed.)

Goodman asks why music can be notated but not painting. His answer concerns articulation. Paintings normally do not resolve into combinations of distinct objects from a finite vocabulary, like the notes of music or the syllables of speech. On the other hand, he takes dance notation to be equivalent to musical notation in its semiotic structure (and potentially as influential). Dances, like music and unlike painting, typically are composed of combinations of a discrete, finite vocabulary. His argument that dance and music have this characteristic hinges on his analysis of performance as the instance of a particular composition. He can walk into the hall where a performance is in progress and say, "That is Beethoven's Fifth" or "That is Giselle." Ballets and musical compositions are "allographic" works, works that retain their identities despite differences of realization. Paintings are "autographic." Ultimately, the reproduction takes second place to the original. With musical compositions and dances, every performance, good or bad, stands in relation to the conceptual construction on its own; there is not one "original."

(Goodman's comparison of dance and musical notations neglects to consider that musical notation has reference to a system of representatives that had already been impressed on singing by the influence of instruments. Some dance styles have vocabularies that also establish a system of representatives for movement, but the most widely practiced dance notation, that of Laban, is not directly keyed to any such system. It is vectorial and keyed to a Cartesian, continuous space, not a stylistic vocabulary. I think, therefore, that labanotation does not meet Goodman's requirements for a notational system and is unlikely ever to have as much influence on dance as musical notation has had on music.)

MODELS

The notation of a text is a model of the text, but not all models are notations.

A sign is a *model* if: (1) the representamen is constructed entirely from a vocabulary of known elements and known relations; (2) we understand the resemblance of the representamen to the object to be such that we can learn about the object by studying the representamen alone; and (3) the actual connection between the representamen and object is immaterial to its semiotic function (i.e., it is not indexical).

A musical notation is a notational model for a performance. A blueprint is a notational model for a house. The conductor's beat is a nonnotational model for a symphonic performance.

A photograph is not a model, first, because we do not know all its elements. For example, in a black-and-white photograph, the various grays and, for that matter, the various shapes cannot be assumed to be known. The second criterion is satisfied: We can learn about the photographed object from the photograph. The third, however, is not: Our reliance on the photograph results from its physical derivation; the actual connection between model and object is not immaterial.

The mathematical equation for an ellipse is truly a model (whether correct or not) for an orbit. In general, we speak of theories as models for their objects.

DIAGRAMS

Diagrams aspire to the status of models. The term "mental diagram" (which we invoked to account for the sense texts make) is a metaphor for a neural data structure of which we don't know the physics. Here I speak in the common, literal manner of invested diagrams.

We professors who, in the midst of complex explanations, wheel around to the chalkboard, circle some words, connect circles with lines or arrows, are living in the dynamics of interaction between natural and artificial language, making a diagram to represent ideas that have not been clearly worked out, hoping that straight lines and right angles will substitute for the clarity *felt* in the relations but not yet actually fingered. The diagrams in Goran Sonneson's book are a good case in point because the book, called *Pictorial Concepts* (1989), features some wonderfully complicated diagrams of schemes of ideas. The schemes make a certain sense, but so far as I can tell, the diagrams do not; their pictorial terms are undefined.

What diagrams do offer is an opportunity to regard all the parts of a system *simultaneously,* which is one key to their psychological power.

Simultaneity is a perceptual construct of consciousness. We know that the brain (like a computer) has to take in its data from the world in relatively small bits and that it builds up a picture of "now" that encompasses a lot more of that data than are simultaneous. The visual sense is privileged in this regard. Hearing has less capacity to detach itself from the flow of time. We see motion in a steady world, but we hear "events" against the flowing seas of time. Diagrams hold steady for consciousness a complex of relations that otherwise would seem to flow by in elusive thought, exceeding the grasp of comprehension. The clarity provided by diagrams is more a sensorial than a logical property.

As a class of sign vehicles, diagrams are very heterogeneous, but they suggest a few frequent traits: Visual diagrams are usually in two dimensions and two colors. They favor straight lines, distinct borders, right angles, and circles or parts of circles. A roughly drawn diagram generally is intended to be seen as a sketch that *could* be rendered with compass and straight edge. In the absence of universal conventions, it is impossible to state universally what constitutes the grounds of visual diagrams, but there are some recurrent quasi-conventions. Typically, line segments in diagrams represent relations between the objects represented at their end points, relations such as inclusion, dominance, cause, or choice. Such visual elements as dividing lines, horizontal or vertical alignment, and proximity or separation tend to represent such nonvisual relations as co-occurrence, temporal order, and category affiliation.

Diagrams have a tone of formality; they *recall* the elements of plane geometry so that they tend as a class to *connote* the articulatory power of artificial languages. Some technical diagrams, such as the formal graphs to be discussed, diagrams of transformational groups in linear algebra, and computer programming flow charts really earn their pay in this regard. But frequently we use diagrams to make our ideas look better than they are. Diagrams readily suggest relations that we cannot explicate. Representing ideas by diagrams gives us feeling of control over them and suggests that we can *play* with them. Even if the feeling is largely illusory, the effect is significant. It shows how a finite combinatorial system (e.g., a system with lines and dots as its vocabulary) creates its own universe, how ready we are to enter it, and how formal systems lead to free play.

FORMAL GRAPHS:
DIAGRAMS AS NOTATIONAL SYSTEMS

While diagrams in general are vague, mathematics constructs some special types that are formally explicit. Formal graphs can be used as notations.[3]

A formal graph, as a mathematical object, is most economically defined as (1) a list of "points" with (2) a list (drawing on the first) of pairs of points. The pairs of points may be visually represented by lines joining labeled end points. If the pairs are ordered, the lines are directed (like arrows). Commonly such points are called vertices, nodes, or dots, and the lines are called arcs, branches, or lines. Every line connects two dots; two or more lines can be connected at one dot.

As a notational system, graph theory permits us to pin down the distinctions among types of hierarchies that were mentioned in passing in chapters 7, 13, and 15. A succession of lines, each connected to the next, forms a path between the extreme vertices of the succession. If a graph has one and only one path between any two dots, the graph is a *tree graph*. In figure 18.1, if there is more than one path, the graph is a type of *net graph*. Graph A is a tree graph. Graphs B and C are potentially synonymous net graphs. Tree graphs can well represent a componential hierarchy over a disjunct series such as hierarchies ascribed to sentences, but not all the componential hierarchies commonly ascribed to music or—as we shall see presently—to narratives or computer programs. The grammatical diagram of boundaries and regions of the tune in chapter 15 (figure 15.3) required a net graph. (It doesn't make a practical difference if the structure analyzed has uniform connections throughout; it's the interruptions at various hierarchical levels that call for a different graphing.) If we take graphs as models of mental diagrams, then different sorts of comprehension of sense are suggested for melodies and sentences in adapting these different models.

COMPUTER LANGUAGES AND NARRATIVES

Flow charts, melodies, and narratives exhibit boundary and region hierarchies.

Vladimir Propp (1928/1968) proposed a narrative grammar for Russian folk tales built from a limited group of character types (hero, villain, etc.) and a limited group of actions (interdiction, violation,

Figure 18.1   Tree graph (A). Equivalent net graphs (B and C).

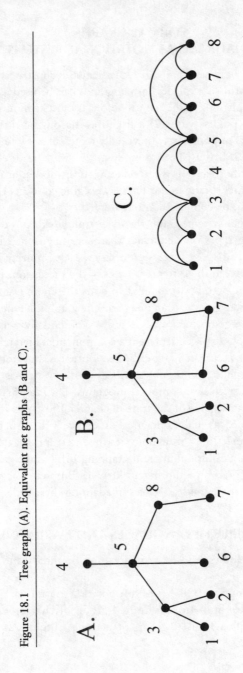

trickery, donation, etc.). His demonstrations in combination with the traditional view of plot, which descends from Aristotle, that the story can be boiled down to a single dominant action, have interacted to engender some very sophisticated and sometimes highly hierarchical models or narrative. In his invaluable handbook, *The Semiotics of Cinema* (1976), Jurij Lotman says that the structure of narrative is parallel to the structure of the sentence. This is why, he reasons, an action always can be paraphrased by a sentence. Another theory of narrative grammar in this vein by Roland Barthes is a good practical tool for analysis. The most abstract and elaborate theory is that of Algirdas Julian Greimas (1987).

These theories all share an error in identifying narrative structure with sentence structure. The distinction missed is exactly the one mentioned for melodies and sentences. In a story, as in a chess game or a computer program, each action takes us from one situation to another situation, and each situation except the first and last connects two actions, the one leading to it and the one that departs from it. Situations and actions or states and transitions make a continuous chain. The structure has no parallel in language grammar for it creates a boundary and region articulation, where situations are like regions and actions like their boundaries (or vice versa!).

Figure 18.2 is a net graph, the more natural diagram for a hierarchy of this type, which portrays a fragment of the outline of *Lady of the Camellias* with actions bounded by situations. (This is the plot of the novel by Alexandre Dumas fils or Giuseppi Verdi's *La Traviata* or the film with Greta Garbo.)

In this hierarchy, the middle lower constituent must not be associated exclusively with either of the two higher constituents. We might call the hierarchy, which computer flow charts and melodies share, a *net hierarchy* as opposed to a *tree hierarchy.*

Figure 18.2   Net graph of plot

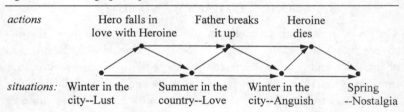

actions	Hero falls in love with Heroine	Father breaks it up	Heroine dies	
situations:	Winter in the city--Lust	Summer in the country--Love	Winter in the city--Anguish	Spring --Nostalgia

The consequence of having region and boundary structure for the art of narrative is that the narrative artist may emphasize action and downplay situations or the reverse, or the artist may strike any balance or variation of these options. In the theories mentioned, the tendency seems always to be to regard descriptions and depictions of situations or characters as embellishments to action. (Lotman comes near to avoiding this.) I think it may be true that elementary storytelling, such as storytelling for children, tends to eliminate the static moments in favor of action, but to suppose that action is therefore more "basic" than situation mistakes a psychological tactic for a logical principal.

Computer languages have two domains of application. On one hand, they represent to computer experts the actions that a computer may take. In this sense they are a true semiotic systems.

The other thing that computer languages do is activate computers. In this function they are the cause of an effect and are not semiosic; they are like DNA or keys in a lock. They are the input replaced by the output with no interpretant arising.

Computer languages are human languages, artificial or not. People think in them. Furthermore, the need to think effectively in and about programming languages has given rise to computer metalanguages. Programming flow charts constitute a diagrammatic metalanguage over programming languages. The flow chart shows alternating "states" and "transitions," which, like note and interval in melody, situation and action in stories, supports a dual hierarchy. These are, in Goodman's sense, notations. Like a musical score, a flow chart indicates a plan, in this case for a program, not a musical performance. Whereas the various realizations conforming to a given musical score differ with respect to nuances and quantitative relations that are not themselves capable of formal notation, the alternative programs satisfying a given flow chart differ logically even though equivalent in function.

CONCEPTS, GAMES, AND PLAY

The problem of inference considers whether there is any logic to the discovery of logical relations. Charles Peirce was fascinated with the problem of inference and gave it a characteristic twist by dividing inference into three types determined by his categories. In deduction we apply a rule to specific cases and reach a *certain* conclusion. With induction we compare specific cases of some type of circumstance to reach a *probable* conclusion about the governing rule. With abduction we consider a specific case in relation to some circumstance and arrive at a *plausible* rule. Terrence Prewitt provided the following example from cryptography to an e-mail discussion group[4]: If he receives a signal and knows the code, he can deduce the message with *certainty*. If he receives a signal and doesn't know the code, he attempts inductive methods. For example if substituting "e" for "q" works in several words, he induces a probable rule. If he is not getting anywhere, he may abduce a plausible hypothesis: "If this is French, maybe I can make sense of it in such and such a manner . . ."

Where do hypotheses come from?

The only conditions Peirce discovered for the tenuous interpretants that constitute abductions were negative. Abduction is plausible if we don't have a good reason to doubt it. He associated abduction with "musement," the free play of thought, a motif he took from Freidrich von Schiller's *Letters on Aesthetic Education*. I believe neither Peirce nor Schiller took note of the power of delimitation and articulation to promote musement. Hypothesis is facilitated by a limited set of clearly differentiated possibilities. Artificial languages are like games; they support play by establishing limitations.

The discipline of the signifier by limitation of means is the unifying theme in this overview of artifice, models, graphs, and notations. These limitations contribute to what I will call *conceptlike* representamina. We may find hypotheses by playing with conceptlike representamina. Representamina are *conceptlike* to the extent that they attribute text structure to their objects—that is, to the extent that they represent their objects as articulated by categories or sets of parts, aspects, and relations. Notations and sentences and formal graphs and, even with their failings, invested diagrams are conceptlike. To the extent that they resist articulating their objects, representamina are *holistic*. Paintings and performances, to the extent that they incorporate unarticulated inflection, are more holistic than formal graphs and notations, but they include conceptlike aspects. The intent of this opposition is to orient a continuous axis of complex mixtures of conceptlike and holistic elements, not to divide signs into two sharp classes. For example, a rag doll is conceptlike in representing the human body as an object defined by a few very articulate, categorical features (eyes, limbs, etc.) but holistic in its unified, "jolly" character. (See Langer's [1942] felicitous opposition of concepts and conceptions.)

Conceptlike representamina facilitate play. Hans George Godamer, in *Truth and Method* (1975), takes pains to emphasize that play is not a subjective condition so much as the property of a situation. Play is movement without strain, "The to-and-fro movement which is not tied to any goal that would bring it to an end" (p. 93). Muscular strain is not at issue here but rather the freedom from consequences that is gained by immersion in a closed and insulated world. This is what it means to make a game of something.

The principles these definitions evoke need not be manifest as pure or absolute. Art is not bound as math and science are to live strictly by the rules of its own artifices. Changing them becomes part of the game. Frédéric Chopin wrote big and little notes in his manuscript, assuming we would guess what he meant even though there was no precedent for such a differentiation in the formal notational system of music.

Artificial languages are playful inventions. Many people are put off by algebra or computers, perhaps from a bad first exposure. Still, anyone who takes a good look at artificial languages will see that these are domains of play and typically attract playful practitioners. You cannot play with the whole universe at once. To play requires focusing, and a closed, artificial world assists that focus.

Focusing and closure both in programming languages and in the languages of art demonstrate the reciprocity of play and formality. The more a system is restricted, the more it invites invention and even caprice. The artist Michael Snow spent five years making compositions from his one cardboard cut-out of a walking woman, and they are exuberantly different from each other. The most outrageously unnatural or confined materials lead to deeply human expression, a principle common to classical ballet and abstract algebras.

19

SIGNS IN THE VISUAL ARTS

Looking at a work of visual art is not like looking at most other things. The artwork evokes semiotic consciousness. We see something that has a double appearance, for example, a thing that looks like marble and that also looks like the head of Julius Caesar. Because it is double, the appearance of the work is available as a sign; it is not merely an unconsciously computed object. The appearance of the material is the *visual vehicle;* the appearance it represents (its object) is the *scene.* (Langer calls it a "virtual" scene and extends this notion in parallel applications to all media.)

Following Sonneson (1989) I will call what we see generally the *lifeworld.* The visual vehicle is seen as part of the lifeworld while the scene is a world unto itself. The semiotic problems of the various visual arts are not identical; in what follows I focus primarily on pictures.

Pictures, as representamina, have structures apart from the structure of what they represent. Typically a picture seems complex but coherent. We may therefore regard the picture as a text. However, at present, we seem to have a much more fragmentary knowledge of what the structures of pictures are than we do of the structures of poems and melodies. Chapter 13 drew attention to the variability of pictorial articulation, a topic that is dwelt on further in this chapter. To my knowledge, no theory of pictorial structure adequately takes into account these essential fundamentals. The concepts of grammar and pattern have application in the visual arts, but they don't always cover much ground. When it is not clear that the vehicle is complex in the most literal sense of having distinct parts (as, for example, sometimes in the works of Constantin Brancusi or Mark Rothko), it is still evident that the vehicle remains complex in the sense that it depends on a combination of *aspects* (size, shape, color, texture, etc.). The general structural problem of treating the relations among perceptual aspects is still a terra incognito.

The components of a pictorial text may include both signs and elements that, taken alone, are nonrepresentational of any apparent object, what Meyer Shapiro (1994) in a justly renowned essay calls the "nonmimetic" elements. In Van Gogh's self-portrait showing his head against a reddish background, the head-figure vehicle represents a lifeworld head, but taken in isolation, the red background does not represent a lifeworld background. It does not show a wall, for example. What it does represent (in context) refers more to an arena of feeling than to lifeworld appearances. Here the scene is, in part, visually vague, like the scene of a story we hear.

THE ARTICULATION SCHEMATA OF PICTURES

In comparison with language, dance, and music, it is striking how much more varied the articulation structures of pictures are. In part this reflects ranges of comparison. When we speak globally of the visual arts, we are likely to summon to mind images that range across the span of history from prehistoric times and images from several continents. When we speak globally of music, many of us will limit ourselves to recent Western culture and perhaps just to a narrow area within that. The wider our horizons on dance or music, the more heterogeneous their articulation appears, but the visual arts still seem special in this regard.

There is no universal articulatory framework for visual art. A mosaic allows an analysis similar to language. A first articulation divides the work into figures (like morphemes). The second articulation is the tessellation with "meaningless" stones or tiles (standing in for meaningless phonemes). It may be that just half a dozen or fewer types of tiles account for the whole work. There is still a difference to consider: In language the first articulation also yields a limited vocabulary, the vocabulary of words. In principle, there might need to be no limitation on the vocabulary of representational figures used in mosaic; any real or imaginary lifeworld object could be represented by an original visual figure. In practice, traditions tend to limit the range of figures and their modes of combination. The analogy between the articulatory structures of mosaic pictures and language is not perfect but holds in some depth.

Something very much like double articulation thus appears possible in pictures, but it is not, as with language, a universal scheme. Every variation occurs. In some styles of Chinese watercolor painting the brushstrokes (sortable by type, color, and direction) form one combinatorial vocabulary, and the represented objects, also formulaic, form another. Much of Vincent Van Gogh's painting approximates a comparable economy of the signifier with a limited vocabulary of brushstroke types and colors, but the vocabulary of represented objects does not suggest closure, for his motifs are not limited to stereotypes. He made a painting of his bedroom and another of his shoes. In John Constable, the signified scene is highly articulated, but the signifier has no readily available, independent articulation; the essence of his "realist" technique is to obscure its syntax. Brushstrokes and color boundaries are hidden, assisting the familiar illusion that looking at his canvases is like seeing the lifeworld.[1] In contrast, in Piet Mondrian or Jackson Pollack, there is no semantic articulation whatsoever (i.e., no depiction). The syntactic articulation stands alone. This is not to say that there is no semantic field due to inflection, but inflection alone is minimally articulate. In Mark Rothko, articulation is suspended. Indeed, the most prominent characteristic of articulation in visual signs is its variability.

DEPICTION

Although some of the key terms are my own, in this section (and elsewhere in this chapter) I have drawn extensively on an impromptu paper John Kennedy presented to the Toronto Semiotic Circle in December 1991, reporting on his then forthcoming book (1993). Anything that does not make sense is my own contribution.

Depiction is the most characteristic relation of reference for visual art although it is neither a necessary nor the exclusive one. In visual *depiction* the appearance of the representamen is partially identified with the appearance of the object. Visual depiction does not belong exclusively to art. Depiction may be purely practical (e.g., in an instruction booklet), need not be inflected, and may be part of a text that is not, as a whole, visually coherent. Furthermore, some visual works of art do not depict anything.

Depiction has recourse to knowledge (as do lifeworld appearances). A picture may depict things that we could never inspect in the lifeworld, such as imaginary beasts or, as a traditional genres of some cultures do, the interior organs of a living animal. The relation between the appearance of the vehicle and the appearance of object need not be a simple isomorphism. A depiction of a face might present a precise edge between a cheek and a nose; the line between nose and cheek, even if it cannot be precisely seen, is still a factor in lifeworld visual perception because knowledge attributes a boundary to the objects.

Seeing depicted objects is a kind of reading, a kind of interpreting that interprets depictions. To see the lifeworld is also a kind of interpretation. Both proceed primarily, but not entirely, by unconscious computation, deploying a *grammar of vision,* which interprets the lifeworld, and a *grammar of depiction,* which interprets pictorial representations.

A grammar of depiction is a specialized subgrammar of the grammar of vision, but it is clearly not the same thing. To grasp this, it is sufficient to consider how we interpret line segments. Line segments are utilized to depict relations in images that do not necessarily show up as lines in the lifeworld. As Kennedy (1993) points out, lines in pictures can represent edges of volumes, edges of color patches, or edges of projections (An example of the latter is a circle or an ellipse drawn to represent a ball.) In a stick drawing, lines depict solid volumes. Lines also may be used as "terms" to show motion or texture. I write terms in quotes because Kennedy has demonstrated that these signs are *not* simply conventional. Congenitally blind persons who draw and who "read" pictures made with raised lines employ some of these same signs that sighted persons use.

The grammar of vision allows us to make sense of the appearance of the lifeworld. This grammar identifies a tree as a tree on the basis of its appearance, and it identifies a picture as a picture. A grammar of depiction adapts or replaces the rules of normal vision to provide an understanding of pictures as signs.

Not all objects referred to by pictures are depicted objects. Two other types are stipulated objects and inflectional objects.

Any object or relation that is depicted by a picture can itself be the representamen of another object, as when a depicted halo or gallows or balance represents sanctity or death or justice. In general, such successive representations depend on conventions. By the vocabulary of part III, the depicted objects that convey these stipulated objects are visual terms. With stipulated objects we entrain also the possibility of connotations, allusions, and metaphors.

Although we each have, fundamentally, one grammar of vision for the lifeworld, we can switch among the various grammars of depiction exploited by different styles of depiction.

VISUAL INFLECTION

Inflection was considered in chapter 14 primarily in relation to gesture. The word has the same sense here. The inflections of a picture include a broad range of phenomena, from optical illusions, to synesthetic values, to distortions in depiction. It may seem deceptive to group these heterogeneous effects under one heading, but they are all holistic elements and not easily separated from each other.

Optical illusions singled out as isolated tricks, such as those drawings in textbooks where one of two equal line segments is made to look longer than the other, are special cases. The same dynamics arise in the energy of line and "movement" of color in pictures. In optical illusions the grammar of vision seems to play a trick on itself or encounter contradictions among its own rules. These illusions blend imperceptibly with expressive devices in the arrangement of the visual vehicle and also with expressive distortions, represented as characteristic of the figure (stylization) or as inhering in the depicted object (such as haptic distortion). When the depicted object is a person, distortion may represent invisible tensions and feelings of the person as a subject. Lacking any designative index, inflections surrounding a representational figure (in the background or drapery) also may convey feelings we attribute to the figure.

Among the synesthetic values of pictures are color warmth and color distance. Although artists speak with conviction about the affective attributes of individual colors, it seems pretty clear that these are not projected intersubjectively without a structural context. Red in the lifeworld does not have the same impact as red in a picture, and the impact of red in a picture depends on everything else in that picture. Although I have not the foggiest notion what makes these effects work, the simple fact that they depend on text structure seems self-evident.

In general, the inflections of pictures are representamina of nonvisual objects—such as feelings—which we may call, collectively, the *inflectional objects* of the picture. So-called nonrepresentational art, which, following our present terminology, would be better called nondepictive, focuses our attention on inflectional objects. In some contemporary work the canvas is given over to inflections.

Visual inflection, as best I can understand it, involves a sense of motion. It is very difficult to know how static images code motion. We will be able to advance another step or two when we take up the same problem in music.

The process of reading inflections is quite different from the process of reading depictions. I speculate that normal lifeworld seeing, on which depiction is based, requires a continuous effort to suppress inflectional information because it is related to the paradoxes and illusions. Attention to inflectional objects requires and induces some entrancement wherein we "willingly suspend" those defenses.

MODALITY AND DESIGNATION IN PICTURES

When the media parade in dress review, it is appropriate to note, as in chapter 14, that a depiction fails to designate its subject as specific or general or to assign it to reality or imagination. In everyday situations, the media are rarely pure. Language comes with pointing and with the situation of enunciation; tunes, often with words. Pictures are situated by commissions and titles. These catalysts are decisive. It is not that other media are subordinate to language (or language to pointing). How we know that John James Audubon's pictures of birds are meant to represent species, not individuals, has to do with how they were published. Yet it also has something to do with how he painted them. The idea of a species is a scientific idea, and the ideal of objective type controls his style, which avoids vagueness, distractions, and ambiguity.

Designation and modality in pictures are inextricably entwined with knowledge in language. "The relation between what we see and what we know is never settled" (Berger 1972, p. 7). Whether we ascribe a unicorn in a painting to the world of facts or the world of fancies depends on whether we believe unicorns are entirely imaginary or simply difficult to find. Yet the painting itself may *suggest* an ascription by a fantastic background or by impossible play of light.

Foreground and background, where they are provided, are sometimes like subject and predicate in a sentence. John Berger contrasts two self-portraits by Rembrandt (pp. 110–112). The earlier, by its background, assigns the subject to the world of socioeconomic relations. The later, where, as in many of his late portraits, everything seems to become a background to the eyes that gaze patiently at us, assigns the subject to the world of inner experience. These assignments are not articulated so categorically as those of language, but they are not altogether different in their consequences from what verbs like "is" and "seems" accomplish. Purely pictorial elements that offer their candidacy for indications of modality are clarity of articulation and vividness of contrast. The earlier of the two Rembrandt portraits has a sharply articulated background and offers more heightened contrast. We may read this clarity and contrast as an assignment to the publicly consensual world; nevertheless Salvador Dalí did not obscure his thought in transporting the same clarity to representations of personal fantasy.

A pictorial factor that links modality (strictly construed as the assignment of an object to a world) and the global interpretant of the whole (strictly construed as a process in consciousness) is the picture's angle of vision, perspective in the conventional sense, which may or may not be unitary. The implied angle of vision establishes communicative functions. We ascribe the supervening angle of vision to the painter as an imaginary "addresser," but we are inscribed in the same angle of vision as perceivers or addressees. Film theory studies this structure in terms of the camera's "gaze."

Andrew Wyeth's well-known painting *Christina's World* is a painting of his imaginary world, not hers, and it includes her as its possession, simply by virtue of her relation to his gaze, the pictorial perspective. In this gaze, the endless, even attention to the grass is compulsive and hypnotic. The depicted object, grass, might be said to be represented realistically, but the process it evokes, a process of seeing, is obsessive; it does not focus or abbreviate. (See Dennett [1991], chap.11.) The gaze that seems disturbing because of its grip on the grass remains suspect, therefore, in its relation to the human figure.

THE PICTURE AS A TEXT AND AS A WHOLE

The picture as *text* has a more or less unitary overall object (the scene) and, for *any one reading,* a more or less unitary significance, its interpretant as a whole.

Even with respect to depiction alone, the difference of part and whole is obvious if we consider a figurative picture that doesn't have a depicted object of the whole or one that, as a whole, depicts an event. Typically, in a picture that shows an event, the individual component figures do not depict events. They are, in that respect, like words in a sentence. In the Van Gogh self-portrait mentioned earlier that shows a head against an inflected but nondepictive background, the painting as a whole does not depict anything more than its principal figure does, but it certainly signifies more.

The distinction between the whole and its parts extends even to works that might seem to have only one part. Michelangelo's David, like a one-morpheme sentence (e.g., "Stop!"), has a depicted object (the person) and also represents a situation. The complication is medieval but obligatory. The sculptural text conveys is a particular view of David at one moment. The illusion on which the work absolutely depends, however, is that we could have seen David at another moment and in a different attitude from the moment and attitude depicted. Beyond the figure, there is the scene that extends it in time. Who has seen Michelangelo's sculpture and not imagined David's next move? The illusion is precisely that the scene and depicted object are not mutually implicational.

A picture as a whole encompasses the arrangement of all of its inflections as a unity. The extant theory of visual art is successful in delineating domains of judgment about the balance of pictures but not in articulating fundamental general principles that explain what such balance is. This is where a new structural initiative is needed. The best we can say for now would seem to be that the structural issue here is not either the rule system of grammar nor the abduction of sets in pattern but has something to do with reciprocities: weight and counterweight, tension and countertension. It does not seem to be a kind of structure rooted in categories so much as in magnitudes.

It is generally characteristic of artistic texts that conceptlike elements are coordinated and fused with holistic elements so that we seem to be given, on one hand, a conception of a feeling and, on the other, the feeling of a concept. For pictures, the fusion often is due to the interaction of inflection and depiction: Van Gogh's inflection of the color and movement of his hair and the serenity of the global geometry of Leonardo's *Last Supper* determine how we view what is depicted.

VISUAL ART IN INDUSTRIAL
DESIGN AND ARCHITECTURE

The semiotics of pictures provides entrée to the semiotics of architecture, fashion, and domestic and industrial design.

The prerequisite is to appreciate firmly the distance between the lifeworld grammar of vision and the interpretation of pictures. We must appreciate how even the most "realistic" paintings are unrealistic. For example, one fiction of realist painting is the comprehensive view. A realist painting shows a scene as it would look *if* we could take it in at a glance, which we can't ever really do. Although we are unconscious of our own eye movements, we are not unconscious of the quality of image that results and its difference from pictures. The "big picture" we walk around in has very fuzzy edges. The "realist" painting collapses immediate perception with memory and inference.

In the lifeworld, not everything has a salient appearance. As you walk along a country road in Ontario with its vast checkerboard of agriculture, you see the edges of fields but can't see the boundaries of farms. All industrial buildings have a shape, but many look shapeless. They were not constructed so as to have a coherent appearance. *Design* introduces the grammars of depiction and the composition of inflection into the lifeworld. A visually well-designed building offers a revealing, comprehensive view. A typical cathedral facade includes a large arch that depicts an entrance. The actual door within the arch is much smaller. John Summerson's *Language of Classical Architecture* (1963) shows how marches of columns and other classical figures are employed to *depict* the structure that the architect wishes the viewer to ascribe to a building. (His word is "control," not depict," but it refers to control of perception.)

A visually designed object is a lifeworld object of which the appearance is constructed as a text. A well-dressed person is more visible than a carelessly dressed person. Real ugliness needs unity of structure to have force. The result of dressing without an eye for appearance is less likely to be ugly than vague and unmemorable. I recall first seeing the Grand Canyon. No picture had conveyed to me a sense of the visual impression its size makes nor given me a mental tool for making that impression coherent; on location, the actual view was marvelously disorienting. I had difficulty seeing it and I have difficulty remembering it with any precision. Visually, the canyon is sublime but not well designed.

20

MELODY

When I was at school, I found it very difficult to cope with [the] confusion about form and feeling. My composition teacher complained that melodies which I had felt lacked form and that those that I constructed carefully were arid and unlovely. When he demanded accuracy in my piano performance and my grandmother complained that I practiced without feeling, I felt that both my technical skill and my integrity as a person were under attack. I was not able to relate correct performance to the right feelings, as did Venda musicians, because "feeling" was some elusive, Teutonic quality that one added to music when one got the notes right. In Venda, however, when the rhythm of an alto drum in domba was not quite right, the player was told to move in such a way that her beat was part of a total body movement. She could then play with feeling precisely because she was helped to experience the physical feeling of moving with her instrument and in harmony with the other drummers and dancers.

—John Blacking, *A Common Sense View of All Music*

On the ground of its connection with motion, performed melody can establish reference in the absence of any verbal text. While my exposition here will be largely limited to music, the ideas developed in this chapter may have relevance for any type of text built as a moving image, from music, to ballet, to theater, to video.[1]

THE MELODY AS A REPRESENTAMEN

When we listen to music we can participate in its continuous ebb and flow. We also can notice entities that are quite distinct within that flow, which enter into relations of similarity and contrast and which change, exit, and recur. Music is both a complex of discrete parts and a union of modulating continuities. Chapter 15 modeled both perceptions. The pattern analysis of "God Save the King" exhibited disjunct entities and yielded a hierarchy of regions; the grammar analysis displayed the modulated continuum of rising and falling conjunct intervals, yielding a hierarchy of boundaries.[2] The images of the melody that these two modes of perception yield are quite different, and their competition is a source of liveliness, whereby even this simple tune gains a discursive character.

The pattern of disjunct elements is highly articulate and assists us to reify the melody. Its units establish the identity and individuality of the melody by displaying its unique vocabulary. The modulation hierarchy is less articulate, like a series of waves on a lake. I think we tend to identify conjunction perceptually with continuity and with processes in consciousness rather than items.

Appreciating the double character of the melodic representamen prepares us for the surprising complexity of its references.

MOVEMENT AS AN OBJECT
OF MELODIC REPRESENTATION

The affinity of music and movement is obvious, and the mapping between sound shapes and body movement has an aspect of precision. We know of this from the role of gesture in conducting, from the role of musical style in determining dance style, and from observations of vocal inflection in speech. It is also clear that the mapping is not one to one. Once you have the right swing you can dance it with your hands or your feet, and you can play it on any chord or scale. Those aspects of the mapping are as a whole more arbitrary.

The word "movement" is used here for bodily movement and posture. "Movement" and "dance" are not interchangeable. Dance is a coherent text made of movements. Dance tends to limit its vocabulary and to emphasize style. Dance presented to an audience is designed to be perceived visually. Dance primarily for participation may rely on a broader complex of perceptual modes and weaker criteria of visual appearance but remains intentional and formal. Movement is a much broader category and is more chaotic. Movement is partly utilitarian and is not, in general, controlled by an overall discipline that correlates intention with appearance. Movement is not, of course, less referential than dance; generally, it is more referential. The character of quotidian movements, hesitant or bold, floating or dragging, spontaneous or self-conscious is instantly informative. In contrast, movement in a dance, where structure competes with reference, can be ornamental and opaque.

Utilitarian and casually expressive movement is characterized in the first instance by its proprioceptive or its kinesthetic values. Proprioception is the inner sensory perception of one's own weight and muscular effort and movement. Vicarious kinesthetic experience is the image we form of what it would feel like to move the way we see another person moving. Vicarious kinesthetic experience is mediated by visual perception and plays a role in the perception of both dance and daily movement. Both visual patterning and kinesthetic patterning participate in dance structure. Vision plays with or against spatial symmetries of reflection, rotation, and translation in three dimensions. Proprioception makes shapes of tension and relaxation, refreshment and fatigue, stress and balance, ingress and egress.

The proprioceptive structure of movement has been studied intensively in a normative mode in this century within the field now known as movement education: work in the traditions of Ida P. Rolfe, M. Feldenkrais, and F. Matthais Alexander. Various semioticians and anthropologists also have been concerned with gesture and movement studies, but their work, to the extent I am familiar with it, is visually oriented. Proprioceptive structure is what I wish to consider here. In the last two decades, Roger Pierce and Alexandra Pierce (1989) have developed a new application of movement education that correlates it with the structures of music, theater, and dance. Their schemata provide the basis for several of the preceding observations and also with the first of the two models I will propose for the objects of melodies.

Pierce and Pierce have worked out their theory primarily as a practical pedagogy for artists. The principal vehicle of their theory is activity in the classroom rather than conceptual analysis. Despite this, the term "model" applies conscientiously to their pedagogy. In their practice, the movement sequence that is predicated of a specific passage of music offers a basis of practical experiment and investigation.

The Pierces' model regards movement as constituting a recursive hierarchy explicitly linked to tonal hierarchy. The same categories can represent either large units or their parts. The natural unit of movement is a phrase. Smaller phrases combine to make larger phrases. The simplest motions are what chapter 13 identifies as *inflections;* that is, they have shape but no sharp interior segmentation into parts. Nevertheless, the Pierces identify functional phases of the phrase: its "beginning," its "climax," and its "ending." The wide boundary between two phrases or where two successive phrases join is a "juncture." A phrase may occur over a background of "beats" to which it can be related in different ways. Each of these units—beat, juncture, beginning, climax, ending, and again juncture—is a period of modulation of effort that concerns balance, support, intention, and attention.

In a formulation reminiscent of that of James Mursell and James Lockhard (1937), Pierce and Pierce construe the beat as a recurring cycle wherein intention is developed and attenuated: An effort that disturbs balance releases a motion that restores balance. A phrase is a large scale imposition on balance. A phrase emerges from a palpable moment of stillness. The beginning of a phrase requires effort, which accumulates toward the climax. The climax sustains another balance different in quality from the equilibrium out of which the phrase had emerged and that typically appears, with practice, as an extended sensation of "throwing" or "overflowing." The ending of a phrase exhibits a decrease of effort but does not fully restore the equilibrium from which the phrase emerges; this balance is fully restored only in the period of junction, which can include a "reverberation" involving the whole musculo-skeletal system in settling its ripples. (Like all movement education—and much music theory—the scheme has a normative component. I am not concerned with that aspect here.)

Pierce and Pierce have developed methods of practice for developing sensitivity to the structure of melody but no neutral substitute for personal experience. Applying their categories according to my own intuition, I would describe the climax of "God Save the King" as beginning at the central first high note (measure 7) and overflowing until just before the hemiola. Reverberation follows the beginning of the last note. The attack of the note signals clearly the end of the melody, but we need to hold on to that last note while all the antecedent sense of motion quiets down.

Recall that the immediate object of the sign is a correlate of the representamen of which we have prior knowledge. It is this role that I attribute to proprioceptive knowledge in correlation with music. We have prior knowledge of what it feels like to move and even prior imagination of the proprioception of movements we cannot really accomplish: running as fast as the wind, jumping as high as a tree, balancing on one toe, or even flying.

While music's representation of motion seems widely evident and foundational, this reference may not be universal and is not the only musical object. Let us identify this type of object specifically, therefore, as the "motional object" of music. Other objects of musical reference are considered in the next chapter.

AN INTERPRETANT OF THE MOTIONAL OBJECT

We may interpret the melodic reference to motion as the expressive behavior of a subject. Pursuing a theme from Edward Cone (1974), Naomi Cumming (1997) has retrieved and elaborated a perspective that is fully alive in many nineteenth-century descriptions of music. Music confronts us as an acting subject, a persona with whom we identify. The culturally sensitive type of interpretation she offers is not what I pursue here, but the phenomena to be described may be an important ground of such interpretations. I will describe a single melodic shape as encoding two simpler, simultaneous contours.

European languages differ in their allocation of reflexive verb forms. In German you have to say "I shave myself" rather than "I shave." The reality we refer to with reflexive structures seems to be one about which we experience some ambivalence as it divides our self into agent and patient. (Consider: "I'm trying to *keep myself* on a diet.") Walking up and over a steep hill, you must first, on the ascent, overcome the resistance of your weight. Descending, the same weight pushes you ahead. We push ourselves willfully and then our bodies carry us along a bit, the two attitudes frequently blending. It seems nonsensical to say "our bodies carry us along," but that division between an effort to make an effort and an effort that takes the lead is marked consistently in everyday talk, as in "I hit my speed."

Figure 20.1 suggests the separation of agent (effort) and patient (momentum, perhaps speed) in our tune. The illustration is intuitive and arbitrary with respect to its proportions. The basic idea is that the momentum line always rises while the effort is positive and falls if the effort is negative (resistive, braking, holding back). Here I associate the release of momentum with the leap to a climactic note and with the rhythmic intensification produced by fourfold repetitions of the same note.

Figure 20.1   Effort and momentum represented by melody

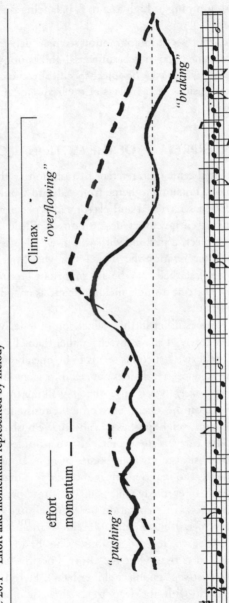

This model envisions the components of the Pierces' movement phrase as conjunct phases of an energy transfer. At the beginning of the phrase, energy is transferred (or force is exerted) from agent to patient. The climax is the phase in which the patient has fully absorbed the effort of the agent and reached a critical momentum from which it will either coast or take off on an accelerating "downhill" of its own, carrying the agent along. The balance within the climax is a balance between effort and momentum. It is the phase of the motion during which the patient's momentum is sustained without strain by the agent and is not reduced by any resistance. In the ending of the phrase, the energy transfer is reversed. The agent absorbs energy, slowing its patient. I believe the capacity of music to represent two contours derives from the independence of its rhythmic and pitch structures; acceleration and deceleration of rhythm play against rising and falling pitch. Acceleration after a highest pitch is quite different in feeling from acceleration before a highest pitch. The first often seems to release momentum, the second to accumulate effort. There is no acceleration at the climax in our tune, but the repetitions of notes that commence there increase the emphasis on rhythm. Without being able to specify the psychodynamics, we can state that melody is complex enough to encode multiple contours. (Indeed, there are many more complications besides those considered in this discussion.)

EMOTION AS AN OBJECT OF MUSIC

The affinity of music with emotion is nearly as obvious as the affinity of music with movement, but talk of this affinity is far more irritating, and for good reasons. Aligning music with emotion is no shortcut to understanding music. Some music is not emotional. It is much easier to express emotion without music—screaming, jumping, crying, pounding, and sighing—than by means of it. Music does something quite different. Unlike "movement," a general term but a clear one, "emotion" is a vague idea confused with mood and sometimes with sensation.

Granting all of this, it remains a fact that music can indicate qualities of feeling and that qualities of emotion are a salient subclass of these. The theory I review here proposes to explain this aspect of musical reference: Music represents specific characteristics of movement that are indices of emotion.

222

Gesture I and Gesture II

Although gesture is a recurring topic in the criticism and philosophy of art
and elsewhere, it is difficult to avoid vagueness while holding to what is intuitively important to us in contrasting the linguistic with the gestural. To
speak intelligibly of gesture, we must distinguish metaphorical extensions
of the word from a literal sense. For example: "the president moved the
Seventh Fleet into the Mediterranean in a gesture of defiance." Obviously,
the way we understand that involves a comparison with something like
clenching your fist.

The reverse does not hold. You can understand a clenched fist without
imagining the whole navy steaming through the Straits of Gibraltar. A *gesture* is a single, molar unit of expressive bodily movement or posture. One
single gesture has no parts that are experienced by the actor or perceiver as
volitionally distinct, that is, as the products of distinct impulses.

Although one gesture is not compound, it is complex. The example in
chapter 14 of Jack angrily slamming, stamping, and whirling around suggested that three different gestures could convey the same feeling. On the
other hand, different executions of what we might call the "same" gesture,
say grasping, as in a handshake, could convey different feelings. A handshake can be firm, aggressive, warm, formal, reserved, or timid. The double matrix of similarity and difference in gestures allows us to construct
and distinguish two concepts. The *articulation of the gesture* (hereafter *gesture I*) is defined by which body parts do what. The *inflection of the gesture*
(hereafter *gesture II*) is determined by its rhythm, its profile of force. It
makes sense to imagine that two differently articulated gestures that carry
a common import (say an affectionate smile and a gentle hug) might have
something in common in their physical makeup, and rhythm is a natural
candidate (not that the opposite view, that these are fully independent
signs, can be dismissed out of hand). Gesture combines cultural and biological factors. I would suggest that those factors of gesture for which language supplies a good analysis are cultural—besides the choice of which
body parts are used, the determination of what occasions are acceptable
pretexts for gestural expression and the overall level of expressivity toler-
ated. Gesture I accepts cultural control; it is capable of notation. The theory we examine here implies that gesture II is biologically determined and
incapable of notation, subject to cultural modification only in that it can
be contextualized, facilitated, or inhibited.

Clynes's Theory of Emotion Expression—"Sentic Forms"

Manfred Clynes is a concert pianist professionally trained in engineering and neurology. His experimental studies in neurobiology were inspired by his own observations of musical expression and depended on the ingenious exploitation of computer recording and averaging of waveforms, especially the cello playing of Pablo Casals.

In 1969/1989 and in succeeding publications, Clynes provided a complex set of hypotheses and experimental measurements regarding emotion expression as well as extensive suggestions relating these to musical expression. Despite their novelty, Clynes's experiments have not attracted a wide professional response. Only some dozen papers deal with it and, to my knowledge, there have been no thorough attempts at replication. In 1992—partly out of frustration with the professional neglect of his work—I undertook to repeat his experiments with some additional controls and had some success (Lidov 1993).

There is no consensual theory of emotions. Clynes's theory portrays emotion as genetically determined and as referencing a neurologically defined, finite lexicon. Clynes claimed to isolate and describe a group of fixed time patterns for neuromuscular activation associated with different emotions. He later reported cross-cultural studies as an indication that the patterns were biologically rather than culturally determined.

Clynes's experimental studies employ a pressure transducer ("sentograph"). The subject presses a button "expressively" and the pattern of pressure is transcribed by a computer as a waveform. In the experiments gesture I is prescribed to the subject (including an uninflected and uncontextualized verbal direction for the target emotion), but each subject must discover and develop gesture II on her own. Clynes's chief finding through experiments such as these is that with unguided practice, the expressive patterns discovered by different individuals tend to converge on a shape that is *distinct* for each of several different emotions but the *same* for most people.

Clynes calls these shapes "sentic forms" (same root as "sentiment"), and I take them to be images of gesture II. Sentic shapes are temporal patterns of fixed duration that describe the growth and decay of muscular effort (and momentum). The quickest is anger, which reaches a peak in a fifth of a second. Those of grief and reverence need a full second to reach their peak and recover still more slowly. The shapes traced as computer averages are easily accommodated by intuitive descriptions: anger flashes; hate jabs; grief droops; love (parental) caresses; sex thrusts; joy skips (literally: the finger after pressing the sentograph button rebounds above its starting level). Clynes does not claim to have found all the sentic forms. The graphs reproduced as figure 20.2 are samples of my own, perhaps somewhat amateurish experiments, which the reader might like to compare with those of Clynes. I do not and did not consider my study sufficiently rigorous or developed to merit publication, and do not mean to use the present context to sell it at the back door. However, it would be a great satisfaction to me if this brief notice encouraged someone else to follow up the work.

Clynes's interpretations of his results entail a number of mutually interdependent hypotheses, including, inter alia:

1. The sentic form is a unit of neuromuscular *behavior* that is biologically correlated with a state of mind and body. The behavior has a set duration and time pattern for the growth and decay of its effort, and may occur several times while the state continues. The state has no set duration. "Feeling" is the appearance of this state in consciousness.
2. The correlation of feeling with gestural behavior is fixed and involuntary. The correlation can be suppressed to some extent but not fundamentally rearranged. You can't accurately fake the behavior without imagining its feeling.
3. Sentic forms are transforms of independently triggered molar actions (single voluntary impulses); the patterns can (in principle) be expressed by any voluntary motor muscles as a transformation of an underlying intentional action.
4. When one person performs a gesture expressive of a sentic form, it: (a) reinforces the feeling of the person who performs it; (b) tends to induce imitation in the person who perceives it; and (c) tends to arouse the same feeling in the perceiver. So long as mimicry is aroused, its external expression may be repressed without loss of the attendant feeling.
5. Intensity of feeling is correlative with the precision (not, e.g., the amplitude or frequency or speed) with which innate gestural forms are executed.
6. Emotion expression is a developing skill that will be self-taught in appropriate situations. Although innate, it is not always instantly or easily accessible.

Figure 20.2 Sentic expression forms. From Lidov (1993)

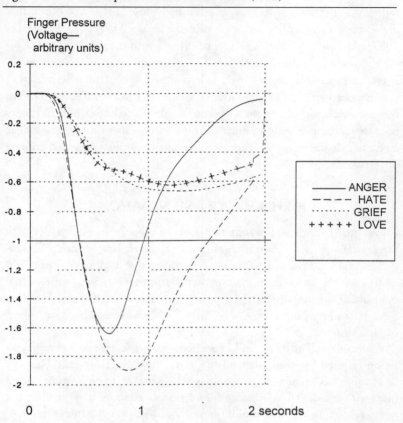

Combined averages of 17 subjects, circa 25 expressions each for each of four emotions (from their sixth sessions).

7. Any art medium can convey the trace of some sentic forms and the sentic form so conveyed retains the capacity to trigger attendant feelings.

I am strongly inclined to accept all of these premises, recognizing that such an opinion is far from consensual. Hereafter I refer to the seven hypotheses collectively as the *gesture hypothesis.*

Clynes provides several examples of musical figures that he identifies as representing sentic shapes. I have published some analyses of music that draw on sentic identifications of musical figures (1978, 1979, 1981b, 1987). Although I make these identifications with conviction, I acknowledge that they are purely intuitive. The advantage of being able to postulate such expressive objects, even as hypotheses, is that they permit us to address a variety of issues that otherwise would be intractable. Regrettably, the gesture hypothesis might suggest a simpleminded push-button theory because it considers only an indexical *component* of artistic expression. The next chapter shows that it lends itself to integration in a very rich context of textual relations.

PERFORMANCE AND NOTATION

The gesture hypothesis holds that intensity of expression is correlative with the *precision* with which innate gestural forms are executed (point 5); sentic forms are incapable of notation. No finite set of distinctive features establishes boundaries for a class of sentic forms. Notation, we recall, is opposite in this respect. When we draw the letter M or the note C it may be neat or sloppy, but it cannot be "more" or "less" intensely M or "more" or "less" intensely C.

Clynes as well as Pierce and Pierce recognize that the gestural representation effected by music depends on how music is performed. The very loyal subject constructed by "God Save the King" may perform her devotions with considerable latitude of inflectional variation. It is possible, but not necessary, to give the second motivic group of the song (measures 3–4) the warmth of an embrace, embodying the sentic shape for (nonsexual) love. The overshooting high note at the end can embody the light skip that characterizes joy. These are variables of performance.

Musical notation does not convey sufficient information to ensure the inflections a musical performance requires. A good reader of musical or dance notation frequently can abduce an interpretation that goes beyond the recorded data. (Here is a passage that would makes sense *if* I performed it as angry.) But these interpretations are not *specified* by the written score, and they invariably involve a precision of shape in execution that lies outside notation *in principle*. On the other hand, just as different body articulations (gesture I) can embody the same particular characterizing time shape (gesture II), different musical figures can embody the same representation of gestural character and the same figure, differently performed, can embody different characters. (In this respect, music approaches the double articulation of language.)

This holds of dance as well. Labanotation, the notational system for dance, was developed by Rudolf Laban for the coordination of mass festivals of choreographed popular dance but was employed subsequently not only for choreography but for the analysis of industrial work.

Laban drew on both musical notation and seventeenth-century choreographic methods in devising a system that is infinitely extendible. It carries, as basic equipment, a generalized mechanism for pinpointing the time and direction of motion at any point of the body. It does not normally attend to the position of the eyebrows, but there is no reason in principle why it could not. The basis for adding refinements of that type is clearly established.

Yet when I talk to people who live with this notation, they are quick to acknowledge that something slips through the net. Laban himself recognized this and invented a less formally explicit system, effort-shape notation (which is not strictly a notation in our sense), to supplement the basic scheme. Just as with musical notation, what we are inclined to call the *quality* of movement is not caught in the sieve of formal notation.

We do not say, of course, that the structures conveyed by notation have nothing to do with performance; yet it seems that in painting, in music, in dance, in all of the arts and even in casual communication we have two planes or streams, one bound up with conceptlike structure, subject to playful manipulations, and one bound up with inflection, subject to inhibition and release. Here I imagine my metaphor "streams" not as separated in a meadow but as ocean currents that might mingle and interact without fixed boundaries. Understanding the interaction of these streams, the topic of the next chapter, is surely a central problem in the semiotics of art.

21

CONCEPT AND EXPRESSIVITY IN ART

We have contemplated two moments in the dialectic of structure and reference: specification of reference through the elaboration of syntax in chapters 14 and 15, and loss of reference as the sign develops toward autonomy in chapter 16.

This chapter, which will seem to recall the first possibility more often than the second, develops interpretations of a symphonic movement by Ludwig von Beethoven and then one of a stained glass by Marc Chagall. I think the reader would be right to feel some discomfort with these two analyses, apart from any due to errors in my logic or evidence, simply because they are asserted too directly.

In reality, those signs, gorgeously elaborated, are so attractive that the arrow of reference looses its head. What we should hope to describe is not its actual flight but rather a possible trajectory. If I could borrow the language of quantum physics, I might speak of distributions of probable objects—like electron clouds—instead of adopting a matter-of-fact tone as a concession to clarity and economy. I hope the reader will indulge me in this abbreviation or if not, then, as we go along, pencil in the missing modifiers of caution, the as-ifs.

Given this caveat, I do insist very emphatically that my reservations have nothing to do with the media of the examples. The same would hold for a novel. What it represents as a whole is not what its parts represent. The meaning of a novel as a whole is as uncertain as the meaning of a symphony. Nor does the principle hold exclusively of art. Even a theory of semiotics has a less and less certain application to the world the more its principles cohere as a whole. Does physics escape this rule? We feel less certain today than ever how the physical world it strives to construct refers to the objective world we live in.

In art holistic elements are framed and manipulated so as to become conceptlike; conceptlike elements are transformed and inflected to convey holistic inflections.

We distinguish a plane of composition, where syntax is established, and a plane of inflection. *Composition* deploys pattern and grammar, is conceptlike, and, in principle, is available to notation. *Inflection* is displayed by unarticulated elements that have a character dependent on their exact shape and that, therefore, are in principle susceptible to continuous graphing (i.e., not notational graphing) but not to notation. The harmony still audible when classical music is played on an out-of-tune piano is part of composition. The differences between two accurate realizations of the same score belong to inflection. To speak of the import of music or dance or theater—and not just of its structure—we must have in mind even if vaguely, some way of performing the work. Otherwise our talk can make no sense.

Various media invite analogous distinctions. In dance the relation between composition and performance is quite the same as in music. Nuances of performance transform the strict requirements of composed postures and movements. In visual art, inflection is embodied in the expressive shaping of line, space, and color. These are transformations of compositional elements, either depictions or geometric schemes (straight lines and round circles). In architecture, the sequence of parts establishes concepts of composition, but the expressive effect of proportions is understood as a body language, as in the "march" of columns. The equation of columns with bodies is exhibited in full cycle from the earliest Attic sculpture to the portico of the Erechtheum, with its graceful row of maidens holding up the roof. There are all sorts or rules for the classical architectural orders, but in the end, their proportions have to be felt by a vicarious kinesthesia. (See Summerson [1963].) In the theater ordinary movements are transformed to become more expressive. In poetry gesture is embodied in breath and intonation patterns, languid or excited, smooth or rippling, quick or slow—evoked by the pronunciations thought or enacted but not, of course, notated. The words—the concepts—are notated.

What is most magical and mysterious in art is the intertwining of expressivity and conceptualization. Chapter 20 broached the notion that melody could represent a subject, but we skipped a more elementary phenomenon. It seems that we comprehend spatial relations, time relations, and force relations in part by projecting body images. Artists attribute motion to line and color—for example, they speak of blue not only as distant but as receding.

We project our own *feelings* into the objects or events that evoke them readily if those events or objects embody expressive physical inflections. The feeling of sorrow provoked by an automobile accident appears to be *about* it, not *in* it. In a Michelangelo *Pieta,* we have an overwhelmingly persuasive sense that sorrow resides in the work itself. Nelson Goodman accepts this phenomenon as a deus ex machina. (He discusses it as "metaphorical exemplification" in *Languages of Art* [1968].)

Here the gesture hypothesis is suggestive. We might postulate that the slowly drooping lines—in figure or drapery—capture the pattern of sorrowful behavior and provoke subliminal mimicry, and that we project the feeling resulting from our own muscular tensions onto the sculpture as a sort of illusion. (This example appears in Clynes 1969/1989.)

Where minimal figures may embody the raw ingredient of expressive inflection, larger syntagma and the composition as a whole convey conceptual, philosophic, and cultural representations. A text must not be said to "mean" what some of its individual figures reference. The references of parts and wholes belong to different orders but interact in diverse and complex ways.

THE FUNERAL MARCH OF BEETHOVEN'S *EROICA*

The continuities of sound by which classical music induces a process and asserts its dominance of consciousness normally include both metrical regularity and polished tone. Beethoven takes the risk of endangering the tonal surface at the outset by his gruff exposure of the double basses. The meter is very compelling and pulls us in, but a tension has been instigated by this arresting glimpse of the sonorous orchestral machinery—momentarily opaque—that will have consequences.

Is There a Sign Object?

The movement before us is less abstract than some others. Even without a title, which this movement has, exceptionally for Beethoven, its sphere of emotional reference would be signaled by its stylistic topics. "Topics" in musicology (analogous to "icons" and "iconography" in visual art history) are residual allusions to contextually labeled styles or stipulated objects. To say that these are what the music is "about" puts the matter too strongly. While we must not lose sight of the intentional repression or sublimation of objects, at the least, topics may orient the character of abstract music. (For virtuosic development of the theory, see Ratner [1980], Hatten [1994], and Monelle [forthcoming].)

Thus the movement is not only titled, it moves in the tempo, the minor mode, and the rhythmic figures of a funeral march. The too-prominent bass imitates the convention of the muted tenor drumrolls and the heavy steps of a military funeral. Later phrases suggest hymn style (measure 17), a recitativo of pathetic speech (measure 27), a possibly conventional sign of tenderness (the syncopated, melodic diminished third of measure 34), and fantasia style (measures 69ff), all relevant to a funereal episode. These stipulated objects belong to the plane of composition (although they can be sabotaged by bad performance).

These conventional references are clues to others that depend entirely on performance, the gestural objects. In the opening melody, quoted in figure 21.1, there are melodic figures readily correlated with grief, but the melody offers the conductor considerable liberty where to draw out a strong inflection and where to fall back on an orderly flow.

The materials of classical music are very neutral in expressive content: bland scales, bland chords, metrically balanced rhythms, symmetrical

Figure 21.1   Beginnings of march melody and trio. Beethoven, Op. 55, ii

forms. The figures into which this material is shaped, short distinctive groups of notes, lend themselves to interpretation as representing gestures. When selected groups of notes are performed in a manner that brings out their gestural characters, they transform the entire musical structure from a merely rational construction into an expressive construction. What groups one selects remains a personal matter. A performance of music in which every phrase was *independently* expressive in this sense would exaggerate. (This exaggeration, called expressionism, is sometimes cultivated, as in Arnold Schoenberg's styles and some vocal blues.) Here the melody includes a number of figures that have the descending contour traditionally associated with the musical representation of a sigh and also suitable in their force and pace to be inflected in the manner of the sentic shape for grief isolated by Manfred Clynes. Yet I personally feel that there is no better locus for this sentic expression than the compositionally unshaped single note that begins the third measure—a note that can be shaded by inflections of loudness.

To say the movement is "about" Napoleon or about his minister's rejection of Beethoven's job application or about Beethoven's confrontation with deafness and his suicidal episode—this is unpardonable fishing. But to suggest that the object is death, or death as a metaphor for defeat, insofar as the movement conveys a perspective on or attitude toward death, is not farfetched or arbitrary.

Is There a Double Articulation?

The criteria of double articulation (discussed in chapter 13) can be considered in relation to performance and composition. The paradigmatic affinity of the composition cells labeled *A* and *C* in figure 21.1 is obvious. In contrast to *B*, the two share rhythm, direction, initial pitch, and syntactic position (as conclusions of their respective motivic figures). But in a performed articulation of expressive inflections, I find them unlike. The first sounds hopeless. (The discussion of this figure in Deryck Cooke suggests this. [1959, p. 220–223.][1]) The other cell, *C*, manages a contrasting instant of repose. Cell *B* which has an utterly different rhythm and pace, making a sort of convulsive gulp, seems expressively close to *A*, or at least far more so than *C* does. Is this an independent semantic articulation or a more sophisticated reading of the syntax? Cell *D* is cell *B* again, but renotated as Mozart might have preferred, and it is evident that it is an ornamented version of *A* after all, rationalizing the affinity, which also extends to the harmony. It seems impossible to establish a double articulation on the basis of compositional analysis alone, but the option remains for performance to impose something rather like one. We can decide to play *A* and *B* or many other sets of figures with comparable inflections apart from the relations established by composition, and the boundaries of inflections need not correspond at all to the boundaries of grammatical forms or units of pattern.

Closure

Syntactically, the world of this funeral march is made one whole by a grammatical form. Overall, despite the magnification of drama that Beethoven achieves, the movement is conventional in its framework. The form is that of march and trio, with the march itself in rounded binary form.[2] Using the standard convention of music theory that represents recurring passages of music by letters, and variants with primes, we have the scheme represented by figure 21.2.

Grammatical closure dominates the movement. Nearly every note is precisely situated and precisely interpreted, with respect to syntax, by thematic, tonal, and metrical grammar. The style of this movement maximizes a tendency of the style of its period to apportion, identify, and correlate its parts so clearly that time seems much like space in its power to manifest position and proportion. The representation by the movement as a whole of an authoritative, monological voice has its first ground in this closure.

Figure 21.2   Overall form of the Funeral March

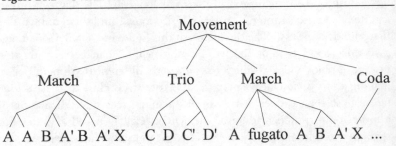

Discourse

Yet the movement is not entirely autonomous and not entirely stable. The stipulated objects that link the work with external styles and conventions are minor leakages compatible with the grammatical form and hardly disturbing its autonomy. But the broad arches of the form show other stresses, distortions that, if they do not upset the grand hierarchy, instill it with the dynamism of unfolding thought. The lengths of the strains marked B and A' in the diagram are skewed by ambiguous extension and contraction. The phrase shown as X is an extra wing on the conventional house, splendid but of uncertain relation to the rest. After the trio, highly irregular in its internal phrasing, the march returns in a far more fluid version. What is least conventional in the overall scheme (although not without precedent) is its progressive loss of articulation toward the end. The neatly repeating sections of the reprise dissolve in the continuous turbulence of the fugato that leads to the disjointed utterances of a long coda. (There are also practical matters at play. In this work, allied in some ways with French neoclassicism, Beethoven has committed us to monumental proportions and a promise of a monumental symmetry. Had he literally followed through, repeating the March in its first guise, the tedium would be vacuous—like an unrelenting video pan, window by window, of the whole facade of the Louvre.)

The March Themes

To model the themes kinesthetically makes immediate sense. In the march tension is accumulated that eventually ebbs but that never obtains a gratifying release; momentum never takes over from effort. The highest notes are prolonged; the descending figures that follow are slow or broken in motion, without enough energy to break the preceding tension. The inability to overcome inertia, thus evinced, is depressive. Depression is a set of dispositions. The predominant depressiveness of the march is the character of the conscious process it evokes, but this does not mean that the music holds to one emotion throughout. The march is modulated by now more strenuous, now more relaxed melodic figures and harmonies, and achieves a hymnlike serenity in the phrase marked B in figure 21.2.

When the fugato takes over from the march in its reprise, there is finally a release of inertial energy into continuous movement, but not with an attendant settling; the fugato gets worked up and collapses in fatigue.

In the larger scheme of the symphony as a whole, Beethoven will not perpetuate depression. The ensuing movements break it off and give full scope to rhythmic vitality. In the slow movement, we are stuck with it. The only glimpse of escape is the dreamlike trio.

The Trio

The march is in minor, the trio in major. Here high registers draw attention. Arpeggio and scale patterns over a steady accompaniment recall the genre of the fantasia. It is always difficult to know what in coloristic associations is cultural and what is biological, but there can be no doubt, whatever the basis of the quality, that the sound is gracious and heavenly, indicating on this ground a transcendence of the preceding and following gloom into a realm of grace. The key sentic gesture is perhaps that of hope (first three quarter notes).

The melody of the trio is interrupted by loud, reiterated chords in a passage that, despite its brevity, I marked separately as D in figure 21.2. It can sound subjectively to the hearer either short or long, for here, in a sense, nothing happens. It is a moment of emphasis on a chord that needs no emphasis, on an obvious rhythm, on a vacuous figure, and it is the summit of the movement. The orchestral medium, at last resolving the clue of the opening gruff basses, becomes fully opaque: The absence of syntactical relations throws us back onto the material of sound. To give the passage a semantic interpretation is all too easy—the spirit of affirmation, the voice of God. To see why this is not arbitrary we must go back to root issues.

Articulatory Contrasts

The march theme is highly articulate; its melodic phrases are disjunct and solid. The first part of the trio (C) evokes continuity; the steady pulse of a flowing accompaniment supports a strain of melody composed of dovetailing, conjunct units. The second part of the trio (D) is pure interruption. There seems to be no substance but the articulation itself, a passage of pure punctuation. Its chords are "articulated"; yet we can hardly call them "articulate."

The most complex patterning of articulation contrasts occurs in the reprise. The articulation of the march gradually erodes. The fugato's conjunct and overlapping figures make a continuous texture. No dominant melody is identified with that continuity as one was in the trio. Division of the texture into melody and accompaniment is suspended. When melody emerges again, the continuity becomes a background phenomenon, an accompaniment, and the articulations of the melody gradually lose their connections.

The patterns of articulatory contrasts develop closure in that the march and trio establish contrary types, each in turn negated. In its changes of articulatory character, the music moves toward or away from the world of speech, suggesting a play of modalities. Reluctant as I am to accord the scheme any universality, it is tempting here to invoke the Greimasian square as a diagram of this closure as suggested in Figure 21.3.

There is no way to certify my grounds for this analogy, but I hear it thus: The articulated march stands to the continuous trio as the world of fact to the world of hope and dreams, the real to the possible. Dreams have, despite their disorder, a sensuous continuity that wakefulness denies. The march stands to the coda as does the permanent to the momentary (the two modal positions of present tense). The broad, balanced phrases of the march, creating a stable time frame, give us, as it were, something like funereal contemplation of death as an eternal fact; the Coda, falling apart, losing its orientation in time, throws us into the present moment, into the

Figure 21.3   Articulation contrasts in the Funeral March

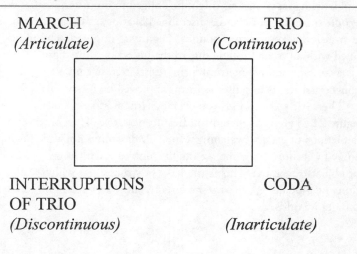

MARCH   TRIO
(Articulate)   *(Continuous)*

INTERRUPTIONS   CODA
OF TRIO
(Discontinuous)   *(Inarticulate)*

fatigue of a burial witnessed. Between these had been the transition of the fugato, its double counterpoint obliterating the distinction of foreground and background and thus interiorizing the feeling that had been objectified earlier. We cannot carry the eternal/actual distinction into the dream world of the Trio. What can interrupt a dream as those chords do, but still stay within it, except the oracular call of the supernatural?

A Hierarchy of Objects and Interpretants

I would not generalize the schema, but for this particular movement, which inherits a strong quasi-linguistic cast from the linguistic rationalism of the eighteenth century, it does seem possible to indicate hierarchy of levels of interpretation.

Some of the shortest figures effect stipulated and/or affective references. They hardly determine interpretants beyond our willingness to sense that a subject's perspective is being evoked. Not all of the music's short figures carry these representations, but figures that would be neutral on their own become assimilated to the feeling tones of others of stronger character.

At the more complex level of longer phrases, social structures are constructed. Both as images of motion and as articulated structures, phrases are analogous to styles of comportment and manners. The phrase is a formal structure that contains, displays, and *constrains* the references of its own motion and of its component figures. At a royal Western European funeral of 1804 mourners would not roll around on the ground, shrieking and bawling (as mourners might be obliged to do in some other cultures). People maintain poise and a disciplined bearing, as the march phrases do. Expression is kept within bounds. Dignity is imposed. The phrase is imbued with an overall feeling due to the inflection of its figures, but it also, via a strict harmonic, metrical form, resists excessive inflection. The phrase conceptualizes its impulses as forms approved by its society.

Thematic sections in this movement (the middle horizontal line of the figure 21.3) are the syntagms nearest to narrative. They are a little bit like depictions of events (watching a funeral, dreaming hopefully, being overcome by feeling, etc.), and we might think of events in general as the sort of objects suggested. This is the level of structure at which the constructions of modalities can arise as interpretants, assigning the references to different worlds.

At the level of its composition as a whole, the movement has resonance with attitude or even what we informally call a philosophy of life, more specifically here a philosophical stance toward apparent defeat. It is not an "expression of feelings." It is more like an argument or sermon. The world it creates and into which its process of consciousness induces us never lets us forget its sense of global order. Here is Beethoven's argument for an aristocracy of spirit, with every image and every shred of evidence fastened precisely in place by the noble arch of its form, an authoritative monologue that brooks no question or rejoinder.

"JOSEPH" IN THE JERUSALEM WINDOWS OF MARC CHAGALL

Marc Chagall's 12 stained glass windows frame and surmount the Holy Ark, the cabinet that holds the scriptures, in the synagogue of the Haddasah University Medical Institute in the Judean Hills to the west of Jerusalem. Readers who have no acquaintance with them may wish to consult the reproductions beautifully annotated by Jean Leymarie (Chagall 1963/1967) whose notes I relied on for much background information. I have sketched some elements of composition in one window, "Joseph," as an aide-memoire in figure 21.4.

The lantern turret that the windows illuminate is a square with three of the windows on each side. The windows are uniform in shape and size, about 8 feet by 11, including their rounded arches. The arc holding the Holy Scriptures is centered beneath them. The 12 windows refer to the 12 tribes of the Jews, named for and descended from the 12 sons of Jacob. The tribes are initially characterized in Genesis by the blessings Jacob accords to his sons in his last days. In accordance with the traditional proscription of human images, the sons are not depicted in the windows. The tribes are represented by a traditional but relatively little-used iconography, which stems from biblical metaphors, especially those of Jacob's blessings and also of Moses' blessings on the 12 tribes pronounced shortly before his death (Genesis 49; Deuteronomy 32). In "Joseph," a tree branches over a wall to correspond with the first verse of Jacob's blessing. The King James Version (like the window) has "bough" instead of vine. I quote here and later the translation issued by the Jewish Publications Society of America in 1917:

Joseph is a fruitful vine
A fruitful vine by a fountain
Its branches run over the walls

And at the top of the tree, a dove holds a bow:

But his bow abode firm
And the hands of his arms were made supple

Other figures in that window carry out the theme of abundance and fruit-fulness without a specific link to the blessings. The figure of two hands holding a shofar (the ceremonial ram's horn trumpet) that crowns the picture does not correspond to any one element in the blessings, but it marks the preeminence of the blessings of Joseph, who received the first and the most elaborate blessings, and the preeminence of his tribe that became the part that represents the whole. Joseph, the chosen son, heralds a chosen people. This is the picture opposite the entrance, the first to be seen upon entering.

The Jerusalem windows merge the functions of symbol, ritual, and art. As spatial ritual (i.e., as a monument), they enable viewers to take their own presence as representing participation in the history and destiny of Israel. As a hierarchical assemblage of symbols, they establish contact with forces of magic. As a work of art, the process in consciousness they induce establishes a mystic perspective of ceremony, prophecy, destiny, and revelation.

The windows do not accommodate a synchronic grammar, but they allude strongly to and enter a dialogue with a traditional practice of stained glass. They contribute to the resurrection of this system. Chagall's assertion of the little developed system of Jewish iconography in these windows also alludes to the Zionist reclamation of Palestine. (Chagall felt some caution here, as his ecumenical remarks on the windows show.) The stained glass window is an ancient form, but its language declined in the seventeenth century. A revival of liturgical arts in post - World War II France drew the participation of Henri Matisse, Georges Roualt, and Fernand Léger among others. Chagall stands apart in availing himself of the full spectrum of traditional techniques, painting and burnishing the glass to make figures, textures, and highlights either through the addition or removal of pigments. With regard to these subtle inflections, so vital to the life of the windows, we would never speak of a grammar, however traditional their basis. What evokes the old grammar is the hierarchic, syntactic articulation with its inclination toward symmetry—the division of the window into plates by heavy frames, the division of the plates by the lead tracery that joins the individual fragments of glass.

The windows are subject to a supervening symmetry and hierarchy, yet they are deeply dialogical at every level. Chagall prepared models, at one-eighth scale. These models give scarcely any indication of divisions by frames and leading. Stained glass windows require the collaboration of the artist with craftsmen: Charles Marq articulated Chagall's models as plates of cut glass. Chagall responded with his final modulations of the glass, which sometimes required its recasting as final colors were negotiated. We shall see that this dialogue in production is emblematic of dialogues invested in the resulting work.

Composition

Articulatory Hierarchies

Discourse is instantiated in the continuous dialogue among the largely independent hierarchies of framing, color, and figure.

Each window is divided into 12 plates by 3 horizontal lines of framing and 2 series of verticals. The verticals, usually not quite aligned, make a different dance in each window, a play worth a study in itself and apparently all due to Marq. Figure 21.4 shows the frames.

The hierarchy of the frames meets insubordination in the leading. The leading, which traditionally is subordinate to depiction and to framing, is not so here. That is, Marq's leads do not correspond primarily to edges of the figures, and edges of the figures are not always represented by leads. (For example, in "Joseph," the shaft of the arrow crossing the bow is depicted by a lead except for its front end and tip, which are painted in grisaille.) The rectilinear preferences of the old windows gives way to broad curves suggestive of shatter patterns. In places, curves of the leading continue across the plate frames as if uninterrupted.

The medium of stained glass divided by framing encourages a distinction of scale between large figures—roughly, those larger than a plate and extensively outlined by leads—and small figures, those of which several may be grouped within one plate and relying more on paint for their articulation.

Figure 21.4   Frame pattern in the windows

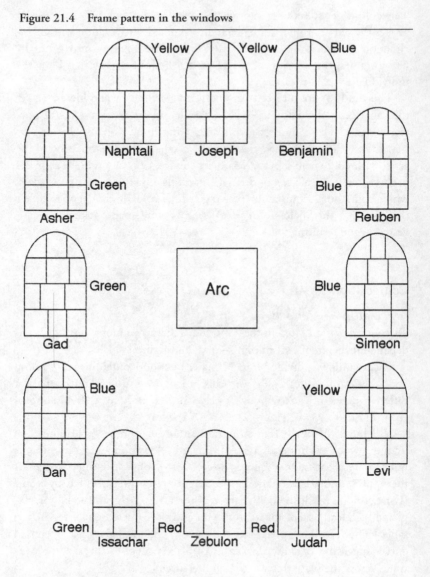

Chagall accepts but argues with this distinction. Some of his smallest figures are cut by the frames.

Large figures are further grouped, sometimes symmetrically, and a group of small figures may be positioned in symmetrical balance to one

Figure 21.5   Sketch of compositional elements of "Joseph"

large one, are all the small animals and the well in the bottom rank of "Joseph." Some figures mediate between the two scales, such as the second tree in Joseph, but these are fewer and vaguer. Medieval stained glass often displays a single large figure that fills most of a window. In this series there are no figures on that very large scale except the abstract wheels of revelation that occur in "Benjamin."

The large figures in "Joseph" are the two trees (the second tree is small enough to be an in-between case), the dove with crown and bow and arrow, a basket of fruit, the hands and shofar, and the well. The smaller figures include a foreground group of animals and some detailed floral work, such as leaves in the tree. The individual fruits clearly belong to the large-scale depictions although as figures they are a bit smaller than some of the small-scale animals.

Pattern

The cycle of 12 windows is not dominated by any one distributional scheme. The groupings by wall compete with the groupings by color. By dominant background colors, there are two reds, three each of various greens and yellows, and four blues. These are distributed around the four walls asymmetrically. The priority of "Joseph" has been mentioned, but other windows are singular in their own ways. The formality of the windows is as arresting as the energy of their colors. Four windows have a very strong vertical axis: "Levi," "Juda," "Issachar," and "Dan"; four others suggest the same more mildly. Two windows have strong circular symmetries ("Naphtali" and "Benjamin.") Symmetries are realized both by symmetrical objects on the axis—candelabra, tablets, crown—and by pairings that cross it—as of arced hands or of comparable figures or comparable patches of color. In "Reuben," where reflective symmetry is weak, four fish are set against four birds, two bright red patches against two bright green plus one muted red and one muted green.

The point is that the force of symmetry and pattern in the windows is highly variable and is always pitted against the expressivity of inflection. Symmetry dominates in "Levi," rendering the whole window ceremonial (for a priestly tribe). Symmetry is subordinated to cross currents in the war scene of "Gad." "Joseph" is medial in this respect. Figures deploying reds, blues, and mauve hint at vertical columns on the left and right while green and heavy black are confined to the central plates, and the dark fruit basket near the bottom and the darkly modeled shofar on top suggest an axis.

But the diagonal swirl of the reds across the axis, fervent and impulsive, has equal prerogative.

Grammar of Depiction and Grammar of Iconography

These grammars are kept in check by abstraction, but they determine objects. Depictions suggest seven categories: animal (including birds and fishes), human (hands and eyes only), plant, Hebrew letters, liturgical objects, architecture, and astronomical objects. There are also a basket, boat, and weapons. The categories are not invoked just by language habits (like the game "20 Questions") but by the abstractive character of Chagall's lines, which blur (but do not eradicate) distinctions of species. Landscape is faintly indicated. Several windows have a horizon line, high, low, or middle, but rarely emphatic. (Strictly speaking, a letter [an allographic sign] cannot be depicted, for what appears is the real thing, not a picture of it; yet these letters are so highly inflected that it is easy to associate them with depictions. Some windows show Biblical verses; others, like "Joseph," only the tribal name.)

Hints of perspective in the arrangements of small figures vis-à-vis large ones and by the suggestion of horizon lines establish a dialogical tension between flat pattern and three-dimensional scenes.

In general, each window depicts an arrangement of symbolic objects associated with its tribe and only loosely suggestive, as a whole, of a lifeworld scene. In several cases, the bottom of the windows are more like the lifeworld than the upper parts; yet, as a scene, the whole might comprise a revelation, a vision. This ambiguity of the scene with respect to its affiliation with the lifeworld or the imagination hinges on the quality of the space between the figures—a space inflected by light.

Inflections

Shapes

The most highly inflected figures, interestingly, are the most abstract, the Hebrew letters. In the case of the letters, sheer liveliness is more apparent than any specific emotion.

It is easy to sense sentic forms in visual inflections, but it is difficult to find an explanation for them, as sentic forms are acceleration patterns in time. We might agree or disagree with descriptions of Chagall's renderings of animals as "tender," but it is certainly not nonsense to talk in such terms.

(To bracket these judgments as "subjective" or "personal" is misleading. They are objective and interpersonal but—to date—inexplicable.) Inflections that strike me as salient in the windows are embracing whorls of tenderness, longer, more shallow curves of serenity, vital thrusting shapes of phallic character, exalted vibrations of color—these last pervasively—and in some windows flashes of rage and terror.

To make such a list is to say almost nothing, but we can go from there to something of more point: Within one given window, figures generally are not contrasted with each other by contrasting inflections. On the other hand, different windows contrast strongly with each other in their overall tone, with a particular blend of sentiments pervading each single window as a whole. In establishing these tones, the dominant background color, its modulations, and the inflections of lines play roles that I do not know how to distinguish from each other.

Although highly sublimated (compare the fish of the wayward Reuben), the phallic propulsion of the blaring trumpet in "Joseph," with the responding upward thrust of tree trunks and their spray of fruit, has a fecund if not sexy vigor that reverberates in the audacious, expansive, and constantly varied yellow ground.

Light

In "Joseph," space between the figures is as prominent as the figures themselves, opening broad areas for the flash and vibration of light. The yellow ground is continuously modulated. The activity of its gradation resists the tendency of yellow in stained glass toward dullness and seems all the more forceful therefore. The most striking variation is that produced by scrapping the outer layer of the glass to reduce the pigment, creating highlights of clear, nearly white light. These highlights occur in all the windows. In "Joseph," several figures, most prominently the Hebrew letters, are surrounded by halos of white light, but there are also highlights unattached to any figure, such as the prominent highlight high up in the empty space between the dove's bow and the second tree. (See figure 21.5.)

A speculation in chapter 2 paraphrased mystical quest as an attempt to peel back the signifier (now we say representamen) to achieve an unmediated contact with its object. Is that enthused dissatisfaction with signs presented here, where the figure is elided in favor of pure light? Was that also what we encountered with Beethoven's massive, supernatural chords, where the musical figure was dispensed with in favor of pure sound?

The Window as a Sign

The Jerusalem Windows are celebratory and mystical documents inducing, as an interpretant, the experience of their objects as wondrous revelations. The object is abstract but not obscure: The windows represent tribal destinies that have become histories. The blessings that orient their iconography are prophecies, at once prediction and ordinance. The modalities in play are those of esoterism: The visible and illusory world of the moment allows glimpses of another world, timeless, transcendent, and more real. Light is both a metaphor and an index of the transcendent world. The two worlds are presented in dialogue, mediated by ceremonies and by horizons.

"Joseph" is ceremonious in the dove's crown, in the still poise of bow and arrow, and in the shofar at its apex. Ceremony labels time so exactly as almost to hold it still, making one moment of all of its moments as the transcendent world makes one time of all times. The horizon is not depicted in "Joseph," implied perhaps with the foreshortening of the second tree, the large foreground group, the hints of hills at a middle height. The background yellow runs in an uninterrupted vertical column through all the central panels. Confident and utopian, the earth and the heavens merge.

Religious revelation is often a world of domineering monologue; not here. These windows, reveling in encounter and accident, give us instead the dialogue of active reception. (At all levels! Are those not Paul Cézanne's apples in the basket in "Joseph"? In the war-phantasmagoria of "Gad," with its Hieronymus Bosch - like beasts, does not the warrior horse enter from the very corner where Pablo Picasso's horse had screamed in agony in *Guernica?*)

UNLIMITED VARIETY

The relations of conceptualization and expressivity in art are infinitely variable. Among the resources of their interaction in a discourse where they continuously transform each other we can consider:

1. The principles of design, repetition, and variation, which permit forms generated under the impress of an inflection to be repeated or varied or articulated in ways that they never could be spontaneously.

The inflection becomes conceptlike. A musical "sigh" can be repeated backward, or consider Tai-Chi.

2. Forms determined by concepts, such as geometrical forms, or symmetrical rhythms can carry inflection by distortions of their elements or relations, by embellishment, and by conflictual contexts.

3. With stylization, either a concept is imposed as a filter in the transmission of an inflection or the converse, thereby inhibiting or at-
   tenuating the inflection. Inhibition makes the invisible visible (as
   when a massive tower makes us aware of gravity by not falling
   down).

4. Style *choice*, personal or societal, takes much of its meaning from
   the relations it imposes between concepts and inflections. An inflection manifests an impulse. The control of impulses is the first
   step in becoming civilized, as Freud and every parent of a two-
   year-old child can attest. In art, the conflict between conceptually
   and impulsively controlled forms is continuously played out and
   becomes metaphoric for cultural attitudes. Compare, in this very
   broad context, modern popular music with its antecedents before
   the 1950s, and this mechanism is instantly clear. Aristocratic society in Europe from the Renaissance to well into our century identified itself with codes that hid and sublimated the body. In early
   twentieth-century avante garde music of Europe, human animality burst forth dramatically, as it did later in the jazz craze and in
   rock and roll.

ARE COMPARISONS ODIOUS?

Regarding what the window or the march signify, I do mean what I have
said, but semiotic theory is not wedded to particular interpretations. The
prize I covet is not to persuade someone to adopt my understanding of
these works. What I would like more would be that another person who
has better evidence or deeper insights should want to explicate a different
understanding through a study of foundational elements and relations of
semiosis. Possibly the comparison this chapter draws is a misleading cue in
that regard.

The two principal examples in this chapter, fragments of analysis of a
musical composition and of a pictorial work, are offered in a frame that
suggests comparison. Such a comparison was surely owed to the reader, for

we began this study with a definition of semiotics as a comparative study. Usually we would either compare pictures with pictures or symphonies with symphonies or music globally with painting (or language, etc.) globally. I do not mean to make a method or advocate the practice of the particular kind of comparison indulged here, although surely it has its own place and moment and logic.

Comparisons are odious if they suggest rigid methods. Semiotic analysis should celebrate individuality. I hope the tools deployed are safe and inviting to play with. They don't amount to a rigid method.

PART VI

Consequences

In this book I have not considered the monumental literature—the writings of Michel Foucault, Jacques Lacan, Julia Kristeva, and others—that explores philosophical, social, and cultural issues in the light of semiotic consciousness; my concern has been to review foundational options in the construction of a semiotic theory. I do think it is the case, however, that our arrangement of distinctions regarding signs can facilitate thought on adjacent topics. I close with two speculative essays that intend to demonstrate that semiotic theory can suggest consequences. Both center on the notion of partially autonomous texts and systems. We cannot plan our cultures, but we do not need to think of culture as entirely hostage to blind forces. Semiotics provides a comparative perspective from which we can rethink issues in education, style, and governance.

22

SEMIOTICS AND THE PROBLEM OF FREE WILL

Our anxiety about free will reflects a conflict between what we logically deduce about ourselves and what we intuitively perceive and desire. Marvin Minsky writes: "Will is an empty postulate in which we are obliged to believe most of the time in order to be sane. All decisions are really due to causes or chance" (1986, p. 307).

In modern philosophy, the dialogue about free will is, in essence, a response to the crisis provoked by David Hume's skeptical analysis. The skeptical analysis reduces free will to illusion by arguments from the theory of cause. Since Hume's time we have seen that this argument can take various routes. If our thoughts are regarded as direct functions of their electrochemical substrates in the brain, then the will is not free because it is a physical resultant. If our thoughts are regarded as direct functions of our biological drives (id and libido), then the will is not free but is a biological (hence, biophysical) resultant. If our thoughts are regarded as an immediate function of economic and social conditions, then our will is not free but is a historical/economic resultant. These familiar modes of determinism need not be rehearsed here.

The attack on free will is surely one of the most unpleasant projects of philosophy. Some recent attempts to salvage volition draw on modern mathematics and physics. But what these offer is slight comfort, merely an argument that our behavior is either indeterminate or unpredictable. Since the elementary particles of physics are probabilistic entities, it appears that randomness is built into the fabric of existence. This maneuver merely substitutes probability for cause. Surely it is no comfort to think we are ruled by a accident rather than by fixed mechanisms! As another palliative, the incompleteness of mathematical and logical systems, established by Kurt Gödel, and along with it elaborate demonstrations of the logically necessary unpredictability of certain types of dynamic complexes, is cited to vouchsafe our freedom.

It seems to be a very secure fact that our complexity makes us essentially unpredictable, but is mere unpredictability any comfort? Madmen, fleas, and guinea pigs are equally vouchsafed unpredictable by the same demonstrations. A sense of freedom entails access to contemplated choice.

The problem of free will has been greatly obscured by the prospect of artificial intelligence. Yet the question might be not whether we can guarantee ourselves a permanent unbridgeable difference from computers even if they improve, but whether my superrobot and I will both have free will or both be deluded.

DELIBERATION

There are different sorts of freedom. I disregard political freedom in this discussion but want to distinguish "decision" and "abandon." As a boy who loved to swim, I knew how to dive well enough that for a split second, the suspension in the air and the falling were exciting and gave me a feeling of freedom. That's quite different, indeed opposite, to my deliberation of the decision to do it. The freedom of decision is followed by a moment of abandon. During the active moment of abandon I feel very free in an emotional sense, although my behavior becomes more or less automatic. During the moment of decision, when I may really exercise a freedom to choose my action, I may, if there is a conflict, feel more pressured than liberated from the emotional standpoint. When these opposite kinds of freedom become confused in politics the consequences can be dreadful; a mob encouraged to identify freedom with obedience. (In art the confusion can be quite innocent and wonderful; we guard against it only for the purposes of analysis. Abandon has more to do with inflection; decision is more elaborated in composition.)

In speaking of free will my focus here is on the deliberations that lead to decisions. Free deliberation is characterized by three traits:

1. Selection among distinct alternatives, such as to dive or not to, to use a flute or oboe, or to vote for candidates A, B, or C. (Quantita-

tive decisions, such as "How much salt?" involve an abandonment to feeling, a determination by the body.)

2. Sensitivity of the choice to effort. We recognize the difference between a careful deliberation and an offhand decision.

3. Belief that this effort, up to a point, could improve the choice.

The desire to claim free will is largely a desire to safeguard *these* attributes of deliberation. We do not wish to believe that the effort we expend in deliberating our actions and decisions is either inconsequential or illusory. The commonsense perception is that it is neither. A semiotic analysis of "reasons" supports this commonsense perception.

REASONS AND INFLUENCES

To deliberate a choice is to determine which among alternatives is supported by the strongest *reasons*. Everyone knows that it is always possible to give reasons, usually good ones, for whatever we elect to do. Therefore, we like to distinguish "real reasons" from "rationalizations." It has been suggested that all our reasons are actually rationalizations. The paradigm case is that of the subject of posthypnotic suggestion who obeys a command that is remembered only unconsciously, inventing new reasons on the spot. (Posthypnotic subjects frequently get cameo appearances in discussions of free will.) For example, I give you a direction, during hypnosis, to turn on your living room lights at noon tomorrow. At noon the next day, although the sunlight is bright, you proceed to turn on the living room lights. A friend asks you why, and you respond, perhaps, "I'm going to the hardware store tomorrow, and I just want to see whether I should get more of the discount bulbs." Here the reasoning comes after the fact.

Let us not trip over the question whether a picture of this sort might correspond to most or all of our deliberations or even whether it constitutes an acceptable report of posthypnotic behavior. First note that the specific rationale offered by the subject is not set by the hypnotist and would seem to be constructed as a quickly *deliberated* response to the conscious and unconscious constraints of the situation. There is no reason not to regard the construction of the rationale as partly a free act. This is the case for rationales generally. The difference between rationales and real reasons is only the scope of their influence.

I will take reasons to include both real ones and rationales. Reasons generally do not fully determine decisions. They *influence* decisions. The difference between influencing and determining is crucial here. At first encounter, we might be tempted to think of influence as a probabilistic version of cause. A probabilistic description is quite another matter. If the weather office says that the chance of precipitation is 80 percent, this does not put in doubt the causes of rain, which are known quite securely. It is metaphorical to say that lowering the temperature of a vapor-saturated air mass "influences" precipitation. The relationships are definite and determining. Some events are definitely determined only with respect to a level of probability, but the determination is still, within that limitation, definite. The effects of reasons could, in principle, be described probabilistically (as all phenomena can), but such a description does not reveal their structure.

The structure of reasons is a potentially infinite network. Let us consider such a network by taking as an example your decision to vote in support of a candidate for election. The action could be reflexive (minimal network), or it might be deliberated at length. Perhaps the candidate belongs to a party you usually support, but a friend lends you a book giving good grounds to take an opposite approach. The book may influence you. Whether it does or not depends on many factors. Concentrating on those most extrinsic to you, the quality of evidence and argument in the book could influence you. The evidence, of course, may come from other books, some of which you might know and some not. You might be curious enough to track down one of the latter, find it full of holes, and go back to position 1. But something opposite to that might happen. In principle, there is no limit to the network of reasons that can impact on a decision of whom to vote for.

This is not to claim that we follow reason up to the point where it decides for us. Accidents can intervene at any point. You might lose the book or get tired of searching for the truth, but we need not suppose that accident will play any determining role. Another type of outcome is that, after a certain amount of research, you will feel well grounded in the issues and capable of summing up the evidence even though you know there are further corners of the matter you could investigate if doing so seemed worthwhile. In arriving at this last judgment, and indeed at every stage of research where you decided not pursue a particular avenue of investigation, you were like a person who stands on a prominence to take an estimate of the way ahead, more likely relying on assessment of what seemed to be individual *dominant* features than a mere statistical amalgamation of the whole.

In *The Roots of Reference* (1974), W. V. Quine suggests that all talk of causes is heuristic and that what we call causes are partial, contributory causes. The force exerted by a reason is always subject to qualification by other reasons in its network. Still, the influence of reasons is very real; it is not random and can never be adequately described by a statistical gradient.

FREE WILL IS NOT A FACULTY OF THE INDIVIDUAL

The rationale invented by the posthypnotic subject, a miniature fiction, appeared to manifest real freedom of choice. What is the source of the rationale? It involves a very special interaction between the facts of the circumstances and the possibilities of culture. Culture and language open up myriad distinct possible responses and with these the networks of reasons for selecting one or another.

Reason appeals to knowledge that is embodied externally to the person exercising judgment. Our fiction of your well-researched vote started with a book and postulated a possible trip to the library. The information can reside in any sign system. The reader who gleans my line of argument can transpose it to his or her area of expertise; it could apply to choices in art, to a football play, or to a business strategy.

To illustrate the relation between deliberation and system, I call on Beethoven one last time, this time for the beginning of the recapitulation of the first movement of the Ninth Symphony. Normally recapitulations in classical symphonies began by exactly repeating the opening. Instead of following this procedure, Beethoven altered the passage. The somewhat vague, subdued, and indecisive opening returns with the character of a terrifying catastrophe. No one could possibly prove that the change was predetermined. Neither is it random. The constituents of the change are few and highly systematic, invoking binary oppositions. The second occurrence of the theme is loud instead of soft, fully orchestrated instead of sparsely, and harmonically complete instead of incomplete, the formerly absent harmonic third now appearing in the bass where it reverses mode and inverts the chord. Also, the context, although providing no fixed determination of the passage in question, offers as many *reasons* for it as we could wish (e.g., to have reprised the opening effect after a heroic development would be aesthetically vacuous, etc.). No one would say Beethoven had to write what he did; no one can doubt that he had good reasons. This is the case generally for decisions reached through deliberation.

Deliberation is constituted here as an interaction between a mind and a semiotic environment of systems and texts. The freedom embodied in deliberation is not a property of the mind alone but of the relationship between a mind and its semiotic environment. In this view, we are not born free. Freedom, in a meaningful sense of the word, requires sign systems of some stability and capable of some autonomy.

BUT ISN'T REAL FREEDOM PHYSICALLY IMPOSSIBLE?

The problem—Minsky's error in the statement cited at the beginning of the chapter—is confusing what is physically possible with what is physically interpretable.

This is a fallacy we need to get out of the way. From a physical perspective, all the events in the universe are either random or determined although in practice they may be indeterminate or undecidable. From the perspective of black-and-white film, all the objects in the universe are black, white, and gray. Physics is no more illuminating about free will than it is about chess games or the real estate market.

Is life a physical phenomenon? There is no such thing as a live molecule or a dead molecule. But nobody says life is an empty postulate. Life is a description of higher levels of organization than physics comprehends. Semiosis is too.

Varela, Thompson, and Rosch (1991), like Maturana (Maturana and Varela, 1980) extend the image of closure to include language, considered as a behavior of the human nervous system; they are thus led to see us as cognitively isolated from each other and our surroundings. Our minds are like dictionaries in consisting of a closed collection of interpretations.

Although the metaphorical relation between a self-producing chemical system and a self-defining language vocabulary is reverberant, the literal extension from one idea to the other fails to take account of an important factor: the consequences of signs becoming physically invested in vehicles that are independent of our biological relations.

As a piece of apparatus, the universal Turing machine (the mathematical model of a computer capable of any computation whatsoever), is not much hardware. The trick is, it has an infinite memory. Once we export memory outside our own brains, we too have, in effect, infinite memories. My memory includes the Library of Congress, and my buddies on the Net say access is improving.

People and their invested signs together are not as constrained as simple biological systems. Texts are available to us even when they exceed our biological capacity to maintain them as neural data. We can calculate sums that we cannot remember or revisit a painting that we recall imperfectly. Without arithmetic we might "know" in some sense that 1 plus 2 is always 3. We would not know that 25 plus 13 is always 38. Numbers establish a genuine extension of our universe and a genuine meeting place of minds. So do other semiotic systems to the extent that they are autonomous, as arithmetic clearly has some claim to be.

Varela, Thompson, and Rosch argue that our experience is closed via a theoretical deduction. If this closure does indeed obtain, it must be invisible to us because we are inside of it. The closure that we study in semiotics is the closure of subsystems in our experience that we actually can look at from both inner and outer viewpoints. These are texts and systems: games, the worlds of novels, grammars of classical arts, algebras, moral and religious codes, even philosophies if sufficiently rigorous.

Paradoxically, these systems and texts that are most severely autonomous are the windows through which we escape from self-closure. We are not wrong to value them highly. Their use to us is that they are not fully determined by our needs or by our perceptions. Every new rhyme or bigger prime number discovered by accident has the potential to poke a hole in our cocoon.

As much as our self-defining, quasi-stable, internally evaluated systems do seem like the autopoetic organisms of Varela, Thompson, and Rosch, our own mental life seems quite different. The difference is that our mental life encompasses a variety of these closed systems as well as many more that are more or less fragmentary and unstable. These constitute a continually changing population. Since semiotic systems may enter our mind from the external environment (as when we read a book or hear a song), we have an unlimited opportunity to choose a path through them. Thus the semiotic universe allows us to participate in free will.

23

SEMIOTICS AND THE
AIMS OF EDUCATION

Chapter 1 suggested that semiotics was topical in part because of our worries about our own cultures. The issues sounded were pertinent to educational policy. By way of conclusion, I reflect on two topics in education to which the view of the function of texts developed in this book seem relevant.

ELEMENTARY CONSIDERATIONS

Schools are too often cruel, but no curriculum is kind or cruel. Teachers and administrators alone can make a school harsh or supportive. My impression is that educated people in Europe and in the Americas have, in the main, adopted ideals for teaching that would, if allowed to guide us, greatly diminish the cruelty we still find in schools. Unfortunately, these ideals seem to have clouded thinking about curricula. Curricula cannot be mean or friendly but they can be rich or vacuous. They cannot do the job of a teacher, but a bad, authoritative curriculum can hobble the work of an excellent teacher.

I take it as self-evident that protecting free will, in the sense developed in the last chapter, is prerequisite to any worthwhile political freedom. If you accept that individual freedom depends on the interaction of the individual with semiotic systems and texts, then freedom requires that sign systems of some stability and with some claim to autonomy be available to the individual. These systems are inherently fragile. Education is a primary locus for the maintenance of sign systems and texts.

Children need quasi-autonomous systems of rules and, if they are well taught, enjoy learning them. Nobody worries about making the rules of hockey "relevant" or providing the rules of baseball with a "context." No child I know ever insisted on knowing what Batman has to do with "real life." Jakobson (1971) analyzed the babbling of a two-year-old falling asleep. The babbling was not random; it was highly routinized, but not fully. It followed the routines of a grammar drill; it was an exercise in combinations and conjugations.

Children are born into a small world. If they are healthy, they exhibit an appetite to enlarge it that they never satisfy. Their eagerness to explore their physical environments is usually difficult to thwart. Their eagerness to explore their semiotic environments is equally passionate but seems easier to ignore and distort. Just as children need toys that they can move, manipulate, examine—in a word, master—they need identifiable and manageable packages of signs: games, alphabets, conjugations, spelling lists, lists of dates; all those drills we may think are boring because they were given to us at the wrong time, in the wrong doses, or in the wrong circumstances. They cannot always be fun (no socially structured work can always be fun), but they need not be discouraging. If they were, that was due to bad teaching, not bad curriculum. It is the teacher's job to know the right-size project for the right student. Anyone who has had a glimpse of a youngster proudly mastering an abstract drill and then displaying his or her new possession will understand this.

Children also need texts that they can fully master: tunes, stories, poems, dances of set form, pictures on the wall that show ways of drawing and ways of designing, and later on, deductive proofs. They need memorizable texts—there is no mastery like memorization, a genuine form of empowerment that returns to mind what has been invested in material. The last thing children need is contexts for their texts. The great advantage of learning mythology early—before a system of modalities has set in like concrete—is that the problems of belief do not arise. Fully acquired texts function at first as closed and autonomous. Then, later, those texts become contexts. We don't have to be told what they mean to us or for us. They lead us out of ourselves. That is how they give us freedom.

Recognizing the importance of closure, we see why the press of education toward practicality is so distasteful. A public school curriculum that teaches "Communication Skills" instead of English or "Quantitative Relations" instead of arithmetic is destructive. Intended as a better wrapping paper, these reforms are degrading adult agendas, with little in them to answer to a child's need for dignity and independence. Once learned, times tables and spelling lists are possessions. Under those reformed curricula, what does the student get to take home to keep in his or her head? To have self-respect as an individual, the student must be able to see that his or her task has a beginning and an end and a shape and a name. If everything is connected to everything, like a "real-life" discourse, the teacher will have a nice theory and the student, empty pockets.

Further, "communication skills" does not require ideas of style, another autonomous value that no child should be deprived of. "English" does. Relating "English" to communication is the job of the teacher (when an individual student needs that), not the job of a curriculum. A curriculum must be an autonomous structure, not too readily seduced by practical purposes. Otherwise it can offer the student no freedom from the compulsions of practical life.

Martinet wrote wrongly: "There is . . . every indication that everybody's language would suffer rapid deterioration without the necessity of making oneself understood. It is this permanent necessity which maintains the instrument in good working order" (1960, p. 19). Our offices, stores, and construction projects are full of bored workers whose language, deprived of the counterpressure of stylistic ideals but still adequate for practical needs, deteriorates toward grunting and pointing. On the other hand, no practical "necessity" accounts for the lively traditions of storytelling that many societies can (or did) carry with pride.

The worst abuse in curricula is a flabby notion of creativity. The concept is not without some dignified history, but the popular version, pervasive and insidious, is equally damaging to education and to art.

The popular notion appears to be that we are born with powers of original creation such that simply given materials and liberty, we will make wonderful new things. The consequences of the theory are a mass consumer industry in factory-made artifacts of "personal identity," art councils enslaved to fashion, and children who, given much opportunity to express their selves and practically nothing to form a self out of, come to age dreadfully deficient in old tunes and stories. There is a rousing critique of creativity within critical theory (See Max Horkheimer and Theodore Adorno 1947/1972) and a sourer but very informative one in Alan Bloom's notorious *The Closing of the American Mind* (1987). These scholars show what a tawdry servo-mechanism of a repressive economy "creativity" is. Horkheimer and Adorno talk about "subjectivity" rather than "creativity," but they unmask the same villain. They show that we have asked children and artists to pick up the tab for a society that excludes human feeling from its processes of production and distribution. Bloom takes the word "creativity" apart, noting its theological origin and making its pretensions patent. Semiotic doctrine foregrounds an alternative.

Like free will, the faculty in question is not ours autonomously; it arises in our interaction with sign systems and texts. The invention and the expressivity and the freshness and refreshing clarity of children is best protected when children are not deprived of an opportunity to encounter structured work. All signs and texts are responses to (interpretations of) other signs and texts and take their bearing from their function of response. This holds, of course, for what is supposed to be pure "creativity." The child who is sent home to write an original story and who returns to school with the next installment of whatever was on television last night is operating with the same constraints as the rest of us but with worse resources. Children's work can indeed seem miraculous, but miracles are not encouraged by discouraging the imitation (reinterpretation) of good models. Children need a repertoire of closed texts that they can make their own.

"MEDIA STUDIES" AND "COMMUNICATION STUDIES"

"Media Studies" and "Communication Studies" have become "fields" in higher education, and in the public school classroom the video monitor and the computer are becoming staple outlets for "resources." In the academies, Communication Studies programs are among the best sponsors of semiotics, but that one tool isn't up to the whole job.

"Communication" means either or both "signification" and "transportation." (Compare "lines of communication" in war.) All semiosis involves both, but the relative emphasis of the two is variable.

The camera, the telephone, the video and the audio recording influence style, but they are, in the first instance, devices of transportation, devices that may be put to the uses of a text but that do not need to be. They transport incoherent signs just as well. The novel, the painting, and the geometric theorem are, in the first instance, devices of signification, of text formation, although they take much of their use from their capacity to be transported. One task in the study of novels is to restore the social context that got left behind with the transportation of the text. A related task is to restore lost performance practices to transported musical scores. The distinction between signifying and transporting is a difficult one to trace because the two functions are always combined, but tracing it is vital.

Minimally, what the new media *transport* are samples—specifically, samples of a wave front for sound and/or light. Samples are the least of signs, if they are signs at all. Samples are extracts, not artifacts. Samples cannot stand alone any more than the word "the." An egg as an uninterpreted (unlabeled) sample might exemplify its color, texture, shape, fragility, amino acid balance, or reproductive function. Samples neither designate nor attribute modality: "Please find me something to match this." "Please find something that goes with (contrasts) this." "See if you like this." "See if you can tolerate this." Which? An example without a concept is hardly a sign.

Significant texts can be constructed out of samples (e.g., significant cinema, photography, etc.). That is not at issue here. Although we have studied how texts are built over inflections and over terms and not how texts are built over samples, the theory is hardly a terra incognita. Such texts involve selection, combination, transformation, framing, montage, grammars, patterns, and so on. Such techniques yield conceptlike structures. But devices of transportation do not guarantee a text structure. Genuine vacuousness is possible. Surveillance cameras in banks don't generate texts—not in our sense of the term. Vacuousness doesn't require new media. There are vacuous études for piano and walls of pointless paintings, but the possibilities with new media are unprecedented.

We have never before been able to transport such engaging samples. The teasing cross-cuts and elliptical dialogue that substitutes for conceptual relations in much television fantasy (extra pleats in thin cloth) fascinates because we get close-ups of real faces and real luxury cars and houses, images that offer possession by sampling.[1] This is essentially subsemiotic.

Of course, samples can be signs. Anything can be a sign. Typically, samples are taken for evidence—Moon rocks for a distant chemistry, fossilized animal droppings for ancient ecologies, newscast photos for social bias. But when its own context does not direct the interpretation of a sample, we simply interpret it on the basis of our established prejudices encoded in prior texts. Merely presenting samples is not signification. The new media are rarely, if ever, so barren as merely to present samples; the problem is how close they can come to that.

Recently I watched a wonderful television broadcast that documented the surgical separation of Siamese twins. Toward its end I felt that no novel or play in my recent experience had matched it for suspense. Wrong comparison! A friend had life-saving surgery three years ago and the suspense was even greater—"real life" was the right comparison. The documentary had not so much signified the surgery as it had transported it. Nonsense, several of you will argue: "You are not appreciating the editing, cutting, selecting, pasting, and framing that I would learn about right away in communication studies." But yes, I do. Images are fragile goods. You cannot transport fragile goods in bad packages. The packaging is very important. And sure, there was a text, a narrative grammar, and a metaphorical pattern of hospital and laboratory images modalizing medical progress. We could theorize on it for days. But all of that pales before the shots as samples: They had a zoom lens in the operating room!

The distraction is not entirely new, but it is easier, at least for us, to see that the gilt is not the painting than it is to disentangle perception from signification in front of a screen.

Heightened competition between transportation and signification devalues texts—case in point, the talk of "resources" that beats out the march for the new instructional aid technologies. Texts are not homogeneous and amorphous "resources" like wood and steel. (An encyclopedia entry, by the way, is a text, a source, not a resource. Humans, too, by the way, even when open-minded, are sources, not resources.)

The preliminary point I am leading to is that semiotics is not an adequate tool for critical study of new media because semiotics regards signification and not transportation, whose full study requires at least the leverage of psychology, sociology, anthropology, and economics. Oh, semiotics is relevant here, to be sure, but too much emphasis on "content" becomes a cover-up for a more violent import.

I want to warn about an idea I see gaining ground in widespread seats of learning, that the marriage of semiotics and media studies represents a coming of age of both. To be vital as modes of inquiry, the first must sustain a mandate for analysis and the second a mandate for criticism, complementary tasks only if they are not confused and do not dilute each other.

At the start of this book I posed the question—Has literacy become a foolish investment? No, literacy remains a good investment, and we need to diversify the portfolio. Don't for one minute oppose the full use and full study of all media in education; they are us. But when the media are not on the side of whole, delimited, and integrated texts, they are not on side. Marshall McLuhan's call to attention, apologizing for and even mimicking the fragmentation of advertising and television in his most popular books got us going (e.g., 1969, 1970). It was okay for a one-night stand, but we must resist erosion of the principles that favor well-structured texts. It is no more old-fashioned or escapist to do so than to resist excesses in nutrition, in exploitation of the environment, or in the distribution of political power. Those who appreciate the importance, complexity, and privileges of elaborate semiosis, especially those in education (which broadly construed should include teachers, advertisers, political leaders, artists, parents, and friends of children,) all need to pitch in.

NOTES

FOREWORD

1. The start-up kit I would recommend today (present work aside) would still be Saussure plus Bouissac's own *Circus and Culture* (1976), and Lotman's *Semiotics of Cinema* (1976). No one will want to settle for empty complications after those three books.

CHAPTER 1

1. Not in occidental science. In some Buddhist psychology they are regarded as perceived by the mind.

CHAPTER 2

1. I see no grounds within semiotic theory to disagree with an uncritical perception (e.g., that the wafer is, rather than signifies, the body of Christ). The definition of sign constructed in part III is explicitly relative in this regard.

CHAPTER 3

1. For introductory bibliographies, see entries in the *Encyclopedia of Semiotics and Cultural Studies,* edited by Paul Bouissac (1998).
2. As customary, references to the Collected Papers of Charles Peirce are indicated by volume and paragraph number.

CHAPTER 5

1. My understanding is that in borrowing this figure, westerners have considerably cheapened it, leaving behind its connotation of links with origins. "The mother of all battles" meant not just the biggest but also a phase of the oldest.

2. Hjelmslev draws out an interesting link with formal logic. The relation between occurrences of elements in one paradigm falls under the "or" of exclusion. The basis of the syntagm is co-occurrence, corresponding to "and." (Hjelmslev's terms are "function," "relation," and "correlation.")

CHAPTER 6

1. The thesis that most art, viewed in a broad perspective, contradicts its own norms can be assessed only in the light of expert historical knowledge. Mukarovsky's expertise was in literary history. The only area in which I have sufficient knowledge personally to test the idea is the history of Western music since the Renaissance. Here, at least for concert music, the idea holds. The framework for understanding that music rests on very brief crystallizations of style such as post-Renaissance strict counterpoint, late Baroque fugue, or high classic form, which rarely occur in "pure" examples.

CHAPTER 7

1. See Piattelli-Palmirini, (1980) for the Chomsky-Piaget debate. For a newer vista, see Sue Savage-Rumbaugh and Roger Lewin (1994) on ape communication.
2. For an account of the types of grammars and their corresponding formal languages, ee G. E. Revesz (1983).
3. See, for example, Nelson Goodman (1968); Ray Jackendoff (1987); and the entry on "Reify" in W. V. Quine (1987).

CHAPTER 10

1. This intellectual strategy is developed forcefully but uncritically in Betrand Russell's *Analysis of Mind* (1921/1956). He introduces the hypothesis of unconscious memory, still a new idea at that time, by reference to the "engram" of Semon. The notion of the engram survives in the popularized movement of psychoanalysis called Dianetics.

CHAPTER 11

1. The first example is the key of Nelson Goodman's (1968) distinction between "autograph" and "allograph"; the couterexample is due to Richard Stewardson (personal communication, 1965).

CHAPTER 12

1. Evan Thompson, 1995 For a semiotic treatment of the relativist position see Louis Hjelmslev, (1944).

CHAPTER 13

1. For more history and detail see Michael Shapiro (1983) especially pp. 15–16 and 74–75.

CHAPTER 14

1. In large part this chapter is a response to the discussion of "discursive" and "presentational" forms in Suzanne K. Langer (1942).
2. I give only cursory treatment to a complex topic. As defined here, modality assimilates tense (past and future worlds). I think is an appropriate stance for general semiotics, but I don't expect instant converts.

CHAPTER 15

1. In previous publications I used the term "design" instead of pattern.
2. For more elaborate musical examples, see David Lidov (1979, 1981a, 1992) and Nicolas Ruwet (1972).
3. The theory of Meyer (1973) offers an alternative and perhaps clearer grammatical description for self-sufficient melodies. I do not invoke it here because his integration of grammatical factors with others that pertain to the psychology of perception is so specifically musical that it bypasses certain abstractions that can contribute, in my view, to comparisons across media.

CHAPTER 17

1. Of particular interest in this connection is Carl Dalhaus (1978), which shows persuasively that for its nineteenth-century European audience, music denied mimetic content signified transcendence.
2. Although our vocabularies are incompatible, the notion of process as interpretant that this chapter constructs seems to address essentially the same phenomenology which Kristeva confronts in distinguishing between the "symbolic" and the "semiotic." In a framework derived ultimately from Peirce rather than Saussure, it is no revolution to understand the body and its sensations as positive factors of the sign.

CHAPTER 18

1. Just as the point of Goodman's formulation is to reconstruct the type-token relation, which he finds unclear in Peirce's exposition, Kari Kurkela finds a parallel imprecision in Goodman's version, which he attempts to remedy in his *Note and Tone* (1986).
2. But not when they are used to notate the real numbers because of his requirement for finite decidability, not discussed here.
3. The whole discussion which follows bears only on formal graphs, not continuous graphs, such as the traces produced by a seismograph or cardiogram or for stock market reports.
4. To my knowledge, Prewitt has not published on this topic.

CHAPTER 19

1. Gombrich's argument (1960) that this is just another code fails to acknowledge the radical difference of masking syntax. In Europe, the masking of visual syntax that develops from the Renaissance in visual art and the rejection of verbal mediation in musical meaning that climaxes in the nineteenth century (I would give it the same period of development) seem opposite at first, but they reflect the same quest for immediacy and transperancy.

CHAPTER 20

1. This chapter is concerned with performance. I do not think this concern is disconnected from those of the anthropology of performance, but space does not permit me to trace the connections. The reader might discover that performance in music and performance in ritual both deploy holistic signs to maintain an objective world that otherwise would not be available to the participants, including performers and audience if any.
2. Is language is completely immune from this structure? The *syllable* resisted theoretical definition in generative grammar. Saussure's definition of the syllable suggests a conjunct series. The analytical graphs of H. Schenker, the most outstanding theorist of the unity of musical flow in tonal composition, are essentially nets. His most penetrating discovery, the "interruption" structure, is aptly modeled by the difference between open and closed nets. See David Lidov (1997). Fred Lehrdahl and Ray Jackendoff (1983) represent tonal hierarchy by tree graphs, thus disassociating boundaries from one of the regions they join; their notation is insensitive to interruption structures.

CHAPTER 21

1. Nevertheless I do not endorse Cooke's theory. His syntactic categories are not well enough distinguished, and his semantic categories are not independent of them.
2. In musicology, a rounded binary form is a two-part form both parts of which are repeated and in which the second part terminates with a variant of the first part: AA; BA, BA.

CHAPTER 23

1. We often make the paltry fact into a resplendent metaphor by pretending to invert the transportation; hence, the answering system here says, "*Welcome* to York University," the TV announcer says, "We take *you* to election headquarters." We *visit* a web site.

REFERENCES

Baer, Eugen. 1975. *Semiotic Approaches to Psychotherapy.* Bloomington: Indiana University Press.

Bakhtin. See Volosinov.

Barthes, Roland. 1968. *Elements of Semiology.* Translated by Annette Lavers and Colin Smith. New York: Hill and Wang.

————.1970. *S/Z.* Trans. Richard Miller. New York: Hill and Wang. 1974.

————.1972. *Mythologies.* Selected and translated by Annette Lavers. New York: Hill and Wang.

Barzun, Jacques, ed. 1951. *Pleasures of Music.* New York: The Viking Press.

Bateson, Gregory. 1972. *Steps to an Ecology of Mind.* London: Ballantine.

Berger, John. 1972. *Ways of Seeing.* London: British Broadcasting Corporation and Penguin Books.

Blacking, John. 1987. *A Common Sense View of All Music.* Cambridge: Cambridge University Press.

Bloom, Alan. 1987. *The Closing of the American Mind.* New York: Simon and Schuster.

Bouissac, Paul, ed. 1998. *Encyclopedia of Semiotics and Cultural Studies.* New York: Oxford University Press.

Bouissac, Paul. 1976. *Circus and Culture.* Bloomington: Indiana University Press.

Brent, Joseph. 1992. *Charles Sanders Pierce: A Life.* Bloomington: Indiana University Press.

Bunn, James H. 1981. *The Dimentionality of Signs, Tools and Models: An Introduction.* Bloomington: Indiana University Press.

Carnap, Rudolf. 1958. *Meaning and Necessity: a Study in Semantics and Modal Logic.* Chicago: University of Chicago Press.

Chagall, Marc. 1962. *The Jerusalem Windows.* Text and notes by Jean Leymarie. Translated by E. Desautels. New York: Braziller, 1967.

Chomsky, Noam. 1966. *Cartesian Linguistics: A Chapter in the History of Rationalist Thought.* New York: Harper & Row.

Chomsky, Noam, and Morris Halle. 1968. *The Sound Patterns of English.* New York: Harper & Row.

Clynes, Manfred. 1976. *Sentics: The Touch of Emotion,* 2nd ed. Garden City, N.Y.: Anchor Press. 1989.

Colapietro, Vincent. 1989. *Pierce's Approach to the Self: A Semiotic Perspective on Subjectivity.* Buffalo, N.Y.: State University of New York Press.

Cone, Edward. 1974. *The Composer's Voice.* Berkeley: University of California Press.

Cooke, Deryck. 1959. *The Language of Music.* London: Oxford University Press.

Cumming, Naomi. 1997. "The Subjectivities of Erbarme Dich." *Music Analysis* (April): 5–44.

Dalhaus, Carl. 1978. *The Idea of Absolute Music.* Translated by Roger Lustig. Chicago: University of Chicago Press. 1989.

Deely, John N. 1982. *Introducing Semiotics: Its History and Doctrine.* Bloomington: Indiana University Press.

————.1990. *Basics of Semiotics.* Bloomington: Indiana University Press.

Dennett, Daniel C. 1991. *Consciousness Explained.* Boston: Little, Brown and Company.

Derrida, Jacques. 1967. *Of Grammatology.* Translated by Gayatri Chakravorty Spivak. Baltimore: Johns Hopkins University Press, 1976.

Eco, Umberto. 1962. *The Open Work.* Translated by Anna Cancogni. Cambridge, Mass.: Harvard University Press. 1989.

————. 1976. *A Theory of Semiotics.* Bloomington: Indiana University Press.

Foucault, Michel. 1972. *The Archaeology of Knowledge; And the Discourse on Language.* Translated by A. M. Sheridan Smith. New York: Dorsett Press.

Frege, Gottlob. 1879. "Begriffs-schrift, a formal language, modelled upon that of arithmetic, for pure thought." In Frege and Gödel, *Two Fundamental Texts in Mathematical Logic, 1879.* Edited by Jean van Neijenoort. Cambridge, Mass.: Harvard University Press.

Frisch, Karl von. 1963. *Man and the Living World.* New York: Harcourt, Brace and World.

Gadamer, Hans-Georg. 1960. *Truth and Method.* Translated and edited by Garrett Barder and John Cummings. New York: Seabury Press. 1975.

————. 1975. *Truth and Method.* Translated and edited by Garrett Barder and John Cummings. New York: Seabury Press. Reprinted, New York: Crossroad, 1989.

Garvin, Paul L., ed. 1964. *A Prague School Reader on Esthetics, Literary Structure and Style.* Washington, D.C.: Georgetown University Press.

Garvin, Paul L. 1981. "Structuralism, Esthetics and Semiotics." In *Image and Code.* Michigan Studies in the Humanities. Edited by Wendy Steiner. Ann Arbor, Mich.: Horace Rackham School of Graduate Studies.

Gombrich, Ernst Hans Josef. 1960. *Art and Illusion: A Study in the Psychology of Pictorial Representation.* Princeton, N.J.: Princeton University Press. 1969.

Goodman, Nelson. 1951. *The Structure of Appearance.* Cambridge, Mass.: Harvard University Press.

————.1968. *Languages of Art: an Approach to a Theory of Symbols*. Indianapolis: Bobbs-Merrill.

Gowri, Aditi. 1991. "The Social Construction of Symbolical Algebra in England of the 1830's: Progress and Cyclicity of Mathematical Reform." M.A. thesis, York University.

Greimas, Algirdas Julian. 1983. *Structural Semantics: An Attempt at a Method*. Translated by Daniele McDowell, Ronald Schleifer, and Alan Velie. Lincoln: University of Nebraska Press.

————.1987. *On Meaning: Selected Writings in Semiotic Theory*. Minneapolis: University of Minneapolis Press.

Hatten, 1994. *Musical Meaning in Beethoven: Markedness, Correlation, and Interpretation*. Bloomington: Indiana University Press.

Hjelmslev, Louis. 1943. *Prolegomena to a Theory of Language*. Translated by Francis J. Whitfield. Madison: University of Wisconsin Press, 1961.

————.1944. *Language: An Introduction*. Translated by F. J. Whitefield. Madison: University of Wisconsin. Republished 1970.

Horkheimer, Max, and Theodore Adorno. 1947. *Dialectic of the Enlightenment*. Translated by John Cumming. New York: Herder and Herder, 1972.

Innes, Robert E. 1982. *Karl Bühler: Semiotic Foundations of Language Theory*. New York: Plenum Press.

Jackendoff, Ray. 1987. *Consciousness and the Computational Mind*. Cambridge, Mass.: The M.I.T. Press.

Jakobson, Roman. 1933. "What Is Poetry." In *Semiotics of Art: Prague School Contributions*, pp. 164–175. Edited by L. Matejka and I. R. Titunik. Cambridge, Mass.: The M.I.T. Press, 1976.

————.1960. "Closing Statement: Linguistics and Poetics." In *Style in Language*, pp. 350–77. Edited by Thomas A. Sebeok. Cambridge: The M.I.T. Press.

————.1961. "Linguistics and Communication Theory." In *Selected Writings II: Word and Language*, pp. 245–252. The Hague: Mouton, 1971.

————.1971. *Studies on Child Language and Aphasia*. The Hague: Mouton.

————.1974. "Coup d'oeil sur le développement de la sémiotique.'" Research Center for Language and Semiotic studies, *Studies in Semiotics 3*. Bloomington: Indiana University Press, 1975.

Johnson, Mark. 1987. *The Body in the Mind, the Bodily Basis of Meaning, Imagination and Reason*. Chicago: University of Chicago Press.

Kalu Rinpotche (Rinpoche). 1990. *Instructions Fondamentales: Introdution au bouddhisme Vajrayana*. (Fundamental Instructions in Vajrayana Buddhism, Translation from English, translator anonymous.) Paris: Albin Michel.

Kennedy, John. 1993. *Drawing and the Blind: Pictures to Touch*. New Haven, CT: Yale University Press.

Kevelson, Roberta. 1977. *Inlaws/Outlaws, A Semiotics of Systemic Interaction: "Robin Hood" and the "King's Law."* Bloomington: Indiana University Press.

————.1996. *Peirce, Science, Signs.* New York: P. Lang.

Köhler, Wolfgang. 1969. *The Task of Gestalt Psychology.* Introduction by Carroll C. Pratt. Princeton, N.J.: Princeton University Press.

Kurkela, Kari. 1986. *Note and Tone: A Semantic Analysis of Conventional Music Notation.* Seura: Suomen Musiikkitietiillinen.

Langer, Susanne K. 1942. *Philosophy in a New Key: A Study in the Symbolism of Reason, Rite and Art,* 3d ed. Cambridge, Mass.: Harvard University Press.

————.1953. *Feeling and Form: A Theory of Art.* New York: Scribner.

Lawvere, William. 1969. "Adjointness in Foundations." *Dialectica.* 23, 3/4: 281–296.

Ledbetter, Huddie. 1967. *Negro Folk Songs for Young People: Sung by Leadbelly.* LP. FC 7533. Folkways.

Lehrdahl, Fred, and Ray Jackendoff. 1983. *A Generative Theory of Tonal Music.* Cambridge, Mass.: The M.I.T. Press.

Levi-Strauss, Claude. 1964. *The Raw and the Cooked: Introduction to the Science of Mythology.* Translated by John and Doreen Weightman. New York: Harper & Row, 1969.

Lidov, David. 1978. "Musical and Verbal Semantics." *Semiotica.* 31, 3/4: 369–391.

————.1979. Musical Structure and Musical Significance—I(Working Paper). Toronto Semiotic Circle [First] Monograph series. University of Victoria in the University of Toronto.

————.1981a. "The Allegretto of Beethoven's Seventh." *American Journal of Semiotics.* 1, 1/2: 141–196.

————.1981b. "Describing a Signified for Music." *Semiotic Inquiry.* 1, 2: 173–187.

————.1987. "Mind and Body in Music." *Semiotica.* 66, 1–3: 70–97.

————.1992. "The Lamento di Tristano." In *Models of Musical Analysis, Vol. I, Music before 1600,* pp. 66–92. Edited by Mark Everist. London: Blackwell.

————.1993. "Biological, Cultural and Formal Factors in Music." Read to the American Association for the Advancement of Science, Boston, unpublished, photocopy.

————.1997. "Our Time with the Druids: What and How We Can Recuperate from Our Obsession with Tree Graphs." In *Musica Significans,* pp. 1–28. Edited by Raymond Monelle. London: Harwood Academic Publishers.

————.1998. Entries on "Aesthetics," "Articulation," "Artificial Languages" "Clynes," "Diagrams," "Nattiez," "Bertrand Russell," "Semiosis," and "Sign" in *Encyclopedia of Semiotics and Cultural Studies.* Edited by Paul Bouissac. New York: Oxford University Press, 1998.

Lidov, David, and James Gabura. 1973. "A Melody Writing Algorithm Using a Formal Language Model." *Computers in the Humanities.* 4, 314: 138–148.

Locke, John. 1690. *An Essay Concerning Human Understanding.* Edited by A. D. Woozley. New York: New American Library. 1964.

Lotman, Jurij. 1976. *Semiotics of Cinema.* Translated by Marc E. Suino. Michigan Slavic Contributions, No. 5. Ann Arbor: Department of Slavic Languages and Literature, University of Michigan.

Martinet, André. 1960. *Elements of General Linguistics.* Foreword by L. R. Palmer. Translated by Elisabeth Palmer. Chicago: University of Chicago Press. 1964.

Matejka, L., and I. R. Titunik, eds. 1976. *Semiotics of Art: Prague School Contributions.* Cambridge, Mass.: The M.I.T. Press.

Maturana H., and F. Varela. 1980. *Autopoiesis and Cognition: The Realization of the Living.* Boston: New Science Library.

McLuhan, Marshall. 1969. *Counterblast.* London: Rapp and Whiting.

———.1970. *Culture is our Business.* New York: McGraw-Hill.

Meyer, Leonard. 1973. *Explaining Music: Essays and Explorations.* Chicago: University of Chicago Press.

Minsky, Marvin. 1986. *Societies of Mind.* New York: Simon and Schuster.

Monelle, Raymond. 1992. *Linguistics and Semiotics in Music.* Philadelphia: Harwood Academic.

———.Forthcoming. *The Sense of Music: Semiotic Essays.*

Morris, Charles. 1938. "Foundations of the Theory of Signs." In *Writings on the General Theory of Signs.* The Hague: Mouton. 1971.

———.1964. *Signification and Significance.* Cambridge, Mass: The M.I.T. Press.

Mukarovsky, Jan. 1934. "Art as Semiotic Fact." In *Semiotics of Art: Prague School Contributions.* Edited by L. Matejka and I. R. Titunik. Cambridge, Mass.: The M.I.T. Press. 1976.

———. 1936. *Aesthetic Function, Norm and Value as Social Facts.* Michigan Slavic Contributions, No. 3. Translated by Mark Suino. Ann Arbor: University of Michigan 1970.

Muller, F. Max, trans. 1962. *The Upanishads.* New York: Dover Publications.

Mursell, James, and James Lockhard. 1937. *The Psychology of Music.* New York: W. W. Norton and Company. Reprinted. Greenwood Press, 1971.

Nattiez, Jean-Jacques. 1975. *Fondements d'une semiologie de la musique.* Paris: Union Generale d'Editions.

———.1990. *Music and Discourse: Toward a Semiology of Music.* Translated by Carolyn Abbate. Princeton, N.J.: Princeton University Press.

Ockham. See William.

Peirce, Charles S. 1867. "On a New List of Categories." Daedalus: Proceedings of the American Acadamy of Arts and Sciences. VII: 287–293.

————.1902. "Law of Mind." In *Charles S. Peirce, the Essential Writings*, pp. 190–215. Edited by Edward C. Moore. New York: Harper & Row. 1972.

————.1931–35. *The Collected Papers of Charles S. Peirce*, volumes 1–6. Edited by Charles Hartshorne and Paul Weiss. Cambridge, Mass.: The Belknap Press of Harvard University.

————.1955. *Philosophical Writings of Peirce*. Edited by J. Buchler. New York: Dover Publications.

————.1972. *Charles S. Peirce, the Essential Writings*. Edited by Edward C. Moore. New York: Harper & Row.

Pierce, Alexandra, and Roger Pierce. 1989. *Expressive Movement: Posture and Action in Daily Life, Sports, and the Performing Arts*. New York: Plenum Press.

Piattelli-Palmirini, Macsimo, ed. 1980. *Language and Learning: The Debate between Jean Piaget and Noam Chomsky*. Cambridge, Mass.: Harvard University Press.

Polanyi, Michael. 1969. *Knowing and Being: Essays*. Chicago: University of Chicago Press.

Propp, Vladimir. 1928. *Morphology of the Folktale*. Austin: University of Texas Press, 1968.

Quine, W. V. 1974. *The Roots of Reference*. La Salle, Ill.: Open Court.

————.1987. *Quiddities, An Intermittently Philosophical Dictionary*. Cambridge, Mass.: Harvard University Press.

Raja, K. Kunjunni. 1963. *Indian Theories of Meaning*. Madras: The Adyar Library and Research Centre.

Ratner, Leonard. 1980. *Classic Music: Expression, Form and Style*. New York: Scribner.

Revesz, G. E. 1983. *Introduction to Formal Languages*. New York: McGraw-Hill.

Rintpoche. See Kalu.

Russell, Bertrand. 1903. *The Principles of Mathematics*, 2nd ed. New York: Norton. Reprinted London: Allen and Unwin, 1956.

————.1921. *The Analysis of Mind*. London: G. Allen & Unwin Limited. Reprinted New York: The Macmillan Company, 1956.

————.1940. *An Inquiry into Meaning and Truth*. London: G. Allen and Unwin. 1951.

————.1959. *My Philosophical Development*. London: Unwin.

Ruwet, Nicolas. 1972. *Language, Musique, Poesie*. Paris: Editions du Seuil.

————.1975. "Parallélismes et déviations en poésie." In *Langue, Discourse, Sociéte: Pour E. Benveniste*, pp. 307–51. Paris: Editions de Seuil.

————.1980. "Malherbe: Hemogène our Cratyle." *Poétique*. 42:199–224.

————.1981a. "Typography, Rhymes, and Linguistic Structures in Poetry." In *The Sign in Music and Literature*, pp. 103–130. Edited by Wendy Steiner. Austin: University of Texas Press.

————.1981b. "Musique et vision chez Paul Verlaine." *Langue Français* 49: 92–112.

————.1981c. "Linguistique et poétique: une brève introduction." *Le Français moderne.* 49, 1: 1–19.

————.1983. "Une chanson d'Alfred de Musset." *Le Français Moderne* 51,1: 18–22.

————.1989. "Roman Jakobson: 'Linguistique et poétique,' vingt-cinq ans après." In *Le souci des apparences,* pp. 11–30. Edited by Marc Donimicy, Bruxelles: de l'Université.

Ryle, Gilbert. 1949. *The Concept of Mind.* New York: Barnes & Noble. 1969.

Salus, Mary, and Peter Salus. 1978. *Cognition, Opposition and the Lexicon.* Toronto Semiotic Circle [First] Monograph Series. No. 3. Toronto: Victoria University.

Saussure, Ferdinand de. 1915. *Course in General Linguistics.* Edited by C. Bally and A. Sechehaye. New York: McGraw-Hill 1966.

Savage-Rumbaugh, Sue with Roger Lewin. 1994. *Kanzi: The Ape at the Brink of the Human Mind.* New York: Wiley.

Savan, David. 1987–88. *An Introduction to C. S. Peirce's Full System of Semiotic.* Toronto Semiotic Circle, [Second] Monograph Series. No. 1. Toronto: Victoria College.

Schapiro, Meyer. 1966. "On Some Problems in the Semiotics of Visual Art: Field and Vehicle in Image Signs." Semiotica, 1/3 (1969): 223–242. Reprinted in his *Theory and Philosophy of Art: Style, Artist, and Society (Selected Papers),* pp. 1–32. New York: George Braziller.

Schmitt, Gladys. 1973. *Sonnets for an Analyst.* New York: Harcourt Brace Jovanovich.

Scholes, Percy. 1938. "God Save the Queen." In *The Oxford Companion to Music,* pp. 408–413. Edited by John Owen Ward. London; Oxford University Press. 1975.

Scruton, Roger. 1980. "Possible Worlds and Premature Sciences." *London Review of Books* (February 7): 14–6.

Sebeok, Thomas A. 1994. *Sign: An Introduction to Semiotics.* Toronto: University of Toronto Press.

Semon, Richard Wolfgang. 1923. *Mnemonic Psychology.* Translated by Bella Duffy. London: G. Allen & Unwin.

Shapiro, Michael. 1983. *The Sense of Grammar: Language as Semiotic.* Bloomington: Indiana University Press.

Shklovsky, Victor. 1917. "Art as Technique." In *Russian Formalist Criticism: Four Essays,* pp. 3–24. Edited by Lee T. Lemon and M. J. Reiss. Lincoln: University of Nebraska Press. 1965.

Sonneson, Goran. 1989. *Pictorial Concepts: Inquiries into the Semiotic Heritage and Its Relevance for the Analysis of the Visual World.* Lund: Lund University Press.

Sontag, Susan. 1978. *Illness as Metaphor.* New York: Farrar, Straus and Giroux.

Spencer-Brown, G. 1973. *Laws of Form.* New York: Bantam Books.

Stapp, Henry P. 1993. *Mind, Matter and Quantum Mechanics.* New York: Springer-Verlag.

Summerson, John. 1963. *The Classical Language of Architecture.* Cambridge, Mass.: The M.I.T. Press. 1966.

Thompson, Evan. *Colour Vision: a Study in Cognitive Science and the Philosophy of Perception.* New York: Routledge, 1995.

Varela, Francisco. 1979. *Principles of Biological Autonomy.* New York: Elsevier North Holland.

Varela, Francisco, Evan Thompson, and Eleanor Rosch. 1991. *The Embodied Mind: Cognitive Science and Human Experience.* Cambridge, Mass.: The M.I.T. Press.

Voloshinov, V. N. [Mikhail Bakhtin]. 1973. *Marxism and the Philosophy of Language.* Translated by Ladislav Matejka and I. R. Titunik. New York: Seminar Press.

Whitehead, Alfred North. 1920. *The Concept of Nature.* Cambridge, Mass: Cambridge University Press.

William of Ockham. 1328. *Ockham's Theory of Terms: Part I of the Suma Logicae.* Translated and Introduced by Michael J. Loux. Notre Dame: University of Notre Dame Press, 1974.

Wills, Gary. 1978. *Inventing America: Jefferson's Declaration of Independence.* New York: Vintage.

Wittgenstein, Ludwig. 1921. *Tractus Logico-Philosophus.* Translated by D. F. Pears and B. F. McGuinness. With an Introduction by Bertrand Russell. New York: The Humanities Press, 1961.

———.1933–4. *Preliminary Studies For The "Philosophical Investigation."* Generally known as The Blue and Brown Books. Oxford: Basil Blackwell, 1969.

INDEX OF PERSONS

Adorno, T., 263–264
Alexander, F.M., 217
Audubon, J., 210

Bach, J.S., 171, 177–178
Baer, E., xvi, 19
Bakhtin, M., 77–80, 176
Balzac, Honore* de 177
Barthes, R., 16, 47, 49, 54, 111–112,
    121, 171, 177–179
Barzun, J., 100
Bateson, G., 152
Beethoven, L. van, 42, 155, 163, 229,
    231–239, 257–258
Berger, J., 210
Bernstein, L., 113
Blacking, J., 215
Bloom, A., 263–264
Bouissac, P., xi, xvi, 269
Brent, J., 87
Bühler, K., 11, 57–60
Bunn, J.H., 16
Bush, G., 155

Chagall, M., 229, 239–247
Chomsky, N., 10, 67–72, 75, 75,
    80–81, 137, 144, 194, 270
Chopin, F., 204
Clynes, M., 223–226, 231, 233
Colapietro, V., 94
Cone, E., 219
Constable, J., 207

Cooke, D., 233, 273
Cumming, N., xvi, 219

Da Vinci, L., 140, 156, 212
Dalhaus, C., 271
Dalí, S. 211
Deely, J., xvi, 27, 38, 118
Dennett, D. C., 100, 117, 211
Derrida, J., xiii, 143
Dumas,fils, A., 201

Eco, U., xii, 1, 7, 41, 171

Feldenkreis, M. 217
Foulcault, M., 63, 176, 251
Frege, G., 30–32, 63, 85, 106
Frisch, K. von, 29, 37
Frost, R., 156

Gadamer, H-G., xiii, 204
Garbo, G., 201
Garvin, P., 59, 153
Gibbon, E., 42
Gödel, K., 254
Gombrich, E. H. J., 272
Goodman, N., 101, 194–196, 202,
    231, 270, 272
Gowri, A., 31
Greimas, A. J., 136–137, 150, 201,
    237

Halle, M., 137

Hatten, R., xvi, 143, 232
Hjelmslev, L., xii, 9, 47, 50–51, 70,
    73, 106, 133, 144, 178,
    270–271
Horkheimer, M., 263–4
Hume, D., 22

Jackendoff, R., 70, 270, 272
Jakobson, R., 1, 26, 35–36, 54–55,
    60–62, 65, 141–142, 151, 153
Jefferson, T., 157–163
Johnson, M., 70
Joyce, J., 42

Kalu, R., 101
Kennedy, J., 208
Kevelson, R., xv, 79, 88, 175
Köhler, W., 133
Kristeva, J., 271
Kurkela, K., 272

Laban, R., 196, 227
Langer, S. K., 203, 205, 271
Lawvere, W., 177
Leadbelly. See Ledbetter.
Ledbetter, H., 21–23
Lehrdahl, F., 272
Leibnitz, G. 30, 193
Levi-Strauss, C., 1, 54, 137, 144, 175
Lidov, D., 153, 223, 271–272
Locke, J., 27–29, 99, 126
Lotman, J., 45, 201–202, 269

Martinet, A., 143, 263
Maturana, H., 125, 258
Meyer, L., 206, 271
Michaelangelo, 212, 231
Minsky, M., 145, 253, 258
Monelle, R., xvi, 232
Morris, C., xiv-xv, 1, 9, 26, 29–30,
    34, 40, 63, 72–73, 109, 137

Mukarovsky, J., 36, 59–60, 62, 90–91,
    270
Mursell, J., 218

Nattiez, J., xi, 64, 167

Panini, 176
Peirce, C., xi-xiii, 1, 9, 11, 26, 29,
    33–35, 38, 40, 43, 63, 74, 85,
    87–97, 99–101,103–112,136,
    179, 181, 194, 202–203
Piattelli-Palmirini, M., 270
Picasso, P., 179, 184–185, 247
Pierce, A. and Pierce, R., 217–221
Polanyi, M., 15–16
Poussin, N., 156
Prewitt, T., 272
Propp, V., 199

Quine, W.V., 67, 257, 270

Ratner, L., 232
Rembrant, R., 210
Revesz, G.E., 270
Ricoeur, P., 73
Rinpoche. See Kalu
Rolfe, I., 217
Rosch, E., 118, 173, 258–259
Russell, B., 8–10, 32, 70, 88, 101,
    128, 173, 270
Ruwet, N., 153, 271
Ryle, G., 80

Salus, M., and Peter S., 143
Saussure, F., xi, 1, 25–26, 32–33, 35,
    41, 46–59, 65, 67–68, 74,
    77–78, 80–81, 84–85, 87,
    90–91, 95, 128,131, 133, 135,
    144
Savage-Rumbaugh, S., 112, 270
Savan, D., xii, 87–8, 109

Schapiro, M., 206
Schiller, 203
Schmitt, G., 19
Schoenberg, A., 185
Scholes, P., 163–164
Schubert, F., xii
Sebeok, T. A., 1, 39
Semon, R. W., 270
Shakespeare, W., 11–12, 21–22, 38, 61, 106, 114, 194
Shapiro, M., 142–143, 271
Shklovsky, V., 186
Snow, M., 204
Sondheim, S., 113
Sonneson, G., 197, 205
Sontag, S., 19
Spencer-Brown, G., 133
Stapp, H. P., 38
Stewardson, R., 270

Stravinsky, I., 183
Summerson, J., 213, 230

Thompson, E., 118, 173, 258–259, 270

Van Gough, V., 206–207, 211–212
Varela, F., 118, 125, 173–4, 258–9
Verdi, G., 201
Voloshinov, V.N. see Bakhtin.

Whitehead, A. N., xiv, 70, 82, 128
Wilder, T., 21
Wills, G., 157, 160
Wittgenstein, L., vii, 47, 49, 108, 113, 150
Wyeth, A., 211

Yeats, W. B., 20, 161

INDEX OF TERMS

This index locates only the passages that construct the technical terminology that I advocate. Not every passage exploiting these terms is indexed nor are discussions of terms or definitions which belong to different semiotic theories cited in the book but not adopted. These latter may be searched by author.

aspects, 132
abstractive duality, 119
articulation (see also dual articulation; double articulation), 131
articulation of a gesture, 222
autonomous, 172

boundaries and regions, 138

categories, 154
classes, 132
communication, 264
complete, 172
composition, 230
concept-like, 203
construct, 106
context
    of a representamen, 109
    of an object, 109
    of an interpretant, 110
contours or inflections, 133

denotation, 150
depiction, 207

design, 213
designation, 110, 150, 151
double articulation, 145
dual articulation, 138

elements (of semiotics), 11
epistemic duality, 119
expressions, 151

factors of a sign, 103, 104
feature, 133–34
form, 154

gesture, 222
gesture I, 222
gesture II, 222
gesture hypothesis, 225
grammar, 74, 154
graph (see tree graph, net graph)
ground, 104
groups, 132

holistic, 203

icon, 93
idiom, 74–75
image, 105
immediate interpretant, 108
index, 93
inflection (see contour), 230
inflection of a gesture, 222
interpretant, 103, 107
interpretant-process, 183

investment, 125
item in consciousness, item, 98

lifeworld, 205

markedness, marked term, 26, 141
material (of representamen), 104
mediation, 175
modality, 110, 149, 152
model, 197

net graph, 199, 201
notation, notational system, 195

object, 103, 105
objective world, 119
object-process, 188
opaque, 8

pattern, 74–75, 154
perspective, 102, 110
phenomenal duality, 120
process in consciousness, process, 98
processive sign, 182

representamen, 26, 103,
representatives (system of), 139

scalars, 140–41
scene, 205
semantic relations, 73

semantic resultant, 145
semiosis, 15
semiotic analysis, 3
semiotic system, 82
semiotic theory, 3
sentic form, 223–225
series, 138
sets, 154
sign (see sign-complex,
        representamen)
sign-complex (sign), 103
sign-designate, 90
signified, 9
signifier, 9, 26
sign-situate, 90
syntax, 73
system of representatives, 139

term, 93–94
text, 74
transformative expression, 151
transparent, 8
tree graph, 199, 201

units, 154

vectors, 140
vehicle, 105
visual vehicle, 205

world (of an object), 109

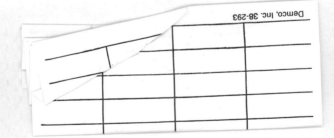
Demco, Inc. 38-293